Album

MITCHELL BEAZLEY

Album

style and image in sleeve design

Nick de Ville

Album
Nick de Ville

First published in Great Britain in 2003
by Mitchell Beazley, an imprint of
Octopus Publishing Group Ltd,
2–4 Heron Quays, London E14 4JP

ISBN 1 84000 605 6

A CIP catalogue record for this book is
available from the British Library

To order this book as a gift or incentive contact
Mitchell Beazley on 020 7531 8481

Commissioning Editor: Mark Fletcher
Managing Editor: Hannah Barnes-Murphy
Executive Art Editor: Christie Cooper
Copy Editor: Mike Evans
Design: Hoop Design
Picture Research: Giulia Hetherington, Claire Gouldstone
Production: Gary Hayes

Set in Serifa
Produced by Toppan Printing Co., (HK) Ltd
Printed and bound in China

Introduction
Style and Image in Design for Music

During the 20th century, design for music was the closest thing the design world of the West had to a living folk art. Which is to say that, as an art form, it was clannish, heterogeneous, disposable, generated from "beneath", amateur, faddish on the surface (although in many ways rooted in symbolic continuity), and firmly part of popular culture. "Folk" is sometimes regarded as an art which is produced by practitioners who, although exposed to the highest stylistic aspirations of their art form, are, nonetheless, unable to emulate them. The reasons for this inability is not seen as a purposeful sense of aesthetic dissent but rather naivety and ineptitude. Some glorious exceptions apart, this is not the case in design for music of the 20th century. Here there is a notable absence of designers overawed or beguiled by the canons of high art.

Instead, album cover design offers us pictorial representations of the self-consciously adopted aesthetic values and worldly interests of specific, identifiable lifestyles, subcultures, urban tribes and other self-determined communities. For these groups the repudiation of the design values of the mainstream is a deliberate act, just as are the particularities of their chosen musical form. The stories of surfers, hippies, mods, rockers, bikers, rastas, punks, skinheads, slackers, crusties and Eurotrash clubbers are all inscribed in the designs featured in this book. Design for music reflects the extraordinary breadths (and highs and lows) of 20th-century popular culture in a way that mainstream graphic design reflects politely, tepidly …at a distance, tempered as it is by the generality of its target audience.

Although many famous graphic designers have turned a hand to the design of album sleeves, much which was exceptional and innovative in 20th-century sleeve design, as befits its folk art status, was done by the itinerant, occasional, or anonymous designer. Many outstanding images were the product of one-off collaborations, often instigated by recording artists themselves, and completed with the collaboration of a variety of specialists: illustrators, artists, designers, photographers, retouchers, make-up artists, typographers, and friends.

Although it was useful in structuring this book to think of design for music as a continuation of folk traditions in modernity, it would be mistaken, as a consequence, to consign album sleeves to a realm of design kitsch, as some commentators have. Although many of its exponents have offered explanations for their intentions in the terminology of folk culture; the field is too full of homages, in-jokes, sly parodies and all manner of elliptical quotations to be as innocent as it sometimes pretends. As a consequence, I hope to show that it is a field of design in which complex stylistic tropes are regularly deployed; half authentic, half bent on complex missions of (re)contextualization.

What gives design for music its particular potency is its contribution to the creation of the modern myths of popular culture, often located at the intersection of youth, beauty, and self-destruction. Design for music may share this quality with other popular arts but the conjunction of visual image, music, and charismatic performer, has given many album sleeves a special iconic potency. They have a capacity to an extraordinary degree

Chicago X.
CHICAGO, Columbia, 1976.
Design: John Berg.
Illustration: Nick Fasciano.

Chicago IX Greatest Hits.
CHICAGO, Columbia, 1975.
Design: John Berg.
Photography : Reid Miles.

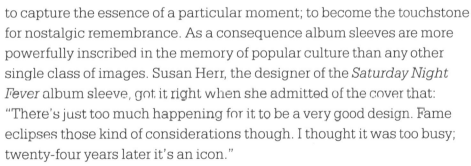

to capture the essence of a particular moment; to become the touchstone for nostalgic remembrance. As a consequence album sleeves are more powerfully inscribed in the memory of popular culture than any other single class of images. Susan Herr, the designer of the *Saturday Night Fever* album sleeve, got it right when she admitted of the cover that: "There's just too much happening for it to be a very good design. Fame eclipses those kind of considerations though. I thought it was too busy; twenty-four years later it's an icon."

Although this book touches on the wider perspectives of design for music – posters, sheet music covers, club flyers – throughout the 20th century, the primary focus is, inevitably, on album sleeve design. In this field the album's front cover is traditionally considered to be the most important element, with all the other elements of package design seen as secondary. Album sleeve books have regularly reproduced solely front covers, even of gatefold designs which were originally intended to be seen opened out, both inside and out. This is often to misrepresent the designers' intentions, something we have tried to redress in these pages. Even so, until the arrival of the promotional video and MTV, it was universally accepted in the record industry that the front cover was its primary marketing tool (aside from the music itself), and the front cover's visual impact has long been a vital consideration.

The inevitable consequence of the emphasis on visual impact is that the album cover has tended, more than other forms of graphic design, towards a minimum of typography. This has led even some designers

working in the music industry to disparage album sleeve design as "another photograph with a bit of typography slapped on it". Generally, it is an unusual front cover which carries more than a handful of words. In fact, over the past forty years there has been an insistent tendency for the most blithely self-confident – from the Rolling Stones to Björk – to banish lettering from their covers entirely. Most other significant forms of graphic design – magazines, posters, book covers – have tended towards a different balance between typography and image, requiring more rigourous formal attention to be paid to their integration. As a consequence, album sleeve designers have often been somewhat less than respectful of the formal niceties of typography usage. Even though there are considerable exceptions to this general rule – jazz in the 1950s and British new wave design of the 1980s, for instance – one suspects that the pursuit of visual impact means that the tenets of design for music are largely incommensurate with design principles in other graphic design fields. The album sleeve's focus on the power – and the power to provoke – of startling images has more than compensated for its frequent lapses of taste in this respect. In short, there are images in this book which, in their day, flouted – purposefully or not – the tenets of "good design". The conventions of good design are not a criterion for inclusion here, rather that a sleeve is fabulous and evocative.

It is sometimes considered that the classical period of the album cover design ended during the 1980s, dealt a double blow by the advent of the promotional video and the change-over to CD jewel cases. Although the

Into the Groove.
MADONNA, Sire, 1983.

True Blue.
MADONNA, Sire, 1986.
Photography: Herb Ritts.
Design: Jeri McManus.
Art direction: Jeffrey Kent.
Ayeroff with Jeri McManus.

Virgin Records.
Original logo designed by
Roger Dean, 1974.

Virgin Records.
Current logo designed by
Ray Kite, 1973.

financial resources devoted to album packaging may have declined since then, there is no doubt that design for music continues to thrive. The inclusion of club flyers demonstrates, as the whole history of design for music attests, that low-budget does not mean boring. Since the '80s influential designers of CDs have changed the rules of album packaging, reducing the emphasis on a single killer image for the front cover, and instead turning the CD booklet into extended visual essays in parallel with the disc's musical contents. 12-inch (30cm) DJ discs still provide the large-scale canvas of album sleeves and continue to be a vital field of design for music. The widespread adoption of personalized single sleeves did not begin to take off until the 1970s. They have their place in this book, not least because many outshine the sleeves of the albums from which the singles were taken, because there was less client pressure and designers were able to be more spontaneous and daring.

Among the attributes that album sleeve design's cast of collaborators have worked towards, the two most important have been identity and distinctiveness. To project identity is to offer a visual equivalent of the character of the music – the genre allegiance of the performer. Distinctiveness offers the possibility of a further refinement: to distinguish that particular album from the work of other performers in the same field, whilst not losing sight of its genre allegiances. The visual means chosen to articulate these two attributes have taken many forms which I hope are comprehensively displayed in the pages of this book. Many of the most successful recording artists have built these attributes by ensuring a strand of visual continuity from album sleeve to album sleeve, a strategy now commonly known as "brand building". The concern to build brands has been of equal importance to record companies – particularly niche players. In both cases, many have employed the tools of brand-building with instinctive *élan* – logos and other consistent typographical elements, themed stylistic tropes and recurring imagery have all been used to build identity and distinctiveness. Practically none have been the product of expensive commissions to branding consultancies. When Lisa Orth was designing the album sleeve for the first Nirvana album *Bleached* in 1989 she approached Grant Alden who was then both editing and typesetting the freebie Seattle music paper *The Rocket*. Orth wanted to put the name of the band on the cover and she asked him to output "Nirvana" in whatever typeface he happened to be working with at the time. It turned out to be Compugraphic's version of condensed Bodoni. It remained the band's logo from then on. Richard Branson tells a similar tale of casual invention about the Virgin signature logo. A designer called Ray Kite was put onto the task. Branson recalls that "as we were talking, this guy (Kite) got up from the table to go to the loo, looked over his shoulder, and just scribbled the now-famous Virgin logo on a piece of paper – then he went off and sent us a bill for it."

A third important consideration in album sleeve design is glamour. In the album covers of Madonna between 1983 and now we can admire the consummate skill with which her progress from New York ingenue, to Hollywood temptress, to post-feminist icon of female empowerment has

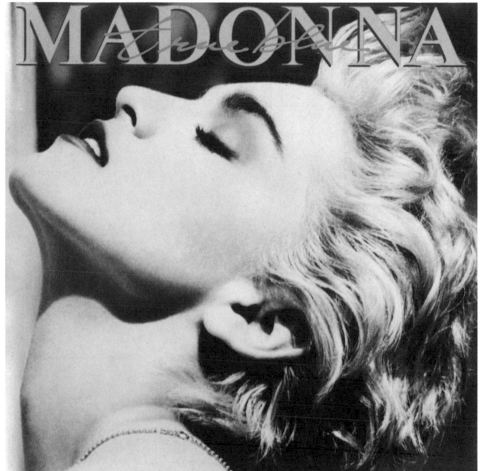

been visually represented. It is true that for some acts glamour is of little importance (at least the poised glamour of fashion plates), and in the music business the tales of the battles by management and designers to discourage groups with shambolic visual images from putting photographs of themselves on their album sleeves are legion. None the less, in pursuit of glamour the music business has not only produced specialist photographers like Mick Rock, Moshe Brakha, and Norman Seeff, but also regularly commissioned the best fashion and show business photographers – Avedon, Herb Ritts, Nick Knight, Mondino, Annie Leibovitz (who started out working as a staff photographer at *Rolling Stone*), Norman Parkinson, Mario Testino…

As already noted, the story of music graphics cannot be told without simultaneously telling other, parallel stories. One of these is of the growth of the recorded music industry since the birth of the long-player record in the late 1940s. Since then the industry has consolidated into a handful of giant international companies. Beneath them a firmament of small, specialized companies has continually come into being to exploit a host of specific niches. Many have shone for a few years only, others have been bought up by the majors, a few have ploughed their individual paths in glorious idiosyncrasy. The major record companies throw an ever-present shadow across this story, and for the purposes of this book they are most often represented, explicitly or not, by their creative art directors. Art directors have fantastic power and can imprint their aesthetic sensibility on a record company's design output, for good or ill. Some art directors

have played an active role in all the design aspects of their company's visual output, others have been gifted commissioners, sub-contracting to a shifting population of staff designers and freelancers. A mid-'70s roll-call of the major labels' art directors would include John Berg at Columbia, John Cabalka and Ed Thrasher at Warner Bros., Bob Defrin at Atlantic, Roy Kohara at Capitol, George Osaki at MCA, Acy Lehman at RCA, Ria Lewerke at United Artists, Dierdre Morrow at Island, and Roland Young at A & M Records. You will find designs by some of them in this book, but the taste and influence of them all are to be found reflected somewhere within these pages.

Over the period to which this book offers a guide there was a constantly changing dynamic between record companies (represented by their art directors), recording artists, and album sleeve designers. A central strand in this story is of the changing importance of the record companies' in-house design studios. They were established early on to service and give visual style to the pioneer companies' musical output. The most coherent instance of this is the story told in this book of the succession of designers who worked for Columbia in the period 1940 to 1960. Although freelance designers have always made a significant contribution, during this period the record companies' control over album sleeve design was absolute. A sea change occurred in the record industry in the early 1960s when stars began to insist on the right to take control of their own artistic output. In America this was vividly symbolized by Frank Sinatra's decision to launch his own record label – Reprise. Soon enough this

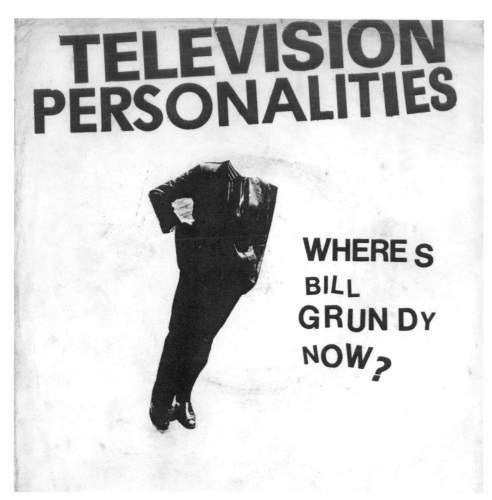

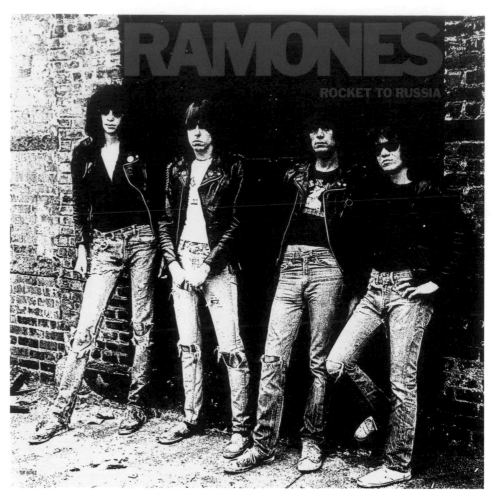

meant that all decisions – including the design of album sleeves – were seen as the prerogative of the artist, and invariably they wanted to work with designers who were empathetic with their music, their artistic leanings and lifestyles. The result was that in-house design studios declined in importance, their activities increasingly confined to repackaged back catalogue, and producing ancillary designs for advertisements, point-of-sale, and merchandising.

As the major record companies grew in size during the '60s, largely on the back of the explosion in rock music, the reliance on designs supplied by a haphazard network of freelance designers became increasingly problematic. Record company executives, with more than enough anxieties caused by the artistic temperaments of their recording artists, sought to regularize this network. Those designers with the necessary business acumen realized that by forming design groups with the specific aim of working with the art directors, and the design studio of record companies, they could help them manage the design process more effectively. One of the earliest of such design groups was London-based Hipgnosis, formed in the late '60s.

Quite soon others followed their example – with varying degrees of success and having longer or shorter life spans – and gradually a network of specialist design groups whose chief clients were record companies appeared on both sides of the Atlantic. Not surprisingly, a significant number of these were started by ex-record company art directors such as Bob Cato and Rod Dyer.

The arrival of punk's self-made aesthetic in 1977 was hailed by many commentators as a profound blow to the increasing professionalism of the music business. As far as design for music is concerned this argument is far from proven. In many ways, from post-punk onwards, the professionalization of the freelance music designer became much more entrenched on both sides of the Atlantic. Whilst this tendency inevitably reflects the needs of both big music and the struggling fringe label trying to make its mark, it has also, to some extent, undermined the folk art nature of design for music.

Some small record labels have sought to project an identity by following a coherent design policy and committing to a single designer or small group of designers. Examples of this are Blue Note in the 1950s and early '60s, Stiff in the late 1970s, 4AD in the '80s, ECM throughout the '80s and '90s, and Ivan Chermayeff's work for Grammavision in the late '80s and early '90s. Single designers have also been given the task of overseeing a specific aspect of a big record company's design output. Erik Nitsche's work for Decca's classical catalogue in the early 1950s and Paul Huf's for the Philips Favourite series of the mid '50s are good examples of this.

Professionalization of the design process can lead to the loss of the album sleeve's folk art attributes, which in turn means a dulling of the visual distinctiveness of different genres of music. One could argue that the reason why so little classical music design has made it into this book is because the composers of classical music have not been around to

Where's Bill Grundy Now?
TELEVISION
PERSONALITIES,
Kings Road, 1978.

Rocket to Russia.
RAMONES, Sire, 1977.
Art direction: John Gillespie.
Photography: Danny Fields.

Back to the s--t!
MILLIE JACKSON, Jive, 1989.

argue the case for artistic control over their album sleeves with record company executives. All too often the result at the major labels — until EMI decided to make classical music sexy and glamorous – was the "Deutsche Grammophon" effect: bucolic landscapes (photographed or reproduced from Old Master paintings) and formulaic lettering. Professionalization has always haunted the story of album sleeve design. Regrettably, since the early 1990s, even for supposed "cutting edge" music.

Having argued here for the diverse origination of the best of album sleeve design, this book is structured around both topic-based spreads – surfers, heavy metal art and so on – and those devoted to individual contributors and collaborations: designers, typographers, photographers, illustrators and art directors. I have attempted to strike an appropriate balance between these categories. Some spreads are dedicated to individuals whose output of designs has been comparatively slight in terms of quantity but whose contribution, none the less, has been seminal. There is an Anglo-American slant to this book. In America's case this reflects the sheer size and importance of the North American market for recorded music. At the end of the century, North America accounted for some 40% of the recorded music market, Europe around 30%, Japan 17%, the rest of the world the other 13%. The recorded music industry is largely an American invention, and American recording companies have always been important players in the development of all forms of music. In Britain's case this reflects its disproportionate influence in the development of rock, pop and street cultures over the

past forty years. In both these countries designers have found themselves at the forefront of innovation in many fields of music, and it is the music which has provided the inspiration for the design process.

Lastly, it is also inevitable that this book recounts the story of popular music in the 20th century as design has sought to express the growing diversity of musical genres which have been made available by the record industry. The intricacies of the many interlinking sub-plots would defy many volumes as large as this. I trust therefore that devoted fans everywhere will forgive the book's many foreshortenings and omissions. They have been unavoidable, and *Album* can only be an adjunct to many others in telling the full story of design for popular music since the birth of the illustrated album sleeve.

SALON DECCA

The Musician's Instrument

An Instrument combining perfection of Tone and extraordinary Station-Getting :: Abilities. ::

L'INSTRUMENT DE SONORITE PARFAITE : IL VOUS OBTIENT FACILEMENT VOS POSTES.

The Supreme Portable.

LE PORTATIF SUPREME: LE CELEBRE SALON DECCA.

DECCA
THE SUPREME RECORD
THE DECCA RECORD CO. LTD.

DT

"WARSAW" CONCERTO (Contd.)
(Richard Addinsell)
(From "Dangerous Moonlight")
MANTOVANI AND HIS CONCERT ORCHESTRA
(Piano Solo by Ivan Fosello)

DR. 6633

B

K P
KEITH PROWSE & CO LTD
LONDON

F. 8021

Manufactured in England   Fabriqué en Angleterre

DECCA
Regd TRADE MARK

1878–1940
Design for Music before the Illustrated Album Cover

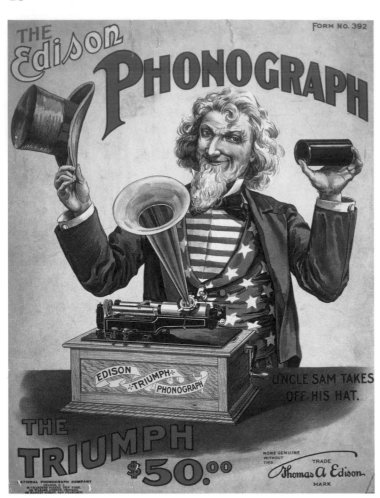

Record sleeve: Salon Decca.
1920s. [previous pages]

Advertisement poster.
Edison Triumph Phonograph.

Before 1940 the visual images with which designers embellished music's glamour, and projected the identity of its stars, were confined to sheet music covers, and to the advertisements and billboards for vaudeville, music halls and musicals. None of these brought music and visual image into the close and telling relationship that album sleeves have. However, the vehicles of visual expression which pre-dated the illustrated album sleeve were, initially at least, important models for album covers, providing their designers with much of their archetypal imagery. This opening chapter, then, looks at these pre-album vehicles for design for music, and sets them in the wider context of the development of the record industry.

The early decades of the 20th century mark the final flourish of an era in which widespread amateur music-making was the sole means by which ordinary people could hear music in their own homes. The new technologies bringing professionally played music into the home, via the radio and the gramophone, were destined to undermine the long-established traditions of do-it-yourself musicianship. Prior to their coming, sheet music of the popular songs and melodies of the day, more often than not scored for the piano, were the means by which a vast participating public could enjoy their favourite hits of the day. At the beginning of the century there existed a vast network of local music shops across Europe and throughout America which catered to the needs of home musicians. Not only did they sell musical instruments, accessories and spares, they also offered a fast-changing library of

musical scores. Like record albums which, largely speaking, were destined eventually to replace them, the sheet music of popular hits was published with illustrated covers designed to attract the music shop browser. Sheet music reflected the changing fashions of the day, the comedy numbers and romantic ballads of the music hall, music to sing along with and to dance to, patriotic songs in time of war and novelty numbers celebrating national events, great and small, and all had illustrated covers designed to tempt the buyer by defining the character – and intensify the experience – of the musical scores they featured.

Looking back, it is curious that the tradition of often elaborate covers for sheet music designed to project the style of their contents and encourage sales did not immediately transfer to the sleeves of records, but that is the case. Sheet music covers offered the fledgling record companies a fully developed iconography that delineated and distinguished the different genres of music from one another. In particular the combination of a portrait of the performer and theme elements (where the former was often photographic and the latter usually illustrational) would become a staple of early album cover design. The sheet music of music hall novelty numbers featured sketch caricatures, and romantic ballads were adorned with willowy lovers, both often rounded out with a vignetted photograph of the singer most closely identified with the success of the song. Show-stoppers from revues and patriotic back-stiffeners all had their appropriate illustrative style. And yet, in the early years of the record industry, marketing records was an

Sheet music:
**There's Always One You
Can't Forget.**
CHARLIE CHAPLIN.

Sheet music: **New Deal
March Song.**
MARGARET D. EVANS.

entirely separate business from music publishing, record companies not automatically adopting the habits of music publishers as they expanded their markets at the expense of the sheet music business. Despite the ready-formed range of visual styles that the covers of sheet music offered, records were instead sold in thin sleeves usually made of cheap paper in a self-coloured pastel shade, with a standard design advertising the record company, not the recording artist.

The invention of recorded sound is usually ascribed to the prodigious American inventor Thomas Edison who founded the Edison Speaking Phonograph Company in 1878. His other interests meant he had little time or energy to devote to improving the sound quality of the phonograph until, in 1888, he was stung to produce his "Improved Phonograph" following the launch of the "graphophone" by a rival company, Tainter and Bell (later to become the Columbia Phonograph Company). The phonograph and the graphophone worked on similar principles, playing music recorded acoustically on reusable wax cylinders and amplified by a soundbox or horn.

The two companies had hardly settled their differences over patent infringements before Emile Berliner had launched a new invention, the gramophone, which instead of using a wax cylinder, played recorded music from a horizontally revolving disc of shellac. Berliner's gramophone was both simpler to manufacture and gave superior sound reproduction to its cylinder competitors. What is more, the flat discs of shellac could be easily pressed in vast qualities, whereas it would not be

until 1901 that Edison would develop an industrial process for moulding cylinders. Despite Berliner's small-scale manufacturing capability, his gramophone and records began to make inroads into the cylinder's market. Columbia took action to prevent Berliner infringing patents originally lodged by Tainter and Bell. Although Berliner was forced out of the American market for a while he was able to market his gramophone in Europe. Here many companies manufacturing gramophones sprang up quickly, notably in Germany and Switzerland. Eventually a legal judgement gave both Columbia and Berliner the right to produce the gramophone. Berliner secured the financial backing to begin large-scale manufacture, and in 1901 the Victor Talking Machine Company was incorporated in Camden, New Jersey. The triumph of the record over the cylinder was swift and Columbia, still manufacturing cylinder-playing machines, admitted defeat and by 1902 had turned its factory over to the production of the gramophone.

The first two decades of the 20th century witnessed a spectacular growth in the sale of home gramophones. By 1924 sales of gramophones in America had grossed $158 million. This was in spite of the relatively poor sound reproduction the simple mechanical amplification these machines gave. Bass frequencies were entirely missing, as was the definition and detail of treble frequencies. Until radio made its appearance the poor sound quality was more than compensated for by the ever-widening range of music available on records. In 1916, American record company Victor initiated the practice of recording symphony

Sheet music: Banjo Song.
FRANK STAFFORD.

orchestras, notably the Chicago and New York orchestras. Then, in 1917 the company began to market the Afro-American jazz of New Orleans in a way that it believed would be acceptable to the metropolitan European American audiences of New York and Chicago. It announced "the very latest thing in the development of music", a recording of "Livery Stable Blues" by a dance band called The Original Dixieland Jass (sic) Band.

The standard 10-inch 78 r.p.m. single held between between two and four minutes per side. The generic paper record sleeve had a hole punched in the centre of sufficient size to allow the record's label to be read without sliding the record out of the sleeve. Although the label carried the name of the recording artist and the title of the song, it was of a standard design and dominated by the record company's logo and manufacturer's information. Only occasionally did it carry a personalized pictogram as, for example, the caricature portrait of bandleader Paul Whiteman which appeared on some of his early recordings for Columbia. So little importance was given to sleeves by the record companies that sometimes retailers would replace the record company's sleeve with one of their own, advertising the shop rather than the record company responsible for the recording.

Lengthier recordings – generally of classical music – and, later, collections of shorter pieces, were sold in "albums" consisting of a set of records, the sleeve of each record (made of card rather than the paper of single sleeves) was bound into the spine of the album. The covers of these albums were generally a generic grey or brown, or sometimes bound in

Poster: Revue Negre.
MUSIC HALL DES CHAMPS-
ELYSEES, 1925.
Illustration: Paul Colin.

Poster: Mistinguett.
CASINO DE PARIS, 1931.
Illustration: Zig Brunner.

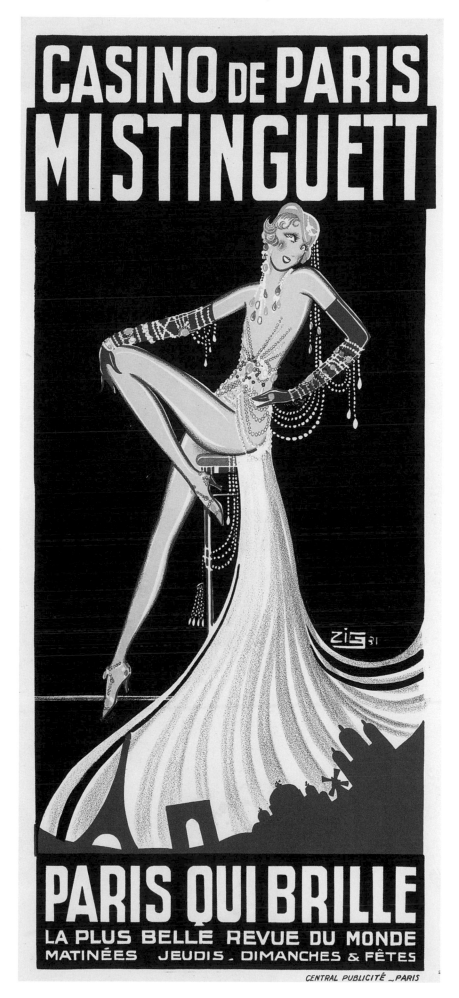

leatherette like old-fashioned books. The only personalizing of album covers was the artist's name and the title in gilt lettering on the spine and, occasionally, a pasted-on label on the front cover. As stock in music shops, albums were generally displayed on shelves with only their spines showing. In many countries the record companies were also the manufacturers of the gramophones on which the records were played. The chief aim of early marketing efforts was to encourage the purchase of gramophones by showing how sophisticated and modern owning a gramophone was, rather than the promotion of individual records or recording artists.

Although publicity and marketing for individual recordings would become an increasingly important aspect of record companies' activities, they were mainly pursued through the well-established formats of advertisements in newspapers and magazines, and on billboards. It would be some sixty years after the appearance of Edison's Phonograph before it occurred to record companies that the personalization of albums might be an important opportunity to establish the distinctiveness and increase the desirability of their recordings at the point of sale, and nearly as many years again before the habit caught on for singles.

By the end of World War I the gramophone's monopoly on music in the home was beginning to come under threat from radio. Radios had developed rapidly from simple crystal set to receivers with multi-tube amplifiers which gave a quality of sound reproduction that the gramophone could not compete with. By the beginning of the 1920s

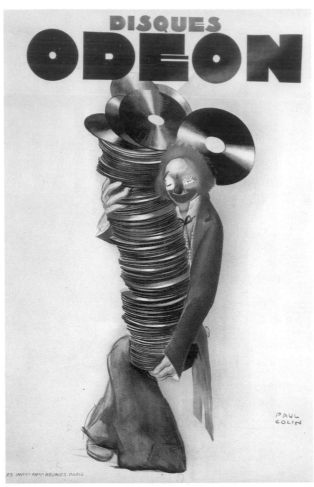

Advertisement: Disques
Odéon.
Illustration: Paul Colin.

Advertisement: Pathé.
Illustration: Cassandre, 1932.

commercial radio transmissions in America had developed to the point where radio stations were launching continuous scheduled broadcasts. The saturation of popular frequencies meant that they were soon fighting one another for air space, and although the resulting cacophony may have been annoying to listeners (Congress eventually stepped in to allocate frequencies), the increasing choice they offered meant that the sales of both gramophones and records began to decline, bringing Columbia close to bankruptcy in 1923.

In Europe too live music was giving way to radio and the recorded performance, although only slowly. In the big cities of Europe and the Americas live popular musical entertainment still continued to thrive. The popular stars of music still performed in theatres and music halls. Their performances were advertised through the press and, most memorably, through posters. The posters of the Parisian music halls are undoubtedly the most sophisticated publicity material from the inter-wars period. The impresarios of the music halls had the services of a number of incomparable illustrator/designers who captured the dazzling spectacle of the musical extravaganzas in which they specialized. L'Olympia, on the Boulevard des Capucines was one of the most celebrated and certainly the most enduring, still going strong as the century ended. Headliners performing there have ranged from Josephine Baker to Edith Piaf, from Jacques Brel to the Rolling Stones and the Beatles. Another celebrated Parisian music hall was the Casino de Paris, and, in the period after World War I, Mistinguett was one of its great stars.

Interior, Radio City Music
Hall, New York.

Mistinguett's favourite designer was Charles Gesmar (1900–28) who joined the Casino de Paris company in 1917. He not only produced posters but also designed sets and costumes for the theatre's productions. After Gesmer's early death, Zig also produced outstanding work for Mistinguett and other stars of Parisian music hall and theatre, during the late 1920s and early 1930s. Paul Colin (1892–1985), who was principal stage and poster designer for the Théâtre des Champ Elysées, was another key exponent of the Parisian Art Deco style.

The continuing popularity of vaudeville in America is vividly illustrated by the opening in 1932 of Radio City Music Hall, housed in one of the fourteen massive buildings of the Rockefeller Center in New York. It was the greatest vaudeville venue to be built between the wars, opening at the height of the Depression with the city nearing bankruptcy. Even so, the theatre was not only a live venue, but also a facility of the radio company NBC and near the new headquarters of NBC's owners, RCA. NBC's frequent radio broadcasts "Live from Radio City" guaranteed their listeners America's top musical acts. Its opulent, dazzling interior and headlining stars made it an immediate nation-wide success. The Radio City Rockettes, America's most celebrated chorus line, devised by "Roxy" Rothafel, stolen from Paramount by John D. Rockefeller, promised its audiences a home-grown version of the spectacle of the Parisian Follies. Their speciality was, in Rem Koolhaas's droll characterization, "the mass high-kick: a simultaneous display of sexual regions, inviting inspection but on a scale that transcends personal provocation".

New York was also home to the Broadway musical, then approaching its high renaissance as the quintessential American art form. The musical was a staple of Broadway theatre throughout the '20s and '30s and the great composers of the American musical – Cole Porter, George Gershwin, Jerome Kern, and Richard Rodgers – filled theatres specializing in musicals, such as the Music Box (Irving Berlin's own theatre), the American Music Hall, the Winter Garden, the Majestic, and the Ziegfeld, year after year. Inevitably the most successful were given the Hollywood treatment, rising to an ecstasy of spectacle typified in the MGM films directed by Busby Berkley.

The first inkling of the development of the late 20th century's vast entertainment conglomerates was made visible to far-sighted Hollywood executives by the logistics of producing and marketing musicals. Vastly expensive, the successful musical demanded a light and frothy narrative with witty dialogue, glamour, spectacular set-numbers and – ideally, at least – hit songs. All these components had to be found and what better way, given the complexities, than to source them from Broadway theatre and from radio, where ideas could be tried out and misjudgements and failure were less expensive.

Although many of the great musical films of the period were spectacular transfers from Broadway, a second group took as their subject tales of theatrical triumph on Broadway – for example Mickey Rooney and Judy Garland's *Babes On Broadway* (1941) or Eleanor Powell and Robert Taylor's *Broadway Melody* (1938). A numbers of others such as *Ziegfeld*

Girl (James Stewart, Judy Garland, Hedi Lamarr and Lana Turner) and *Rio Rita* are directly inspired by the exploits on Broadway of one of its greatest showman, Florenz Ziegfeld. MGM also produced *The Great Ziegfeld* starring William Powell, announcing "now, in one flashing musical comes all that the great Ziegfeld gave the world in his crowded lifetime! American girlhood glorified…great Ziegfeld stars…the melodies he made immortal…and a new 'Follies' with all the lavishness of Zeigfeld. You follow his fabulous private life…his tempestuous romance with Anna Held…his deep and ardent love for Billie Burke…All in MGM's biggest musical triumph!"

Musical posters and advertisements for Hollywood's musicals did not achieve the stylish daring of Parisian revue posters, however. Unlike the French poster designers of the inter-wars period, there are no distinguished individual practitioners catering to the Hollywood musical. The posters were, largely speaking, the anonymous product of publicity departments of the film studios. They were also constantly subject to interference from the distributors who insisted on posters carrying a profusion of details, including extravagant headlines. The poster designers relied on a traditional and somewhat humdrum iconography already established by vaudeville and circus posters. But although they worked within recognizable conventions, they successfully found ways to crystallize the complex message of storyline, hyperbole, and spectacle they were required to project. The posters were a combination of illustration and photography – photography being generally left to convey subsidiary

detail such as vignette portraits of the stars – usually firmly held in place by an architecture of lettering: "Remember the tune they were singing …the night we fell in love?" (George Stevens' *Penny Serenade* from Columbia, starring Irene Dunn and Cary Grant.) "Your dreams of perfection come true! Surpassing even their amazing *42nd Street*, Warner Bros. now bring you the magnificent climax of screen grandeur! See 'The Stairway to the Stars' and 6 other vast spectacle scenes! Learn 5 new song hits! Thrill to a fun-filled story!" (*Gold Diggers of 1933*). 20th Century-Fox produced *Down Argentine Way* starring Don Ameche, Betty Grable and Carmen Miranda. The poster revealed the film's "irresistible rhythms of Rhumbas and Congas! The glamorous spell of the Argentine! A cast of stars as brilliant as the Southern Cross! Show-stopping new personalities! Romance – the South American way!" Whilst at MGM they were serving up "Victor Herbert's greatest – the big musical of all time! A glamorous pageant of drama, mirth and beauty…mightier than any musical yet seen on the screen! You'll thrill to its glittering extravagance …you'll laugh at its bright comedy…and you'll cheer those new sweethearts, Jeanette MacDonald and Nelson Eddy, who found their love under a creole moon. It's the screen's musical masterpiece!" (*Naughty Marietta*, a W.S. Van Dyke production).

The various competing ways in which popular music was being brought into people's everyday lives in the early decades of the 20th century meant that the youthful record industry was far from having things its own way. As already indicated, it was slow to respond to the

Window card: "Gold Diggers of 1933".
Warner Bros/Vitaphone, 1933.

threat of radio. Although serious research had already begun as early as 1919 to develop a new generation of gramophones based on electrical, rather than mechanical, sound reproduction, the company at the heart of the research was not a gramophone manufacturer but the Bell Laboratories of American telephone company AT&T. Their research team led by Joseph P. Maxwell and Henry C. Harrison subjected every aspect of acoustic reproduction to scientific examination and by the mid-1920s they had surmounted all the engineering problems of an electrical gramophone. The turntable was now driven by an electric motor rather than a hand-wound mechanism. Not only was the quality of the gramophone's sound reproduction much improved, so was the level of amplification – for the first time recorded music could be played loud! Equally important, their research speeded the introduction of the microphone which allowed for revolution in the way in which recordings were made. When, in 1924, representatives of the Victor Talking Machine Company were given a preview of the results of the Bell Laboratories' work, they were not unduly impressed by what they heard and declined to adopt the new technology. By the following year, with record sales still falling, Victor was forced to undergo a change of mind. The company's adoption of recording by microphone and electrical amplification for its Victrola phonograph came only just in time to halt the precipitous fall in the company's sales. The improved technology adopted by Victor, and subsequently by Columbia and the rest of the industry, led to a boom in record sales during the latter half of the 1920s.

Even so, the Radio Corporation of America (RCA) was growing rapidly. By 1929 its annual production of radios had reached almost four million. Radio was in the ascendancy and the inevitable happened: Victor was taken over by RCA. This speeded the process by which recorded music became increasingly just one activity of the big media conglomerates that came into being during the following decades.

Victor's purchase by RCA did not come a moment too soon. The Wall Street collapse in October of that year heralded the Great Depression, and the market for records and phonographs collapsed. In a time of economic hardship the cost of buying records and replacement needles made the gramophone seem like an expensive and unwieldy means of listening to music in one's home, particularly when compared to radio, still a novelty and offering an ever-expanding choice of music, brought into the home for free. In the '30s radio was a much more important medium for popular musical entertainment than records, and reached a larger public than even Hollywood's prodigious output of films. Bing Crosby first appeared on radio in 1931, aged 28, and quickly rose to become America's most popular radio star. At the time he was contracted to the Brunswick record label but was later poached by the British label Decca, whose head, Edward Lewis, was ambitious to expand into the American market. It reflects the depressed state of the market for records in the mid-'30s that, although Bing Crosby was one of America's highest-selling recording artists and on an annual retainer of $40,000 from Decca, his earnings from radio and Hollywood were far greater.

As the Depression abated, record sales began to grow again, significantly aided by a new development: the growing number of jukeboxes installed in bars and restaurants. The jukebox had its roots in the coin-operated phonographs to be found in "phonograph parlours" across Europe and America in the last decades of the previous century. The most famous European parlour was Le Salon du Phonographie run by Pathe in the Boulevard des Italiens, Paris. Customers could sit at individual desks equipped with both listening and speaking tubes. Through the speaking tube the customer could order one of 1500 tunes to be played through the ear tubes from the library of cylinders stored in the room below.

Although the phonograph parlour was a successful idea for a while, it was soon superseded by the coin-operated mechanical piano which could be listened to without ear tubes and produced music of a volume sufficient to compete with the noise and bustle of bars and restaurants. Mechanical bands such as the Seeburg Solo Orchestrion and Wurlitzer's pneumatic Pianorchestra had entirely taken over from the phonograph parlours, and the earliest primitive coin-operated phonographs appeared by the end of the first decade of the 20th century. The engineering of mechanical orchestras was complex and most highly developed in America.

Once the initial technical problems of electrical amplification were overcome these industrial manufacturing skills were to be put to work to develop the coin-operated phonograph into what soon became the familiar visual extravagance of the jukebox.

Record sleeve:
Bluebird, 1928. [opposite top]

Record sleeve: London shop,
1930s. [opposite below]

Record sleeve:
Melotone, 1928.

For recorded music to take the fight to the coin-operated mechanical orchestras required the development of electrical amplification and reliable record-changing and playing mechanisms. By the late 1920s both these had been developed, and from then onwards there was a huge expansion in the market for jukeboxes which, in turn, increased the demand of records. The great names of jukebox manufacturing are all American: Seeburg, Rock-Ola, Wurlitzer, and AMI. Their machines are not only extraordinary from a mechanical point of view, they are also total style statements, the companies vying with one another to produce the most extravagantly decorated cabinets which are one of the glories of Art Deco design. Although they were considered standard equipment in most American bars and diners, they made little impact anywhere else before the end of World War II. A few, mostly second-hand, were imported into Britain in the late 1930s, but elsewhere the jukebox only made its appearance in the wake of American overseas forces.

RCA Victor rode out the Depression years comparatively unscathed in the care of the RCA radio business. Columbia was not so lucky. In 1926, Columbia had taken over OKeh (the Otto Heinemann Phonograph Corporation) whose catalogue included Mamie Smith, Clarence Williams, King Oliver, Louis Armstrong, Lonnie Johnson, Bix Beiderbecke, Frankie Trumbauer, Eddie Lang, and Bennie Moten. In 1934, Columbia and OKeh were bought by ARC-BRC (American Record Company-Brunswick Record Company). Once a serious competitor to RCA Victor, by the mid-1930s Columbia had become just one more label in the hands of a media

company called Consolidated Film. Edward Wallerstein, who had been head of record production at RCA Victor, persuaded William Paley, the head of the radio broadcaster CBS, to buy Columbia along with all Consolidated's other record production and make him the head of the label. Thus began the resurgence of Columbia. Edward Wallerstein's strategy at Columbia was comprehensive: produce high-quality recordings, modernize production, reduce the price of records and extend the company's catalogue. He began to sign the top jazz acts of the era, Count Basie, Duke Ellington, Benny Goodman, Woody Herman, Harry James and Billie Holiday among them. Columbia's roster soon also include Fred Astaire, Harry James, the Philadelphia Orchestra, the Budapest String Quartet, and more.

In 1940 Wallerstein's nose for innovation led him to be persuaded by Alex Steinweiss, Columbia's newly appointed head of design, to issue four 78 rpm records of *Smash Song Hits by Rodgers & Hart* as an album with a pictorial front cover. The marketing department was soon enthusing about Steinweiss's innovation. The sales of albums with his individually designed covers would go on to dramatically outstrip the sales of albums issued in Columbia's traditional plain covers. Such was Steinweiss's success that within a year the other two American major record companies – Decca and RCA Victor – were forced to follow suit and issue all albums with personalized covers, setting the scene for the story that this book tells: how design for music became inextricably linked to the album sleeve.

NEW ORLEANS JAZZ **KID ORY** AND HIS

CREOLE
• JAZZ •
• BAND •

COLUMBIA
records

flora

set C-126

copyright, 1947, columbia recording corporation

1940–49
The Birth of the Album Cover

New Orleans Jazz.
KID ORY, Columbia, 1947.
Design: Jim Flora.
[previous pages]

This is the Army.
ORIGINAL CAST,
Decca, c.1944.

The development of the recording industry in the 1940s is almost entirely an American story. While record sales in Europe were badly affected by World War II, in America they were on a steadily upward trend, both during the War and in the boom that followed its end. Between 1944 and 1946 sales tripled from $66 million to $200 million per annum, and that was despite disruptions caused by material shortages, disputes over copyright fees for composers, and strikes in aid of unemployed musicians put out of work by the talking movies. The big bands, which had been one of the mainstays of the recording industry in the late 1930s, continued to be enormously popular, particularly as the anchor for radio programmes. The Glenn Miller and Benny Goodman orchestras were two of the biggest selling recording acts of the War years. As the 1940s progressed other kinds of recording stars became increasingly important. The success of Frank Sinatra, who sold more records during the decade than any other artist, epitomized the increasing popularity of the solo vocalist. In the War's aftermath classical music, musicals like *Showboat*, latin music, congas and rumbas, barbershop melodies and, of course, jazz, were the increasingly important mainstays of the American record industry.

Europe and the European record industry was in a dire state in the immediate post-war period, laid low by the War's devastation. In contrast, America was the shining, glamorous personification of modernity. RCA Victor, Columbia and Decca were the "big three" of the US recording industry, although the decade saw the launch of new

Favorite Hawaiian Songs.
BING CROSBY, Decca, 1944.
Design: unknown.

The Voice of Frank Sinatra.
FRANK SINATRA,
Columbia, 1946.
Design: unknown.

competitors Capitol (1942), Mercury, and MGM Records (both in 1946). In 1945 Decca, the American subsidiary of British company EMI, which had been built up during the 1930s to become one of the big three, returned to American ownership as part of British war debt repayment (although EMI soon returned to America with the London record label and the subsequent purchase of Capitol in 1955). American recording artists, promoted through Hollywood films and American forces radio stations, dominated the international scene. A high percentage of all records sold in Europe were by US stars. When EMI issued Glen Miller's "Moonlight Serenade" in Britain after the War it sold nearly half a million copies.

The record company majors with international reach increasingly focussed their efforts on mainstream acts guaranteed to sell the greatest number of records. Such popular music made up 90% of all record sales, yet the increasing size of the overall market meant that there was room for numerous niche recording companies specializing in more experimental or esoteric forms of music, or aiming to promote regional talent. New forms of jazz, like bebop, more radical than the big band jazz of the wartime years, were being fostered in the inner cities of North America and western Europe. In Los Angeles, New York, Paris, London, and Berlin there were discerning bohemian audiences eager for the music of Dizzy Gillespie, Charlie Parker, and Stan Kenton. It little mattered whether those communities were just one aspect of a broader society at large, or based on a self-identified sense of difference, they created markets for innovative forms of music. And innovative forms of music led to different

Frankie.
FRANK SINATRA,
Columbia.
Design: unknown.

**A Presentation of
Progressive Jazz.**
STAN KENTON AND HIS
ORCHESTRA, Capitol, 1947.
Design: unknown.

styles of album covers designed to characterize the increasing range of musical genres which was becoming available, and – most important – to differentiate those different genres from one another before a note of the music on an album was ever heard.

Notable amongst the niche American record companies launched at this time specializing in jazz were Prestige, Blue Note, and Atlantic on the East Coast, Pacific Jazz, Contemporary, Clef and Norgran (later Verve), Emarcy, and Bethlehem on the West Coast. Such was the rate at which new record companies were being established that when Ahmet Ertegun was looking for a name for the new record company he was launching in New York he found that every name he tried to register had already been taken. He recalls: "I'd heard of a label that called themselves Pacific Jazz at that time. So in desperation, I said, 'Look, they call themselves Pacific, let's call ourselves Atlantic'".

Once Alex Steinweiss's perseverance at Columbia resulted in the launch of illustrated covers for record albums, the practice was soon universally adopted, in America at least. Although the design of these covers was to become an increasingly important issue for record companies, the designers who produced most of them were employed in their in-house design studios and their work, at least initially, was seen as an extension of the anonymous, artisan skills of printers. As a consequence, individual designers are almost never credited. The designers who produced covers for Columbia are an exception, mainly since they are instantly recognizable because of the individuality and consistency of

Sleeve and Label:
Atlantic Records, c.1948.
Design: unknown.

their styles. Partially for this reason – but also because of the importance Columbia placed on good design – many of the acknowledged pioneers of album cover design at work in the 1940s are associated with the company. Columbia had three accomplished art directors during the decade   Alex Steinweiss, Jim Flora, and Robert Jones. Other notable designers working for Columbia's design studio at the time were Sydney Butchkes, Jim Amos, and George Maas. Between them they created an array of styles appropriate to the label's extensive and varied catalogue.

Album cover design during the 1940s generally relied on illustration. Album designers drew on both music design's existing repertoire of styles and the wider traditions of poster and book design. The immense catalogue of compositional devices that the figurative and abstract painting of the inter-wars years had explored was also rapidly appropriated. One of the reasons why illustration was preferred to photography was that, for most forms of music, black-and-white photographs were considered too stark and documentary, certainly when used unadorned. The main exception to this prohibition on black-and-white photography was jazz where, towards the end of the decade, covers for the more progressive forms of jazz began to use documentary-style photographs of the recording artist captured in the milieu of the recording studio or the concert venue.

To circumvent black-and-white photography's perceived lack of glamour, on most forms of album sleeve they were used in conjunction with illustrative elements designed to soften the original, and to give

added colour. Photographs would often be a relatively minor element within the whole – and often under-printed with a tint to mellow the effect of the original black and white. The more prominent elements – figurative, symbolic, or abstract – were drawn. Typography was often treated in playful manner, as if to catch the music's syncopated rhythms; letter forms scattered across the cover, and undulating between the other graphic elements.

The 1940s brought two important technical innovations in the record business, the tape recorder which was to revolutionize the recording process, and the 33 rpm long-player microgroove record, which was to do the same for the marketing of recorded music. Again it was Edward Wallerstein's instinct for innovation that in 1948 led Columbia to launch the LP. For a while Columbia held the sole right to this technology but eventually it was adopted as a standard by all record companies. Not only did the lower revolutions per minute – 33⅓ rather than 78 – and the microgrooves of the LP allow for longer playing time, they were also pressed in vinylite plastic rather than in brittle shellac. Again Steinweiss, in his role as Columbia's design guru, was brought in to provide a design solution to the packaging of the new format. The first batch of records had been packaged in paper sleeves which had been too insubstantial to protect them from damage. After much experimenting, Steinweiss perfected the cardboard sleeve to which a wrap-round front and back cover printed on paper could be applied. Although this allowed LPs to have the same personalized sleeves that were now universal for the

Paganini, Concerto no 1 in D.
PARIS SYMPHONY
ORCHESTRA, RCA
Victor, 1940s.
Design: unknown.

D'Indy, Symphony No 2.
SAN FRANCISCO SYMPHONY
ORCHESTRA, RCA
Victor, 1940s.
Design: unknown.

albums of 78s, such was the rush to get the new format on the market that for its first series of releases the company reverted to the kind of generic sleeve design that Steinweiss thought he had banished for all time. Once properly launched, though, the LP brought about a rapid expansion in record buying. Its durability, convenience, and long playing time gave rise to the modern music industry, and it is from this point onwards that the story of design for music begins to take on the complexity with which we are familiar today.

1

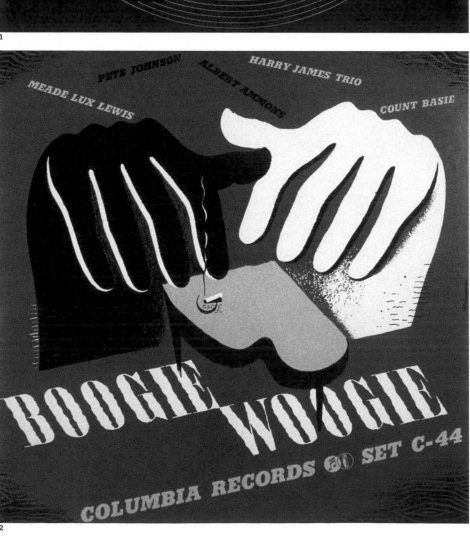

2

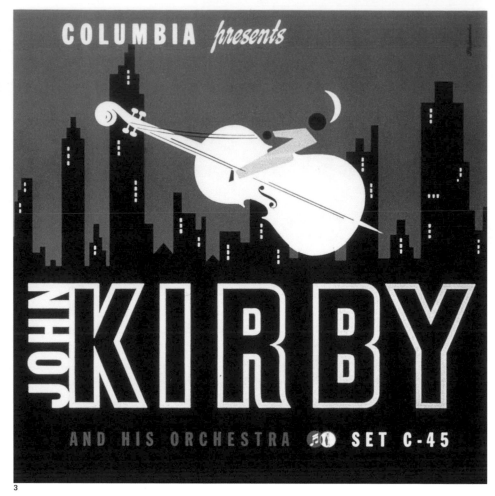

3

Alex Steinweiss was born in 1917 in Brooklyn. He was responsible for the invention of the personalized album cover and also one of the great pioneers of album sleeve design. As the art director for Columbia Records from 1939 until 1943, and later as a freelancer, he designed many hundreds of sleeves for Columbia. He also designed for numerous other record companies. In the late 1940s he devised the protective card sleeve for Columbia's first long-playing record, creating the packaging solution adopted by all the record companies. His designs are characterized by bold, simple forms and show the influence of 1930s French and German graphic arts. Steinweiss's later work of the 1950s draws on many sources, but notably the work of European abstract painters of the inter-war period.

In 1930 Steinweiss enrolled at the Abraham Lincoln High School where he had the good fortune to have his early interest in design fostered by Leon Friend who, in Steinweiss's own words "allowed me to discover a creative spark in myself that has always renewed itself". Friend, who was co-author of *Graphic Design* (1936), the first comprehensive book on modern American graphic design, taught a design program at the school. Among Steinweiss's contemporaries were future designers Gene Federico, Seymour Chwast and William Taubin. Collectively they were known as the "Art Squad" and they designed publications, posters and signs for the school. Friend laid great emphasis on technical accomplishment and an early Steinweiss creation

encouraged by him was a set of beautifully articulated marionettes.

In 1934 Steinweiss gained entry to the Parsons School of Design where, after a difficult start, he studied until 1937. On graduation, he found employment in the design studio of Joseph Binder. While working there, Steinweiss met Robert Leslie who owned a gallery which exhibited designers. Leslie so admired his design work he encouraged him to launch his own design practice. Subsequently he recommended him for the post of art director at Columbia Records, an opportunity Steinweiss was delighted to accept.

On moving to Bridgeport to begin work for Columbia, Steinweiss discovered that he was the only designer working for the company. As he remembered it, "When I came to Columbia I was 23 years old, and I had to do everything, and there were fifty jobs across my desk every week. Fifty jobs! Not done by a computer. Done by hand with pens and brushes and T-squares and triangles. You had to think and draw and paint all by hand. That took time, so most of the time I worked till midnight." The design work consisted of point-of-sale promotional material, posters and catalogues.

At this period albums – collections of three or four 78 r.p.m. records packaged together – were generally sold in plain covers in brown or grey with embossed gold lettering on the spines. Steinweiss's response was: "Listen guys! This is no way to sell beautiful music", and he was soon proposing to the head of Columbia, Edward Wallerstein, that albums should have illustrated covers to reflect

EVEREST
oody
oody
Prelude Ala Cha Cha
Love Song Ballad
Original #2
Bamba Samba
featuring "Summer Sequence"
Woody Herman and his orchestra with Charlie Byrd, guitar

their musical content. Although Wallerstein was the most innovative record company boss of the period, initially he was reluctant to bear the additional production costs that personalized covers for albums entailed. However, Steinweiss was given the chance to prove his point, and the marketing department was soon enthusing about his innovation. The sales of albums with individually designed covers by Steinweiss dramatically outstripped the sales of albums issued in the traditional plain covers. Steinweiss's first cover design was for *Smash Song Hits by Rodgers & Hart* issued in 1940. Such was the success of his pioneering design work for Columbia that within a year the other two American majors – Decca and RCA Victor – were forced to follow suit and issue all albums with personalized covers.

During World War II Steinweiss went to work for the US Navy Training Aids Development Center in New York, although he continued to freelance at Columbia at night. After the war he resumed his work for Columbia, now as a consultant. Among his other clients were National Distillery, Schenley Distributors, White Laboratories, *Print Magazine* and *Fortune*. In 1948 Wallenstein asked him to develop the packaging for the new long-playing 33 r.p.m. records that the company was developing. His design of a thin board sleeve lined with printed paper was to soon become the industry standard. As a freelancer, Steinweiss was able to work for clients other than Columbia, including other record companies.

Personnel changes at the top of Columbia and the departure from the company of his old colleagues Jim Flora and Bob Jones, and the appointment of Robert Vandervelde as the new art director, resulted in Steinweiss's gradual estrangement from the company in the early '50s. He continued to be much in demand as an album sleeve designer elsewhere throughout the decade. He undertook many hundreds of design assignments for the RCA, Decca, Remington and London labels. So prodigious was his output that he sometimes designed under the pseudonym "Piedra Blanca".

In 1958 he helped to launch Everest Records, taking responsibility for the label's art direction. He retained a strong commitment to hand-drawn illustration in his '50s output, although occasionally he incorporated photographic elements into his designs. He assimilated many influences, but was particularly attracted by the work of abstract artists such as Klee, Kandinsky and Mondrian.

However, improvements in photography and full-colour printing were gradually telling against Steinweiss's approach to sleeve design, and increasingly he found more reliable and lucrative employment for his design talents in other graphic fields. But, in addition to the sheer exuberance of his pioneering album sleeve designs, his lasting legacy was Columbia Record's commitment to inventive album design which was notably continued by art directors Bob Jones, S. Neil Fujita, Bob Cato and John Berg.

9

10

7 **Moody Woody**, WOODY HERMAN, Everest, 1959.
Design: Alex Steinweiss. [opposite]

8 **Stravinsky, Firebird Suite, Chant du Rossignol**, BERLIN RADIO SYMPHONY ORCHESTRA, Decca, 1954.
Design: Alex Steinweiss.

9 **Mozart, Piano Concerto no 21 and Piano Concerto no 17**, BERLIN PHILHARMONIC ORCHESTRA, Decca, 1954.
Design: Alex Steinweiss.

10 **Bing**, BING CROSBY, Decca Records, 1954.
Design: Alex Steinweiss.

11 **Music of George Gershwin**, ANDRE KOSTELANETZ AND HIS ORCHESTRA, Columbia, 1950.
Design: Alex Steinweiss.

8

11

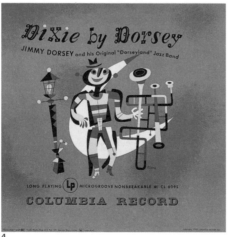

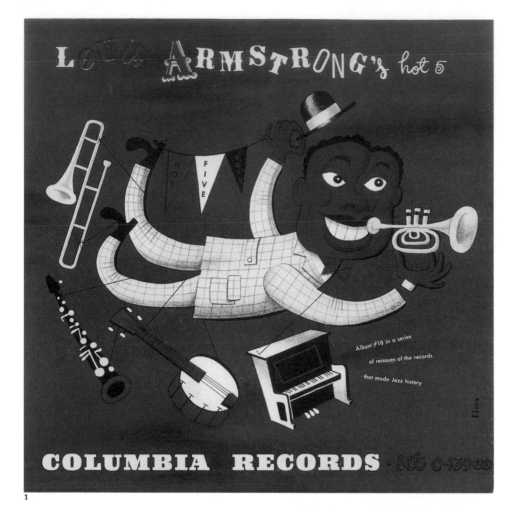

Jim Flora was born in 1914 in Bellefontaine, Ohio. Flora originally hoped to be an architect but he was unable to take up the scholarship he won in 1933 to attend the Boston Architectural League because he was unable to find a job to help support himself while studying. Having saved some money he was able to accept a place at the Art Academy of Cincinnati in the following year. During his summer vacations he worked as an assistant to the mural artist Carl Zimmerman who was to be a continuing influence. Flora completed his studies in 1939 and remained in Cincinnati working as a freelance illustrator and designer. He was a great jazz fan, and in 1942 his admiration for Columbia's jazz recordings led him to send Pat Dolan, the advertising manager at Columbia, a portfolio of cover designs inspired by the archive of jazz recordings that the company was then re-issuing. Dolan showed the portfolio to Alex Steinweiss. Steinweiss was still handling Columbia's design requirements more or less by himself and in urgent need of assistance in the design studio. They agreed that Flora's style complimented Steinweiss's own artistic proclivities, and Flora was duly hired to join Columbia's design studio in Bridgeport. His designs were such a success that Steinweiss soon assigned to him responsibility for Columbia's jazz and popular music output, retaining for himself responsibility for classical music.

Flora was not as versatile a designer as Steinweiss, his album sleeves always being based on his distinctive style of illustration. This was a decorative melange of semi-abstract painting styles – Klee, Miro, Kandinski – but given a comic book twist. It also owed something to the pre-Columbian, Aztec-influenced wing of the Mexican muralist tradition that he had come to admire though the mentor of his student years, Carl Zimmerman. Flora's light-hearted, but knowing, take-a-line-for-a-walk style of illustration was very influential, and it was one of the acknowledged inspirations for the styling of the Mr Magoo and Gerald McBoing Boing animated film cartoons.

In 1943 Steinweiss left Columbia to undertake war work for the Army and it was not long before Flora had taken over from him as company art director. Unusually Flora was both a great designer and a good company man, so it was no surprise that he was offered Pat Dolan's old job and moved up to become advertising manager and subsequently Columbia's sales promotion manager. His old post as art director was given to Bob Jones. In his new role of advertising manager, Flora's work became increasingly involved with executive decisions about Columbia's publicity budget, and he had less and less to do with hands-on design. Tired of his new role, he eventually resigned in 1950, taking a sabbatical of more than a year, living in Taxco, Mexico, where he devoted himself to his painting. On his return to Connecticut he set about establishing himself as a freelance illustrator. During this period he produced both covers and many other illustrations for *Fortune* magazine.

In 1953 his old friend from his days at Columbia, Bob Jones, who had resigned from Flora's art director's post not long after his own departure,

was appointed art director at RCA Victor in 1953. By the following year he was commissioning Flora to produce album sleeve designs for the company. Jones gave Flora complete license to design as he wished, and he produced some of his most outstanding work during the two years that this arrangement lasted. But finally his style, although still popular, began to fall out of fashion, and the tide was turning against album sleeve design based on illustration. RCA Victor's executives sent an emissary to Jones instructing him to commission more photography-based design, not Flora. The marketing departments of record companies were increasingly preferring the graphic portraiture and wider possibilities that photography provided to promote their recording artists. And some of the striking photographic documentary sleeves being produced by other designers were beginning to make Flora's zany cartoonisms look dated. Flora designed his last record sleeve in 1956; it was time for him to apply his talents to other fields, and children's books could not have been a better choice. He wrote and illustrated seventeen books for children between 1954 and 1982. At the same time he also fulfilled a constant stream of commissions from magazines and newspapers for illustrations. He retired to devote his time to painting in the early '80s, a pursuit he was still actively engaged in at the time of his death in 1998.

1   **Louis Armstrong's Hot 5**, LOUIS ARMSTRONG, Columbia, 1947.
    Design and illustration: Jim Flora.
2   **Collaboration**, SHORTY ROGERS AND ANDRE PREVIN, RCA Victor, 1955.
    Design and illustration: Jim Flora.
3   **Music of the Bonampak Mexican Ballet**, RCA Victor, 1954.
    Design and illustration: Jim Flora.
4   **Dixie by Dorsey**, JIMMY DORSEY, Columbia, 1949.
    Design and illustration: Jim Flora.
5   **Mambo for Cats**, VARIOUS ARTISTS, RCA Victor, 1955.
    Design and illustration: Jim Flora. [opposite]

Mambo For CATS

RCA VICTOR
LPM-1063
A "NEW ORTHOPHONIC" HIGH FIDELITY RECORDING

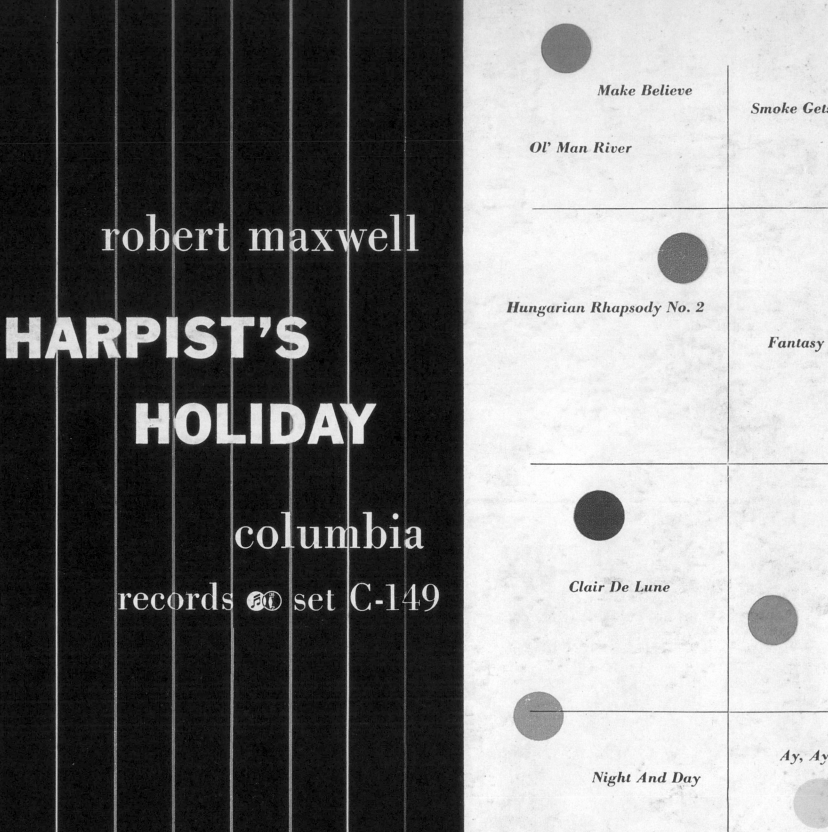

robert maxwell

HARPIST'S HOLIDAY

columbia

records set C-149

Make Believe

Ol' Man River

Smoke Gets In Your Eyes

Who?

Hungarian Rhapsody No. 2

Fantasy On Chopsticks

Clair De Lune

Harping On A Harp

Night And Day

Ay, Ay, Ay

In terms of album sleeve design, Columbia was the most innovative of the big American record companies through the 1940s. As we have already seen, it pioneered individual designs for the covers of albums, and developed the 33 r.p.m. LP microgroove record towards the end of the decade. These initiatives provided Columbia's design studio with an ever increasing work load, particularly the re-issuing of much of the company's catalogue in the LP format. Towards the end of the war there was a considerable period when record production was severely restricted by the redirection of shellac to the military effort followed by a prolonged musicians' strike that lasted a year and a half. When Columbia's design studio finally began to get busy again art director Jim Flora began to hire designers, with Bob Jones and Jim Amos being among the first. The now-freelance Alex Steinweiss also returned to design for the company. Eventually Flora accepted promotion to advertising manager, and was replaced in his old job by Bob Jones. Jones, who had been recruited from a design post at *Life* magazine, ran the design office for the rest of the decade and also designed sleeves for many of the company's

popular music and jazz releases of the period. Jim Amos, Sydney Butchkes and George Maas also made important contributions to the company's design output during the second half of the decade. Although more designers than ever were now working for the company – there were six designers by the time long player records were first marketed – the design studio still maintained a cohesive style, under Jones's watchful eye, largely continuing the Steinweiss tradition based on bold, drawn illustration, geometrical abstract designs and the inventive use of typography.

Jones was born in 1913 in Goff, Kansas. His childhood was spent in Salt Lake City and he later moved to San Francisco to study at the California School of Fine Art. After his studies he returned to Salt Lake City where he had a number of different jobs, taking whatever employment he could find, however vaguely related to design. He worked in the publicity office of a department store and took photographs for a newspaper called the *Desert News*. In 1939 he was employed to organize the exhibition programme at the Salt Lake City Art Center funded by the Roosevelt-inspired Works Progress Administration of the Department of

Employment. In 1941 he got the break he had been waiting for and left for New York and a design post at *Life* magazine. However, the war began almost immediately, interrupting his employment at *Life*, and he was drafted into the army where he spent the next two years designing information and publicity material. He returned to *Life* magazine in 1944 but was almost immediately recruited to Columbia Records.

Jones remained at Columbia until 1950, when he cut his links with the company and his role was taken over by Robert Vandervelde. Jones went freelance, undertaking some album sleeve design, particularly for Decca, and worked extensively on magazine design.

In 1953 he joined Columbia's great competitor, RCA Victor, as art director, a post he held until his retirement in the mid-1970s. Throughout most of his career Bob Jones devoted his spare time to his private publishing venture Glad Hand Press, which specialized in high-quality limited editions through which he was free to indulge his lifelong love of typography, a subject on which he continued to publish and lecture on during his retirement. Jones died in 1993.

1   **Harpist's Holiday**, ROBERT MAXWELL, Columbia, 1947.
Design: Sydney Butchkes. [opposite]

2   **Sextet Sessions**, BENNY GOODMAN, Columbia, 1946.
Design: George Maas.

3   **Boogie Woogie**, VARIOUS ARTISTS, Columbia, 1947.
Design: Bob Jones.

4   **You're My Thrill**, DORIS DAY, Columbia, 1949.
Design: Bob Jones.

5   **Songs by Sinatra**, FRANK SINATRA, Columbia, 1947.
Design: Sydney Butchkes.

6   **Duchin Plays Tchaikovsky**, EDDY DUCHIN,
Columbia, 1948.
Design: Jim Amos.

2

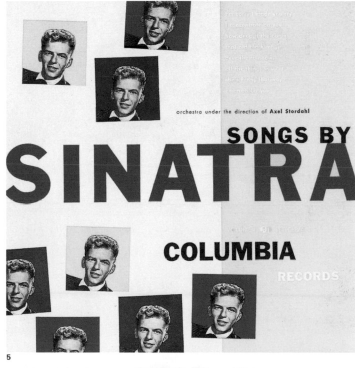

5

3

4

6

Gene Vincent
and his blue caps

BLUEJEAN BOP!

1950–59
The Pioneering Years of Album Sleeve Design

Blue Jean Bop!
GENE VINCENT AND HIS
BLUE CAPS, Capitol, 1956.
Design: unknown.
[previous pages]

**Beethoven, Sonata no 14 in
C Sharp Minor.**
RUDOLF SERKIN,
Columbia, 1950s.
Design: unknown.

Chicago Style Jazz.
VARIOUS ARTISTS,
Columbia, 1955.
Design and illustration:
Ben Shahn.

The catalyst which led to the following decade being a period of rapid change and innovation in album cover design was the launch of the LP at the very end of the 1940s. It was a period when the album sleeves of some key genres of music – particularly classical music, rock'n'roll and jazz – began to assume more distinctive iconographies.

At the start of the 1950s the world record industry was still very much dominated by the American market, and here RCA Victor, Columbia, and Decca were still the "big three", although second tier companies such as Capitol, Mercury, Atlantic, and MGM Records were growing fast. In fact, by 1955 the "big three" had become "the big four" with Capitol (now the American arm of British record company EMI) joining the major league. What is more, the second tier companies were introducing new forms of music to mainstream audiences – country music and new forms of jazz, then rhythm & blues and rock'n'roll – and, in the process, taking a larger and larger slice of overall sales. Such was the climate of competition that in 1953 CBS launched Epic Records in direct competition with Columbia, its existing label. Epic specialized in up-market jazz and classical music, and its bright-yellow and black "Radical Sound" logo was a sign of the unease of the major record companies at their slipping market share.

The early years of the 1950s were still the heyday of album sleeve illustration: both the stylized pictograms typical of designers like Steinweiss and Flora, who were both still very active in the first half of the decade, and the characterful line drawings of the likes of Ben Shahn, David Stone Martin, Pauline Annon, and Burt Goldblatt. Technical

Wizard of the Vibes.
MILT JACKSON,
Blue Note, 1952.
Design: unknown.

B.G. in Hi-Fi.
BENNY GOODMAN,
Capitol, 1955.
Design: unknown.

developments and changing aesthetic fashion were to have a major effect on album sleeve design over the decade. The growing preference for photography over illustration in all branches of graphic design was, to some extent, an indication of technical advances, both in photography itself and also in full-colour off-set printing. But the preference also reflected a growing appreciation of photography's ability to project, unmediated by the illustrator's hand, a recording artist's persona. What is more, clever photographers were able to convey the nuances of the record artist's musical proclivities as part of that persona. Album sleeve design articulated around hand-drawn motifs largely drawing on the traditions of poster and book illustration, and the vocabulary of recent styles of painting began to fall out of fashion. In its place emerged design solutions more orientated towards the photographic image, created by a new generation of designers. The gradual change-over from illustration to photography-based design can readily be traced in the work of those designers, such as Burt Goldblatt, who were willing, and able, to adapt. Those LP sleeve designers for whom illustration was implicit to their way of working, such as Jim Flora, found themselves gradually squeezed out.

It was the designers of jazz album sleeves who first adopted black-and-white photography. The moody, stark documentary qualities of photographs by the likes of Francis Wolff and Bill Claxton were a particularly apt reflection of the underground and "authentic" reputation of jazz. Their photographs were a potent starting point for those sleeve designers able to make a virtue of the limitations of black-and-white

Provocative Percussion Vol. III.
VARIOUS ARTISTS,
Command, 1959.
Design: Josef Albers.

Jazz for Moderns.
DUANE TATRO,
Contemporary, 1955.
Design: unknown.

photography and a restricted palette of additional colours. The 1950s became the great period of jazz album sleeve design in which the daring and inventive integration of photographs and typography led to what the celebrated Blue Note album sleeve designer Reid Miles termed "the period of the renaissance of type". Although Miles's designs for Blue Note in the second half of the 1950s and the early '60s were extremely influential, he was far from alone in creating visual magic out of such apparently limited means.

Designers Reid Miles, Bill Claxton, David Stone Martin, Burt Goldblatt, and their like made the '50s a golden age of jazz album sleeve design. And yet it should not be concluded that their work was typical of the period. Although the decade saw a ferment of LP sleeve experimentation, the great majority of covers were conservative adaptations of existing formats. Despite this tendency, especially notable at the major record companies, there was a recognition that variety in the visual appearance of album covers played an important role in differentiating the growing range of musical genres from one another. As the decade proceeded, this enlarged design vocabulary became more settled and there was an increasing tendency to corral designers within the newly defined conventions for commercial reasons. It is worth noting, for instance, that Rudolph de Harak, designing for Columbia in the early '50s, was free to insert the company's name in a typeface he felt to be appropriate to the rest of a cover design, rather than required to use a fixed corporate logo. Such an idea would be unthinkable by the end of the decade. Much in-

Kismet.
THE MASTERSOUNDS,
World Pacific, 1958.
Photography: William Claxton.
Design: Hap Crippen.

**Brahms, Symphony no 4
in E Minor.**
LONDON SYMPHONY
ORCHESTRA, Decca, 1950s.
Design: unknown.

house design was undertaken by anonymous designers perfectly happy to work to fairly undemanding formulae, including pasting lettering on to studio, or alfresco, portrait photographs. Such design solutions were efficient, low cost and, although not adventurous, in retrospect had a directness which gives them considerable period charm.

The growing perception of the need to enhance the point-of-sale impact of album sleeves was one more reason why illustration lost out to photography. In fact, those branches of album sleeve design which did not succumb to the advance of photography became ever more esoteric, reflecting increasingly austere aesthetic influences. The influential Swiss modernist style of graphic design, which can be seen at work in the elegant early '50s designs for Decca of Swiss-born Erik Nitsche, placed an emphasis on a refined formalism (characterized by the popularity of the sans-serif typeface Helvetica), and a propensity for using letter forms as an important component of its abstract language. From the mid-'50s on this school of design was also increasingly inflected – in America at least – with the pervasive influence of the New York school of abstract painting. In time this would develop into a kind of album sleeve classicism, of which the work of Ivan Chermayeff is a distinctive example. The subtlety of this restricted design vocabulary did not appeal to the record companies where marketing was becoming an ever-more influential consideration and record covers were seen as an opportunity for a hard sell. The strategy that Paul Huf pioneered for Philips of featuring a glossy, full-colour photograph of a glamourous fashion model as the dominant pictorial

Rock and Rollin'.
FATS DOMINO, London, 1956.
Design: unknown.

element began to be adopted everywhere. Photography-based sleeve design increasingly conformed to a picture-centre and text-periphery oppositional model. To be sure, refined formalism and inventive typography continued to occur in album sleeve design through the subsequent decades, but mainly it graced the covers of classical music, experimental jazz, and other "difficult" forms of music. This marked a significant parting of the ways for high modernist design and design for album sleeves, with the latter increasingly inclined towards overly overt and rumbustious forms of image-heavy design.

As already noted, photographic film technology was in a state of constant improvement during the '50s. This was particularly true of colour photographic stock which was becoming increasingly flexible, reliable, and affordable. Colour photography was perceived to be a more glamorous medium than black-and-white photography, and appropriate to a wider range of album sleeve genres. Allied to the increasing prevalence of full-colour separation printing, full-colour photography was gradually to eclipse black-and-white photography in album sleeve design as the decade proceeded. The connotations of early colour photography were entirely different from those of black-and-white photography. Gone was the mystic and moody, "documentary" feel of the monochrome image. Early full-colour album sleeves tended to have pastel colours, little chiaroscuro, and an informal snapshot-like air. This type of photography has become particularly associated with the jazz musicians of America's West Coast. The consequences of the switch from black-and-white to

Tchaikovsky, Symphony no 5.
THE PHILHARMONIC
SYMPHONY ORCHESTRA OF
NEW YORK, Philips, 1956.
Photography: Paul Huf
Design: Herry van
Borssum Waalkes.

Gettin' Together.
ART PEPPER,
Contemporary, 1960.
Photography: Roger Marschutz.
Design: Guidi/Tri-Arts.

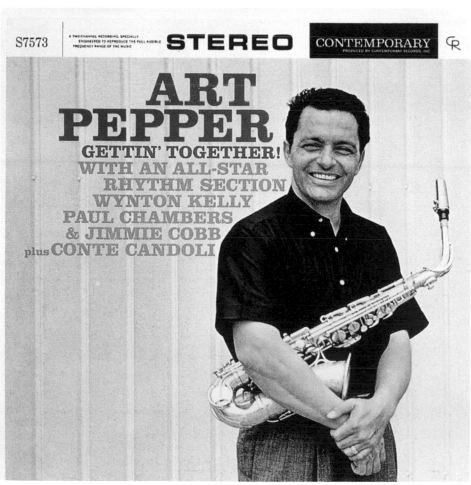

colour can be clearly seen played out in the development of Bill Claxton's photography for Pacific Jazz. Whereas his black-and-white photographs are moody and elegiac – attributes pre-eminently crystallized in his photographs of Chet Baker – once he adopted colour photography his photographs invariably took on a sunlit, anodyne, and faintly suburban aura.

Although many of the "informal" album covers of this period seem artless now, at the time this artlessness served the purpose of promising that the music contained within the sleeve would be consonant with the aspirations of an increasingly affluent peace-time society, where relaxation and the devotion of time and money to recreational activities was an everyday possibility. The record business was, after all, a recreational industry and it sought to reflect the ideals of a leisured lifestyle and stress the casual, relatively unstructured activities of time-off. As far as America was concerned – and this was chiefly an American phenomenon – the final flowering of this "informal" style occurred on the West Coast surfer albums of the early 1960s. As we shall see, these covers usually featured informal group portraits shot on the beach with little artifice. Bands like The Beach Boys were casually posed, accompanied by their surfboards and the other accoutrements of the sport. What would consign the "informal" cover photograph to the sleeves of low-cost compilation albums would be the worldwide arrival of British pop from 1963 onwards, which raised album sleeve design to new heights of symbolic sophistication.

1

2

1 **Boogie Woogie Classics**, ALBERT AMMONS, Blue Note, 1952.
Design and illustration: Paul Bacon.

2 **Jazz Classics Vol 2**, SIDNEY BECHET, Blue Note, 1954.
Design and illustration: Paul Bacon.

Francis Wolff was born in 1907 in Germany. With Alfred Lion, he managed the Blue Note record label through its life as an independent company. A trained photographer, he chronicled the working lives of Blue Note musicians from 1939 to 1967. His photographs are a vivid record of their world. Important jazz musicians recording for Blue Note over the period included Fats Navarro, Clifford Brown, Lou Donaldson, Herbie Hancock, and Jimmy Smith. Blue Note album sleeves were largely responsible for creating the visual look of East Coast bebop and hard bop, and many of Wolff's photographs were used as a central element in their design.

Wolff came from a well-to-do, cosmopolitan Jewish background in Berlin. He met his future partner at Blue Note, Alfred Lion, in the early 1920s. The two young men went into partnership in a jewellery business but it was not a success and Lion left to work in Chile, later moving to New York where eventually he launched the Blue Note record company. Meanwhile Wolff, who had studied photography, established a career as a photographer but was eventually forced to leave Germany in 1939 as a consequence of the Nazi

terror increasingly directed against the Jewish community. He sailed in the last ship bound for New York, and took up residence in Lion's apartment. He was soon working as a manager for the infant Blue Note label, and became the company's in-house photographer.

Blue Note effectively ceased its operation for the duration of the War, but after the armistice recording began again under the watchful eye of producer Ike Quebec, and took off rapidly with the arrival of the LP Blue Note is particularly associated with bebop jazz stars such as Thelonious Monk and Bud Powell, and later with the hard bebop of Horace Silver and Art Blakey. The label was a small-scale operation and most of their releases sold only a few thousand copies. Everything was done on a shoestring budget, and most of the initial photographic material for the company's album sleeves was supplied by Wolff. Two important early designers employed by Blue Note were John Hermansader and Paul Bacon. A sometime trumpet player, Hermansader met Wolff and Lion when he was chairman of the Hot Club of Newark for which he edited a magazine called *Jazz Notes*. He subsequently began to design

covers for Blue Note in the late 1940s, as did his friend Bacon. Bacon then went on to become a distinguished art director for the Riverside record label. Meanwhile, Hermansader continued to design for Blue Note, having established a studio after returning to New York City from a spell in Memphis in the early 1950s. Such was the pressure of work that he took on Reid Miles as an assistant in 1952. Miles became increasingly involved in the design of Blue Note sleeves, and when he left Hermansader's studio for a job with *Esquire* magazine he effectively took the Blue Note account with him. Miles had demonstrated to Lion and Wolff that he had the perfect design outlook for their label, and they were happy from then on to depend on him for the design of almost all of their releases. Although Hermansader continued to design for many clients, increasingly he devoted himself to his interest in abstract painting.

Francis Wolff continued to take photographs, although he stopped completely when Alfred Lion retired in 1967. He continued his association with the Blue Note label as a record producer until his death in 1971.

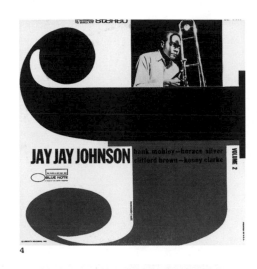

4

5

3 **The Jazz Messengers at the Café Bohemia Volume 2**,
THE JAZZ MESSENGERS, Blue Note, 1955.
Design: John Hermansader. Photography: Francis Wolff.

4 **The Eminent Jay Jay Johnson Vol 2**, JAY JAY JOHNSON,
Blue Note, 1956.
Design: John Hermansader. Photography: Francis Wolff.

5 **Modern Jazz Series Vol 2**, HOWARD McGHEE,
Blue Note, 1953.
Design: John Hermansader. Photography: Francis Wolff.

3

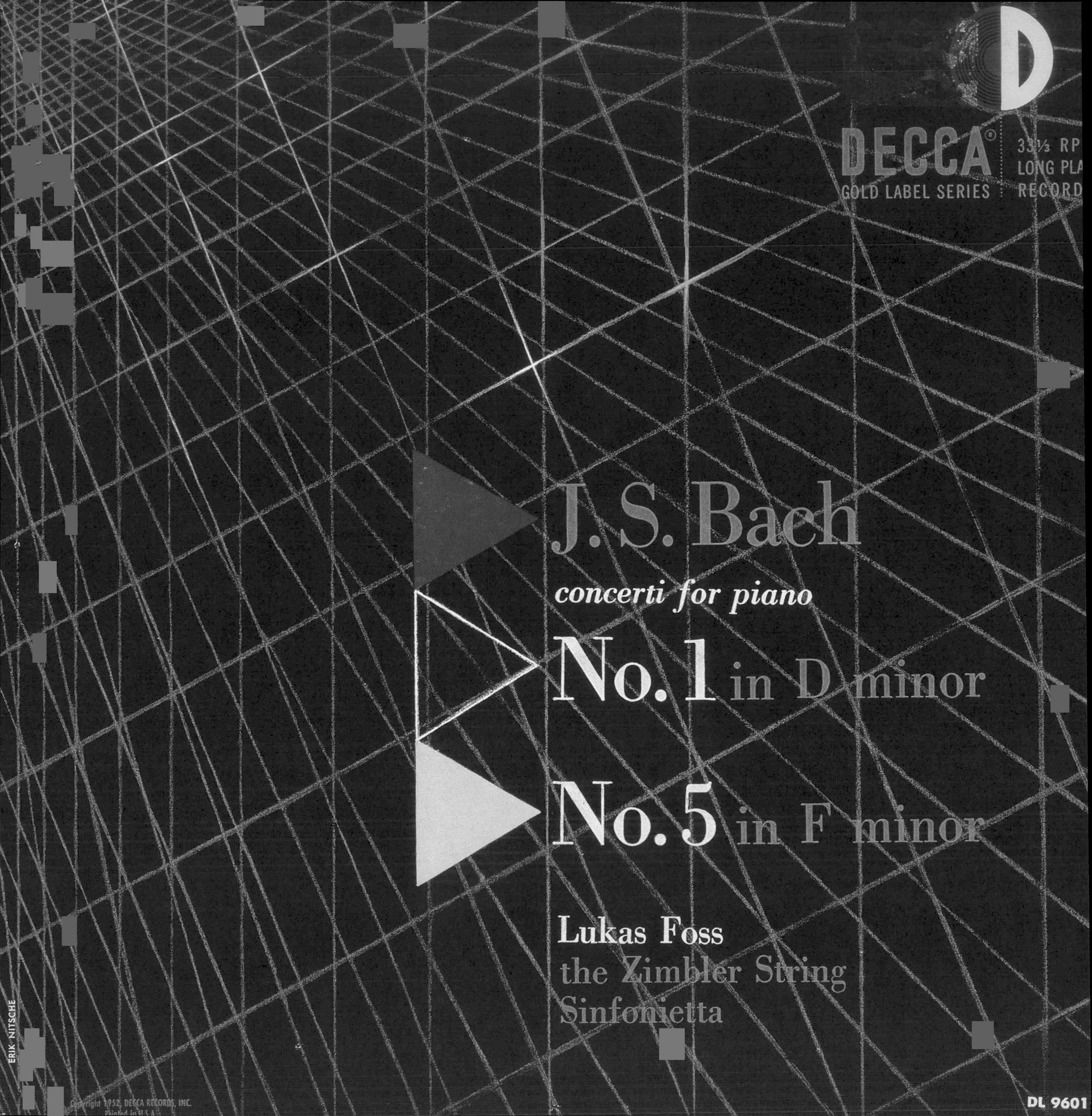
DECCA®
GOLD LABEL SERIES
33⅓ RP
LONG PLA
RECORD
J.S. Bach
concerti for piano
No. 1 in D minor
No. 5 in F minor
Lukas Foss
the Zimbler String
Sinfonietta
ERIK NITSCHE
Copyright 1952, DECCA RECORDS, INC.
DL 9601

ERIK NITSCHE

DECCA
GOLD LABEL SERIES | 33⅓ RPM
LONG PLAY
RECORDS

schubert

sonata in A minor, opus 42

valses nobles, opus 77

Lili Kraus, piano

MONTEVERDI

Vocal and Instrumental Ensemble

under the direction of NADIA BOULANGER

CHARPENTIER

excerpts from MÉDÉE

NADIA BOULANGER

Richard *Tauber* Favorites

DL 8518

2

1 **J.S. Bach, Concerti No 1 and No 5,** LUKAS FOSS, THE
ZIMBLER STRING SINFONIETTA, Decca, 1952.
Design: Erick Nitsche. [opposite]

2 **Schubert, Sonata in A Minor, Valses Nobles,**
LILI KRAUS, Decca, 1951.
Design and illustration: Erik Nitsche.

3 **Monteverdi,** VOCAL AND INSTRUMENTAL STRING
ENSEMBLE DIRECTED BY NADIA BOULANGER, Decca, 1951.
Design: Erik Nitsche.

4 **Marc-Antonie Charpentier, Excerpts from Médée,**
VOCAL AND INSTRUMENTAL STRING
ENSEMBLE DIRECTED BY NADIA BOULANGER, Decca, 1953.
Design: Erik Nitsche.

5 **Favorites,** RICHARD TAUBER, Decca, 1952.
Design: Erick Nitsche.

The Swiss-American designer Erik Nitsche was
born in 1908 in Lausanne, Switzerland. In a
varied and highly successful design career, his
contribution to album sleeve design came from
a commission by Decca to redesign their
Masterworks series that the company was
reissuing on the new LP format. Such was the
success of this original commission that he went
on to redesign Decca's entire classical catalogue,
producing in all over three hundred album sleeves
for the company over the space of three years from
1951 to 1954.

Nitsche studied at the College Classique in
Lausanne and then at the Kunstgewerbeschüle
in Munich, Germany. In Paris he studied with
Maximilien Vox and worked with the Draeger
Frères printing firm from 1929 to 1932. He moved
to America in 1934, where his distinctive approach
to design quickly brought him success. He
established a studio in Ridgefield, Connecticut,
and soon had an extensive list of clients and was
producing layouts and covers for fashion and
lifestyle magazines, including *Harper's Bazaar,*
Vogue, Fortune, House Beautiful, Town & Country,
Vanity Fair, and *Arts & Decoration.* He became art

director for Saks Fifth Avenue in 1938, also
working for other stores including Bloomingdale's,
Ohrbach's and Macy's. He supervised national
advertising campaigns for Douglas Aircraft and
Rolls Razor and designed packaging for Revlon.
After the war a spell as art director of *Record
Review,* published by RCA Victor, brought him into
contact with the record industry. When he landed
the Decca Masterwork commission he was
working on advertising campaigns for 20th
Century Fox, producing publicity material for *All
About Eve* and *No Way Out.*

Decca's commission to Nitsche marks the first
attempt by a record company to use album sleeve
design to provide brand coherence to a particular
musical form. Nitsche's album sleeves not only
differentiated Decca's classical music output from
all its other album releases, it also distinguished it
from its competitors' recordings. Nitsche was well
chosen for the task. The signature style of abstract
forms and integrated typographical elements that
he developed for Decca reflects the virtues of his
Swiss Modernist design training. He was extremely
good at turning the lexicon of European abstract
painting – Klee, Kandinsky, Miro, Mondrian – into

decorative arabesques. His work was elegant,
measured, playful, and inventive, yet across the
series he retained the sense of a unified design
sensibility to a remarkable degree.

During his time working for Decca he continued
to work for other clients, most notably for the
Museum of Modern Art for which he acted as a
consultant co-ordinating the design of publicity
displays and publications. By 1954 he was
becoming increasingly occupied with design
for General Dynamics. In 1955 the company
appointed him as design consultant and his work
for Decca ceased. Over the following ten years
Nitsche concentrated his formidable design skills
on honing the corporate identity of General
Dynamics, and in particular produced their
memorable poster campaign "Atoms for Peace".
His job there was terminated in 1964 following the
death of company president, Frank Pace Jr. From
then on he undertook many freelance commissions,
focussing on book design. He also designed more
than twenty postage stamps, not least a series on
"The Romance of Stamp Collecting". He was
elected to the Art Directors' Hall of Fame in 1996,
and he died in 1998.

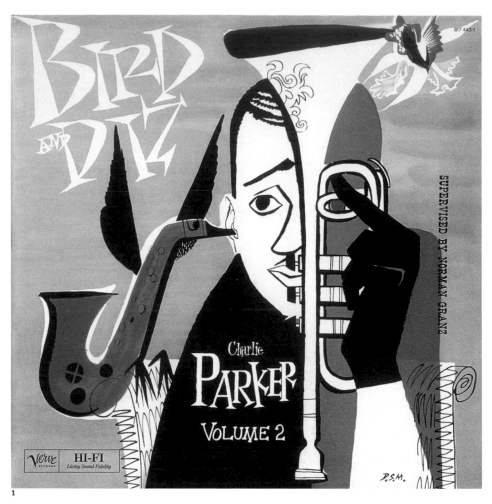

1 **Bird and Diz**, CHARLIE PARKER, Verve, 1955.
Design and illustration: David Stone Martin.

2 **Jamming with the Greats, New Volume 4**, VARIOUS
ARTISTS, Columbia, 1953.
Design and illustration: David Stone Martin.

David Stone Martin was born 1913 in Chicago. He is celebrated for his blotted ink line drawing technique. The fast, fluid ease of his drawings is highly evocative of the jazz milieu and during the 1950s he produced some of the most subtle images of jazz's most glamorous era. His drawing style was much imitated and an important influence on (among others) the early work of Andy Warhol.

Martin graduated from the Art Institute of Chicago in 1935. In 1940 while undertaking a commission for CBS he met artist Ben Shahn who became an important influence. Ben Shahn had been an assistant to Diego Rivera when he was painting his monumental mural for the RCA building at the Rockefeller Centre, New York. Shahn persuaded Martin to move to Jersey Homesteads, an artists' colony established through Roosevelt's New Deal support for the arts. They both worked for the Art Department of the Office of War Information during World War II, producing several important government advertising campaigns. Shahn went on to develop a successful career as artist, designer and photographer and himself designed many album sleeves for folk and classical music.

Martin was awarded his first commission to design an album cover in 1944 through his friendship with jazz pianist Mary Lou Williams, who recorded for the small Asch label. Asch Records was run by Moses Asch, born in Warsaw in 1905, the son of the Jewish author, Sholem Asch. Asch's chief interests were folk music and

jazz. He released records by members of the left-wing folk music movement such as Woody Guthrie, Pete Seeger, Leadbelly and Burl Ives. Jazz was represented by the likes of James P. Johnson and Coleman Hawkins, as well as Williams. Asch liked Martin's work so much he appointed him art director for the label. Unfortunately the job did not last long. In 1947 Asch tried to expand his company into the mainstream and he signed Nat King Cole on an expensive contract. It was too much for the strained finances of the company and it went bankrupt (although Asch went on to launch his famous Folkways record company).

Martin's work for Moses Asch had brought him to the attention of jazz impresario Norman Granz whose series of "Jazz at the Philharmonic" recordings were issued through Asch. In 1948 Granz launched his own record company Clef, and he invited Martin to become art director for the company. Granz launched a second label called Norgran for which Martin also designed sleeves. Subsequently Clef and Norgran were amalgamated to form Verve, again with Martin as art director. Granz had originally worked in the Hollywood film industry and in 1951 he moved the company's headquarters to Los Angeles. Martin followed, living on the West Coast until 1955. He worked for Verve throughout the '50s, always on a freelance basis so that he was free to work for other clients. He designed for other record labels, notably Atlantic, RCA Victor, Mercury and Dial, and also undertook work for a wide range of other show business and publishing clients, including the

magazines *Life* and *Time*. He designed over two hundred record sleeves during the decade, and his close association with Verve only ended in 1960 when Granz sold the company to MGM. As with Flora, the move away from illustration as the mainstay of record cover design meant that from the late 1950s onwards Martin's talents were increasingly used in other spheres. He also taught at Parson's School of Design and the Art Student's League for a spell in the mid-1960s. He was working on a series of portraits of musicians when he died in 1993.

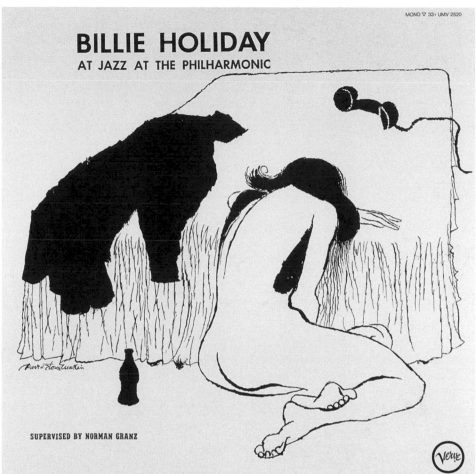

3 **Lester Young Trio**, LESTER YOUNG, Norgran Records, 1955.
Design and illustration: David Stone Martin.

4 **Oscar Peterson at Carnegie**, OSCAR PETERSON, Verve, 1950.
Design and illustration: David Stone Martin.

5 **Billie Holiday at Jazz at the Philharmonic**, BILLIE
HOLIDAY, Verve, 1952.
Design and illustration: David Stone Martin.

1 **Solo Flight**, ERROLL GARNER, Columbia, 1952.
   Design: Rudolph de Harak.

2 **Benny Goodman Combos**, BENNY GOODMAN,
   Columbia, 1951.
   Design: Rudolph de Harak.

1

2

Rudolph de Harak was born in 1924 in Culver City, California. In the late 1940s he was founding member of the Los Angeles Society for Contemporary Designers along with Saul Bass, Alvin Lustig and Lou Danziger. In 1950 he moved to New York and became one of the post-Steinweiss designers at Columbia who helped to steer a new direction for the company's album sleeve design output in the early '50s. It was a style which featured bold typography and abstract forms, and where photography increasingly supersceded illustration. Despite his innovative work for Columbia, de Harak found it increasingly difficult to earn a living and in 1952 he began to teach design at Cooper Union. By 1954 he had ceased to design for Columbia. His career improved markedly in the latter half of the decade, and he produced many sleeve designs for niche labels specializing in jazz, particularly Circle and Westminster for which he designed over fifty sleeves. By the 1960s he had established himself as an accomplished book cover designer, and his work for McGraw-Hill is particularly notable.

The end of de Harak's time designing for Columbia coincided with the arrival of a new art director at the company, S. Neil Fujita. Fujita was born in Hawaii of Japanese parents and had pursued a career as a designer in Philadelphia before being recruited by Columbia. He was appointed at a time of considerable change in the art department following differences between Columbia and its parent company CBS about the company's future direction. A subsequent shake-up had resulted in CBS launching a new label, Epic, in 1953 to search out new talent and which took on Chermayeff, Brownjohn and Geismar to design many of its album sleeves. The onus was clearly on Columbia to be more innovative itself.

During his time with the company Fujita continued to take design in the direction initiated by de Harak. He continued to wean the design studio off the illustration design solutions which had been such a feature of Columbia's design tradition in the 1940s. From the beginning Fujita's designs show the influence of the more hard-edge design approach that was typical of the small, specialist labels, perhaps most notably at Blue Note where Reid Miles was now the art director. Among the freelance designers that Fujita employed was Burt Goldblatt. The consolidation of the new approach espoused by Fujita had the effect of distancing Columbia's design output from that of rival RCA Victor, where one ex-Columbia art director with a penchant for illustration – Bob Jones – had just employed another – Jim Flora.

Fujita brought not only a new attitude to Columbia, he also decided that album design should be more orientated toward point-of-sale marketing. He ensured that all Columbia LP covers would have the artist's name and title at the top so that they could be easily read when displayed in record shop racks. Fujita had two spells at Columbia during the 1950s, the first for some three years. After a break he returned to see out the rest of the decade, sharing responsibility with Loring Eutemey, after which Bob Cato took over as art director.

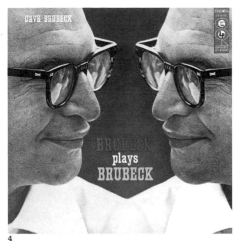

3

4

3 **Chet Baker & Strings**, CHET BAKER, Columbia, 1954.
Design: Neil Fujita. Photography: William Claxton.

4 **Brubeck Plays Brubeck**, DAVE BRUBECK, Columbia, 1956.
Design: Neil Fujita. Photography: Jay Maisel.

5 **The Jazz Messengers**, THE JAZZ MESSENGERS,
Philips, 1956.
Design: Neil Fujita. Photography: Don Hunstein.

5

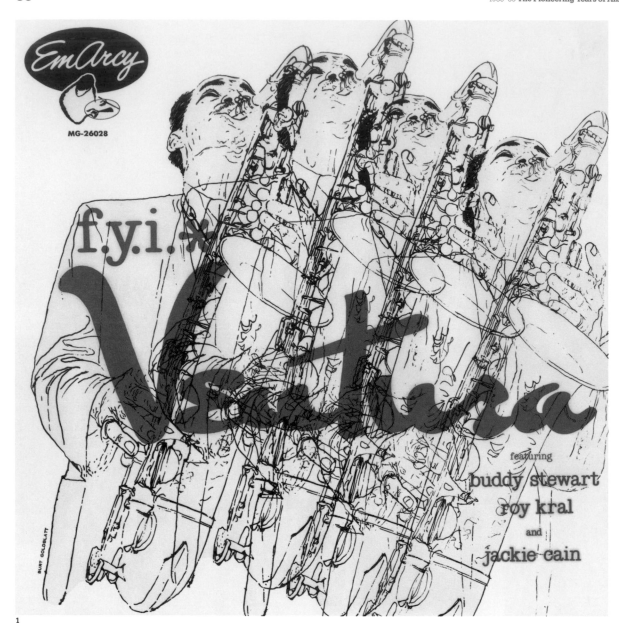

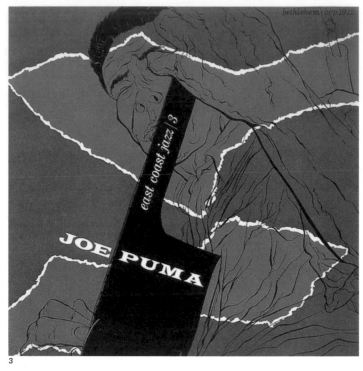

1   **F.Y.I.**, CHARLIE VENTURA, Mercury, 1954.
    Design and illustration: Burt Goldblatt.
2   **Lulu's Back in Town**, MEL TORMÉ, Bethlehem, 1955.
    Design: Burt Goldblatt.
3   **East Coast Jazz Vol 3**, JOE PUMA, Bethlehem, 1954.
    Design and illustration: Burt Goldblatt.

Burt Goldblatt was born 1925 in Dorchester, Massachusetts. He studied design at Massachusetts College of Art where he was already devoting his energies to album sleeve design. After graduating in 1950, he went to work at a printing company where he mastered the technical aspects of the printer's art. He won his first commission to design an album sleeve by answering an ad in the *Boston Globe* placed by Columbia, who were seeking freelance designers. He was employed at a small design agency in Boston for a while and designed some sleeves for Storyville before deciding to move to New York, where he quickly found work designing for small labels such as Roost and Savoy and even a bootleg operation called Jolly Roger Records. Between then and the late 1970s he designed over three thousand record covers for record companies, many for Atlantic, Columbia, Emarcy and Bethlehem. Much of Goldblatt's most innovative work was for the Bethlehem label for which he was both the art director and only designer. Goldblatt was extraordinarily adaptable, making the change-over from illustration to photographic-driven sleeve design with consummate skill.

For some of his early designs for Bethlehem he produced line drawings reminiscent of the blotted ink line illustrations of David Stone Martin and Andy Warhol. As photography became increasingly prevalent, he experimented with a variety of photographic montage techniques, using photography in a subservient role to a strong, formal sense of design. His photographic style of the middle 1950s demonstrates a considerable sympathy with the design ideas being developed by Reid Miles at Blue Note, although there is evidence in his work of an underlying technical understanding of photographic processes which is not a characteristic of Miles's work. Goldblatt was adept in the use of photographic effects – the overlapping of transparent photographic elements, close-ups and image cropping. His portrait of Bud Freeman montaged from tiny saxophones for his 1955 release on the Bethlehem label is a good example of his inventiveness. His technical interest in photography even led him to borrow an x-ray machine from a dentist friend in Boston who took care of Duke Ellington's teeth, to produce an x-ray image of a saxophone for the

cover of Charles Mariano's album *Mariano* (1954). Goldblatt was a genuine fan of music, particularly jazz, and it is not surprising that jazz – because of its experimental credentials – was his favourite form of music to design for. Goldblatt was a friend of many musicians, and the great pianist Bud Powell marked their friendship by writing a tune in his honour called "Burt Covers Bud" for the album *Bud Powell Trio Plays* for which Goldblatt designed the sleeve.

When designing covers for musicians he has confessed, "whenever I did try to keep my distance from them, it was when I didn't want them to tell me what to do. I would tell them, 'I don't tell you what songs to record or what group you should have. Why should you tell me what the graphics should say?'"

Burt Goldblatt continued to design for many record companies in the 1960s, in particular Scepter, Columbia and RCA, and also began to gain a reputation as a portrait photographer. However, he effectively retired from album cover design in the following decade in order to concentrate on book design and other more personal projects.

bethlehem bcp 1023

you'd be. . . .

so easy to. . .

love,

so easy. . .

to idolize. . .

all others above,

Carmen Mcrae

so worth. . .

the yearning for. . .

so swell. . .

4

4 **Carmen McRae**, CARMEN MCRAE, Bethlehem, 1955.
Design and photography: Burt Goldblatt.
5 **Mariano**, CHARLIE MARIANO, Bethlehem, 1955.
Design: Burt Goldblatt.

5

Paul Huf, the Dutch fashion photographer, was born in 1924 in Amsterdam. In the mid 1950s Philips, the Dutch electronics company, was eager to expand the European market for the new LP records. It commissioned Huf to devise album sleeves for a budget series of 52 long-playing records of classical music called Philips Favourite Music, and in so doing created a visual format for covers widely admired and copied. The series established Huf's reputation as a pioneering fashion photographer, and was particularly innovative in the Dutch context where in the 1950s the graphic design tradition was oriented toward the inventive use of typography and largely ignored the newly developing possibilities of colour photography.

In the early '50s Philips were major manufacturers of a new generation of record players able to play the relatively new long-playing records and were keen to expand the market. Sales of long-players had been slow to take off because of their perceived high cost. Philips had a considerable back catalogue of their own classical recordings, and had also recently entered into a marketing agreement with Columbia Records to distribute their recordings in Europe. The marketing department at Philips proposed to release some of their combined back catalogue in an affordable budget series drawing on the traditional light classical repertoire.

When in 1950 Philips began to manufacture LPs it released them in a standard format sleeve which offered no visual guide as to the character of the music it contained. When the company finally adopted individually designed sleeves, the designs were notably unmemorable, tending to rely on stock black-and-white photographs provided by the recording artists themselves. When, in 1954, Margreet Korsman, who was the recently appointed art director for Philip's classical music, was given the task of commissioning the album sleeves for the Philips Favourite Music series, she approached the young Amsterdam-based photographer Paul Huf with the intention of giving them a special flavour of their own. Colour photography was still a comparative rarity in Holland and Huf learned how to process Kodak film stock from Carel Blazer, one of the few people in Holland with any experience in handling the film. Huf's proposal for the series was to feature the same model on all the covers, using her in different guises to capture the mood of each album. A Spanish Gypsy look would be created for "Bolero", and for Rimsky Korsakov's "Scheherazade", an Arab harem ambiance. Typography was supplied by designer Herry van Borssum Waalkes. Huf selected twenty-one-year-old English model Ann Pickford for the role, and over fifty images were produced for the series in which her image remained resolutely "Home Counties" prim.

Philips launched the first twelve albums in the series at the Phonogram Disco Dealer Day in Hilversum, Holland. The use of a glamorous model to adorn the front cover of classical music records provoked moral outrage in some quarters, but the retailers had enough images to devote entire window displays to advertising the series, and it was an instant, although comparatively short-lived, success. Philips Favourite Music helped to make Huf's career as a photographer and his covers turned Ann Pickford into a celebrity in Holland. Her success even provoked a comedy song called "The Cover Cat" that Philips released as a single. Huf died in early 2002.

2

3

4

5

1

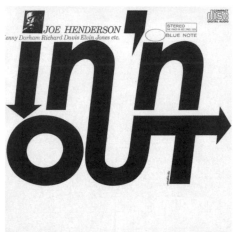

2

3

4

1   **Right Now!**, JACKIE MCLEAN, Blue Note, 1965.
Design: Reid Miles.

2   **In 'n Out**, JOE HENDERSON, Blue Note, 1964.
Design: Reid Miles.

3   **The Sidewinder**, LEE MORGAN, Blue Note, 1963.
Design: Reid Miles. Photography: Francis Wolff.

4   **Midnight Blue**, KENNY BURRELL , Blue Note, 1967.
Design: Reid Miles. Photography: Francis Wolff.

5   **Cool Struttin'**, SONNY CLARK, Blue Note, 1958.
Design: Reid Miles. Photography: Francis Wolff. [opposite]

R eid Miles was born in 1927 in Chicago. After a spell in the Navy at the end of World War II, he enrolled at Chouinard Art Institute (now Cal Arts). In the early 1950s he moved to New York where he secured a post as assistant to John Hermansader, the art director of the agency which designed for Blue Note Records. Blue Note founders Alfred Lion and Francis Wolff liked Miles's design work so much they became regular clients. This began his long involvement with album sleeve design, with his chief claim to fame being the fusion of imagery and dynamic typographic elements which over a period of fifteen years in the '50s and early '60s became the defining iconography of Blue Note jazz.

The records distributed by small, innovative labels like Blue Note were made on tight budgets. There was usually little time for rehearsal. Rudy van Gelder's studio in Hackensack, New Jersey, was a popular choice for recording because of the spontaneous, authentic atmosphere of the recordings produced there. Album sleeves were also paragons of economy, in Blue Note's case generally based on the numerous black and white photographs Wolff habitually took at recording sessions. Their documentary-like spontaneity, the nightclub atmospherics, his portraiture with its sharp contrasts of light and shade gave his photographs a moody *film noir* look which was intensified by Miles's crisp and vigorous use of typographical elements. The two men enjoyed a close rapport and Wolff was understanding when Miles sliced up his images or reduced them to

postage stamp size. Colour too was restricted because multiple colour printings were too costly. Miles's positive attitude to the limitations placed on him is revealing: "Two colours didn't hurt at all. The few full colour covers I did were not as strong as the ones with black and white and red." Since Wolff was constantly photographing Blue Note's artists it is not surprising that this ready material was the dominant imagery used on the company's sleeves, although Miles would sometimes employ other collaborators, famously commissioning Andy Warhol to produce illustrations for a number of covers. He also employed the painter's mother, Julia Warhola, to produce lettering in her distinctive calligraphic style.

Miles was extremely prolific. During his time at Blue Note he designed some five hundred sleeves for the label as well as working for other record labels, notably Prestige. He also designed for a variety of magazines and design agencies, although his insistence on retaining creative control meant that his relationship with many of his employers was stormy and short-lived.

Finally, in 1961, Miles bought a camera. Encouraged by Art Kane and Melvin Sokolsky, he became increasingly proficient as a photographer. In 1965 Lion and Wolff decided to sell Blue Note to a bigger rival, Liberty. Although they continued to work for the new owners, and Miles to design for them, change was afoot. Album sleeves were now full colour and Miles even used his own glamour images to adorn his sleeve designs. In 1967 Lion retired, tired of trying to prevent Blue Note's

identity becoming lost within the larger company. Miles cut his ties with Blue Note in the same year, though continuing to design for other companies, notably Columbia. By this time he was travelling so frequently to the West Coast that in 1971 he decided to return there and acquired a permanent photographic studio as his working base.

In the final period of his career, Miles is most remembered for the incident-filled genre photographs which became his speciality. They are reminiscent of 1930s *Saturday Evening Post* covers by the likes of Norman Rockwell, and are best characterized by his cover photograph for *Chicago's Greatest Hits* (1975) with band members hanging off a collapsing gantry. He continued to supply advertising and editorial material for countless major clients, and even became involved in the production of commercials for television. Miles died in 1993.

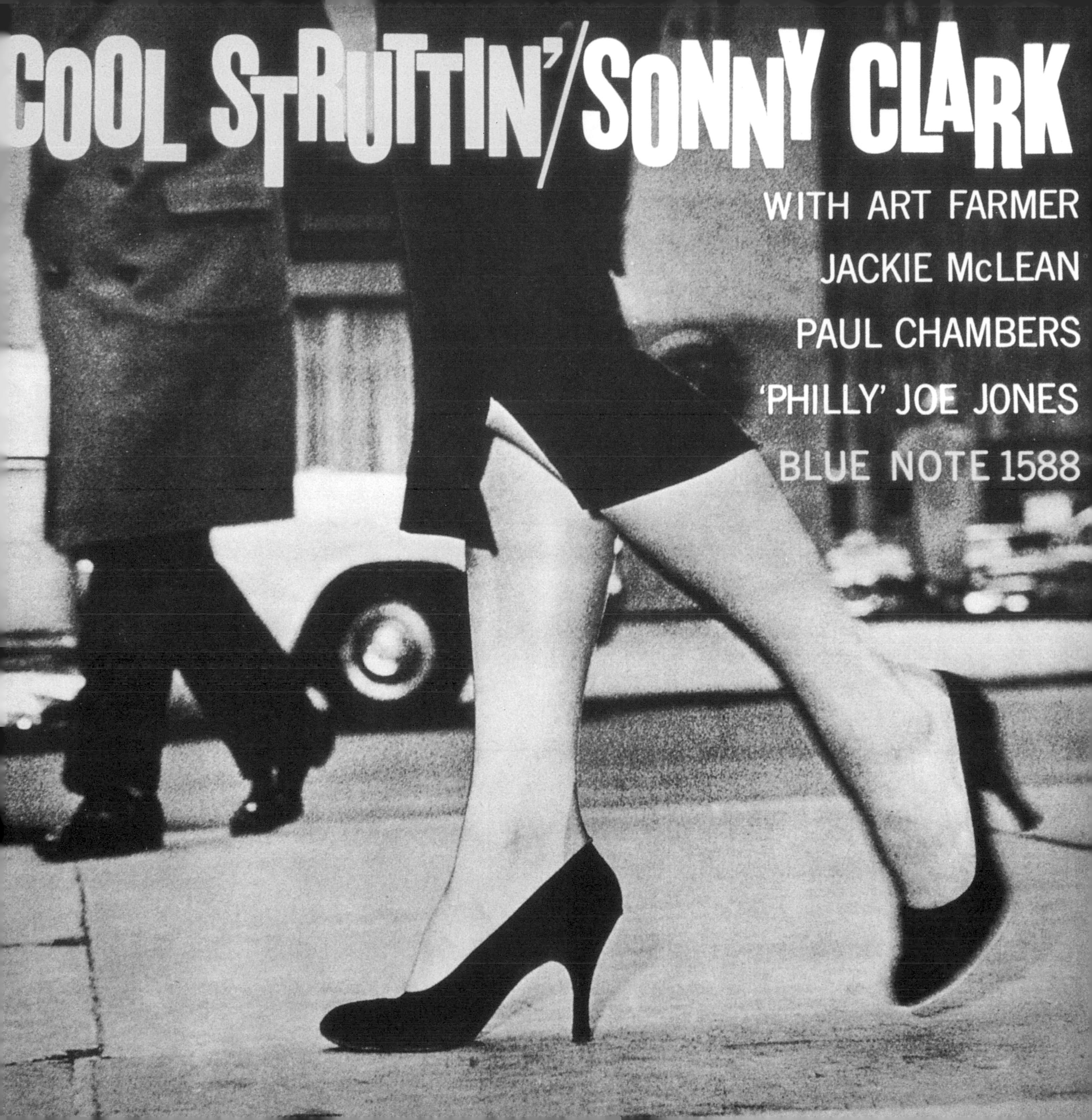

COOL STRUTTIN'/SONNY CLARK

WITH ART FARMER

JACKIE McLEAN

PAUL CHAMBERS

'PHILLY' JOE JONES

BLUE NOTE 1588

CHICO HAMILTON QUINTET IN HI FI

WORLD PACIFIC RECORDS

1 **Chico Hamilton Quintet in Hi Fi**, CHICO HAMILTON, Pacific Jazz, 1956. [opposite]
Photography: William Claxton. Sculptor: Vito.

2 **Bud Shank**, THE BUD SHANK QUARTET, Pacific Jazz, 1956.
Design: William Claxton. Illustration: Pauline Annon.

3 **Jazz Guitar**, JIM HALL, Pacific Jazz, 1957.
Design and photography: William Claxton.
Illustration: John Altoon.

William Claxton was born in 1930 in Southern California. He was uniquely responsible for giving a visual identity to the West Coast jazz scene of the 1950s. It was his photographic album, *Jazz West Coast*, published in 1955 which brought into focus the notion of a distinct West Coast strand of modern jazz promoted by new jazz labels like Fantasy, Contemporary and Pacific Jazz. As Claxton himself observed "At first, many critics and musicians on the East Coast said there was no such thing.... Which in a sense was true at that time. Many newly arrived jazz stars like Dave Brubeck in San Francisco, Gerry Mulligan in Los Angeles, Shorty Rogers, and Clifford Brown were from other parts of the country but happened to be in the right place at the right time. But the name 'West Coast Jazz' did not go away." Claxton's album sleeves emphasized the informal, outdoor enjoyment of the Californian littoral and reflected the cerebral, scored, studio-based West Coast jazz, in contrast to album design for East Coast jazz which sought to capture its more spontaneous, urban, nocturnal character.

Photography was always Claxton's main love. He began to take photographs of the jazz scene when he was a student at the University of California at Los Angeles studying psychology and art in the late 1940s. At a Gerry Mulligan performance in 1952 in a Los Angeles club called The Haig he met Richard Bock who was about to launch a record company called Pacific Jazz. Claxton was rapidly recruited as the company's art director and photographer, and subsequently

became a partner along with Bock, Roy Hart and Phil Turetsky. The company's first offices were above Hart's Drum Shop on Santa Monica Boulevard in Hollywood. He designed numerous album sleeves for the label over the next six years, creating a number of distinct looks. His early work was dominated by black and white photography, and at its best is worthy of comparison with Reid Miles's synthesis of typography and photography. He later began to use colour photography and developed an informal snapshot-like approach to his subjects which was more purposeful than it seemed, being eloquently suggestive of the relaxed Californian lifestyle which was to become such an important model for the post-war leisure industry. Particularly evocative is his photograph of Chet Baker hanging off the sail of a yacht for *Chet Baker & Crew* (1956). His photographs of Chet Baker are iconic: photogenic, the style of both his trumpet playing and his singing disarmingly unaffected, the embodiment of the Californian *dolce vita* masking a "pretty dangerous little bastard" devoted to feeding his drug habit. Claxton's most memorable photographs are those of Baker with his lovers, Lili, and his second wife, Helima, both of whom he mostly treated atrociously.

Claxton was also responsible for a series of sleeves for Pacific in which the interaction between jazz, improvisation and the abstract art of the period was given its most explicit expression. The series was called West Coast Artists Series and, in Claxton's words, "we would

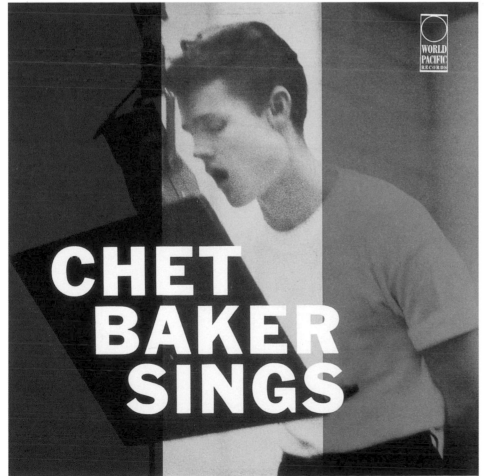

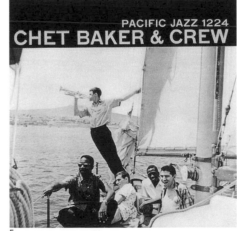

4 **Chet Baker Sings**, CHET BAKER, Pacific Jazz, 1954.
Design and photography: William Claxton.

5 **Chet Baker & Crew**, CHET BAKER, Pacific Jazz, 1956.
Design and photography: William Claxton.

6 **Jazz West Coast Vol 3**, VARIOUS ARTISTS, Pacific Jazz, 1957.
Design and photography: William Claxton.

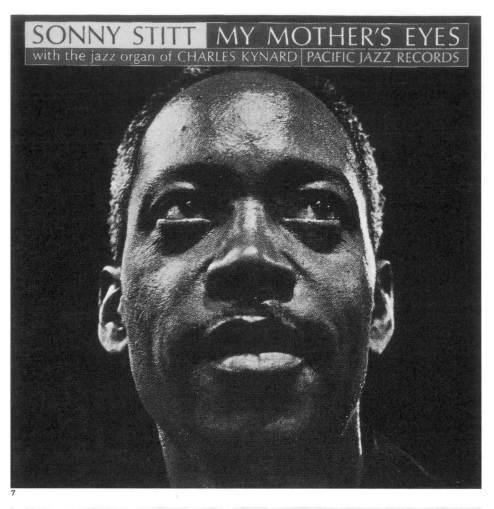

7

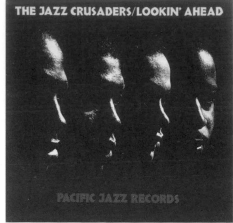

8

7 **My Mother's Eyes**, SONNY STITT, Pacific Jazz, 1961.
Design and photography: Woody Woodward.

8 **Lookin' Ahead**, THE JAZZ CRUSADERS, Pacific Jazz, 1962.
Design and photography: Woody Woodward.

9 **This is the Blues Volume 1**, VARIOUS ARTISTS,
Pacific Jazz, 1960.
Design and photography: Woody Woodward.

10 **First Time Out**, CLARE FISCHER, Pacific Jazz, 1962.
Design and photography: Woody Woodward. [opposite]

9

either give the artist a recording of a specific jazz artist or group to work with, or we would actually have the group play for the artist at his studio to 'inspire' the painter." Jim Hall's *Jazz Guitar* (1956) where John Altoon is seen at work, and *Chico Hamilton Quintet in Hi-Fi* of the same year, where the sculptor Vito is featured, are characteristic examples of this series.

Claxton also worked for most of the other record companies in the Los Angeles area, both the majors Capitol, Columbia, RCA and Decca, and also the small labels, most notably for Contemporary where he often provided photographs for album designer Robert Guidi of the Tri-Arts studio.

Claxton also worked with Pauline Annon, one of the few women illustrators working in the jazz field. She was a well-known Hollywood sketch artist and illustrator, and produced a number of album sleeves both for Contemporary and Pacific Jazz in the 1950s and 1960s.

As already noted, Claxton is as highly regarded for his photographs of the '50s jazz scene as he is for his album sleeve designs. Claxton had an eye for glamour and it was not unexpected that he also worked as a fashion photographer and married Peggy Moffitt whom he met modelling at a fashion shoot. At the time the record industry was seeing a swing towards the fashion for putting glamour models on the front covers of album sleeves. As Claxton observed, "all the record companies decided, with so much competition in the recording market, a jazz musician's personality

and his music were perhaps not enough to insure sales, so the thinking was to put sexy and pretty women on the covers. So, Pacific Jazz did it too." He featured Moffitt in a number of cover shots.

By the late '50s he was more and more pre-occupied by his freelance work, and in spring 1958 he gave up his art director's role at Pacific and sold his partnership back to Richard Bock. His role as art director at Pacific was taken over by Woody Woodward, who had been working at the company in an executive capacity since 1955. He had a background in photography and like Bock himself, was already in the habit of providing photographs for Pacific sleeve designs. Woodward proved to be an extremely capable replacement for Claxton, and continued to develop the Pacific look into the '60s.

Although Claxton continued to provide photographs for album covers and photograph musicians, his time was increasingly devoted to fashion photography for magazines such as *Vogue, McCall's, Harper's Bazaar*, and *Life*. He is particularly well known for his work with the fashion designer Rudy Gernreich, who is best remembered for his topless swimsuits. Claxton took many photographs of his wife, modelling Gernreich's topless swimsuit, and both she and the photographs have become indelibly associated with the topless look.

Richard Bock finally sold Pacific Jazz to Liberty in 1965, and two years later Liberty was itself bought by United Artists.

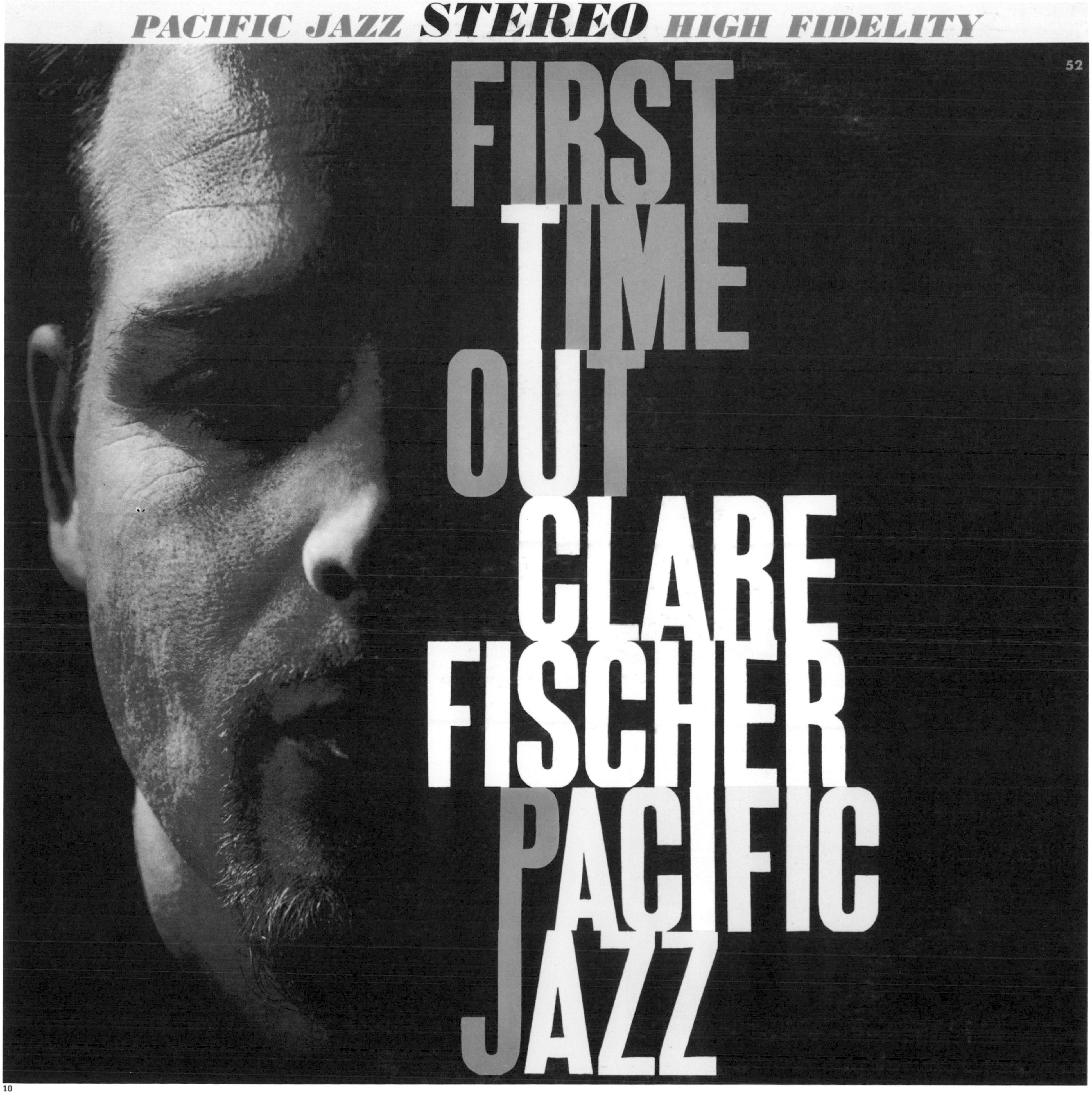
PACIFIC JAZZ STEREO HIGH FIDELITY
52
FIRST TIME OUT
CLARE FISCHER
PACIFIC JAZZ

1

2

3

4

1   **The Man with the Golden Arm**, soundtrack/ ELMER
BERNSTEIN, Decca, 1959.
Design: Saul Bass.

2   **Bunny Lake is Missing**, soundtrack/ PAUL GLASS,
RCA Victor, 1965.
Design: Saul Bass.

3   **Saint Joan**, soundtrack/ MISCHA SPOLIANSKY, Capitol, 1957.
Design and illustration: Saul Bass.

4   **Advise & Consent**, soundtrack/ JERRY FIELDING,
RCA Victor, 1962.
Design: Saul Bass.

5   **Anatomy of a Murder**, soundtrack/ DUKE ELLINGTON,
Columbia, 1959.
Design: Saul Bass. [opposite]

Saul Bass was born in 1920 in New York City. Although designing album sleeves was little more than an aside in a varied design career, the few Bass produced were pivotal in enabling the film soundtrack to emerge as a major new genre of recorded music during the 1950s. His designs combined strong, stylised forms with a consummate ability to capture the essence of a film in an arresting symbol. His perception that for films other than musicals the soundtrack album sleeve could be part of an integrated graphic "look", was to become a significant element in Hollywood's advertising and marketing strategies.

Bass studied at the Art Students League and at Brooklyn College. After working as a designer in New York for a number of years, he moved to Los Angeles and founded Saul Bass & Associates in 1946. In the late '40s he was a founding member of the Los Angeles Society for Contemporary Designers along with Alvin Lustig, Rudolph de Harak and Lou Danziger. Although his design career spans an enormous range – film credits, packaging, corporate identity – it is the powerful animated graphics of his film credits for which he is best remembered. His most famous film collaboration was with director Otto Preminger. He first worked with Otto Preminger on *Carmen Jones* (1954), but it was his designs for *The Man With the Golden Arm* (1955) that first brought his radical approach to film credit design to people's attention. In Bass's own words: "Motion picture photography was always about ten years behind. That's what distinguished my initial work in films. I was bringing to bear the visual standards that I had developed in the graphic field. That was very startling, and that's what made the work I did then look so wild." The film was controversial for its unsparing look at drug addiction. Bass's image of a downthrust arm with its crabbed hand was originally commissioned for media advertisements, but Preminger was so struck with it that he asked him to produce the film's opening credit sequence.

So closely tied to the meaning of the film did the image become that it was used unaccompanied by a title or photographs of the films stars, Frank Sinatra, Eleanor Parker and Kim Novak, on the Broadway cinema's marquee for the film's premiere. Elmer Bernstein's music for the film was released by Decca in its entirety on three LPs. Bass designed three sleeves, each of which featured the same downthrust arm image, but in each volume the image was framed by different colour combinations.

Thereafter, soundtrack albums designed by Bass became a fixed feature of Preminger's film releases, among them *Saint Joan* (1957), *Bonjour Tristesse* (1958), *Anatomy of a Murder* (1959), *Exodus* (1960), *Advise and Consent* (1962), *The Cardinal* (1963), *Bunny Lake Is Missing* (1965), and *Skidoo* (1968).

Bass's work with Preminger led to Alfred Hitchcock employing him to design the credits for *Vertigo* (1958), and subsequently work as visual consultant on *North by Northwest* (1959) and *Psycho* (1960). He later designed the elaborate epilogue title sequence for *West Side Story* (1961) and the famous maurarding cat sequence for *Walk on the Wild Side* (1962). In all he created titles for over forty movies, and logos for another sixty, many of which graced soundtrack albums.

Bass also made a major contribution to the re-badging of American corporations, counting AT&T, Bell Systems, Warner Communications, Exxon, Esso, BP and United Airlines among his clients. He died in 1996.

MUSIC BY DUKE ELLINGTON · FROM THE SOUND TRACK OF THE MOTION PICTURE

OTTO PREMINGER'S

ANATOMY OF A MURDER

3

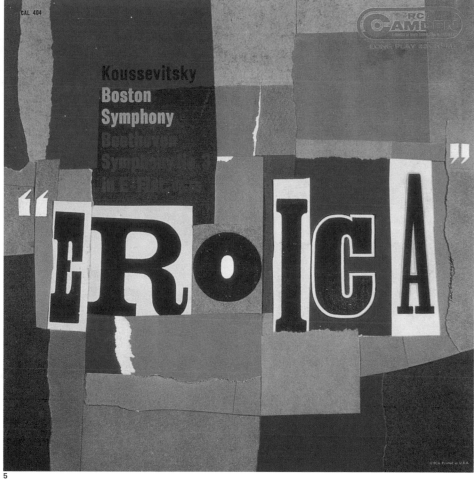

5

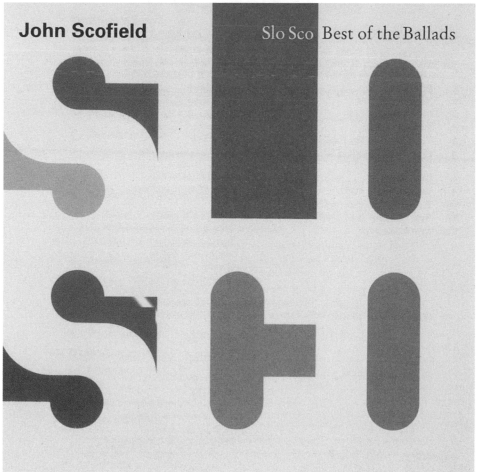

4

Ivan Chermayeff was born in 1932 in London, son of the famous Russian architect Serge Chermayeff. His father eventually emigrated to America to take up a teaching post at the Chicago Institute of Art, where Chermayeff also studied for a while. His design studies also took him to Harvard University and the School of Art and Architecture at Yale University. In 1955 he became assistant to the famous book designer Alvin Lustig. In 1957, in partnership with Robert Brownjohn, who had studied with his father in Chicago, and Thomas Geismar, he launched the design studio Brownjohn, Chermayeff & Geismar. In the first few years of its existence the studio designed extensively for record companies, particularly for the CBS label Epic. Unfortunately much of their work was not credited, and no comprehensive record of the partnership's designs for CBS exists. In 1960 Brownjohn left the partnership for a post in London as art director at J. Walter Thompson. He cut a mercurial figure in 1960s swinging London, and one of his last commissions before his premature death in 1970 was the sleeve of the Rolling Stones' album *Let It Bleed* (1969).

In New York the two remaining partners continued their partnership, renamed it Chermayeff & Geismar Inc., and it became one of the city's most successful design studios taking on new partners such as Stephan Geissbühler and John Grady.

Chermayeff & Geismar Inc. have largely specialized in the design requirements of large corporate clients such as Pan-Am, Chase

Manhattan Bank, and Mobil, and have been adept at re-casting American corporate identities in the minimalist geometric vocabulary of the Bauhaus. Chermayeff has the perfect modernist designer's pedigree and was well aware of the pitfalls of sterility that over-strict adherence to Bauhaus design tenets can produce. Nevertheless, the design output produced under the imprint of the various partnerships of which he has been a part, whether produced in the 1950s or the 1980s, has all the rectitude of classical modernist design, though often laced with playful quirks or humour.

Although not central to the output of Chermayeff & Geismar Inc, Chermayeff has been responsible for the design of numerous album sleeves over the studio's long life. They have often drawn on the vocabulary of painterly minimalism strongly associated with the New York School of abstract artists. His austere integration of simple geometrical forms and abstracted typeforms is sometimes reminiscent of the graphic style of Josef Albers, a European precursor of the New York School who was the director of the Design Department at Yale in the period 1950–53. His output of album sleeves has largely been undertaken for clients concerned to project sophisticated, high art values. His designs offer an invaluable check list of forms – playful and austere – that have been paradigmatic for niche record companies and their designers, evoking esoteric types of music from archaic folk and mediaeval madrigals to musiqué concrete and atonal jazz.

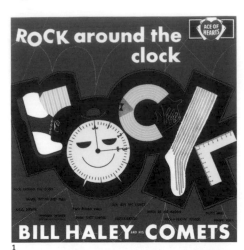

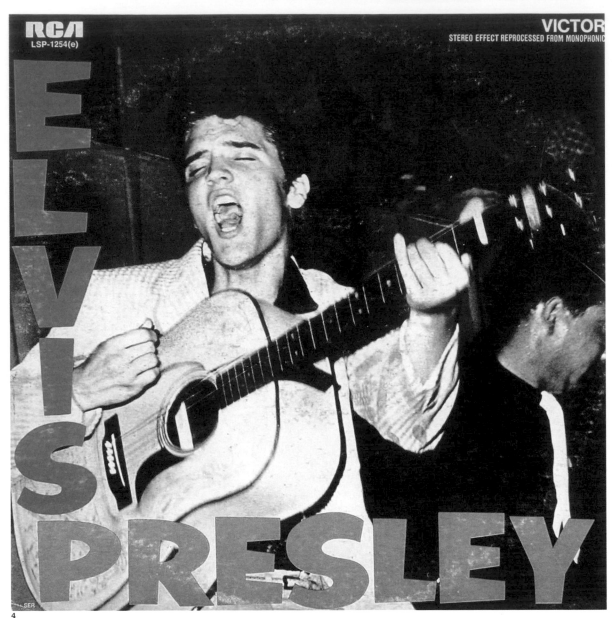

1 **Rock Around the Clock**, BILL HALEY AND HIS COMETS,
   Decca, 1956.
   Design: unknown.

2 **The Fabulous Little Richard**, LITTLE RICHARD,
   Specialty, 1959.
   Art direction: John Ewing.

3 **The "Chirping" Crickets**, THE CRICKETS, Brunswick, 1957.
   Design: unknown.

4 **Elvis Presley**, ELVIS PRESLEY, RCA Victor, 1956.
   Art direction: Colonel Tom Parker.

5 **Ricky** , RICKY NELSON, Imperial, 1957.
   Design: unknown. [opposite]

Rock culture is one of the most extraordinary phenomena of the second half of the 20th century. It roots can be traced to many different sources, and once it took form it grew in wild profusion, nevertheless there are no doubts that its greatest debt is to black American musicians and rhythm & blues. The date of the big crossover into the mainstream is generally identified as 1955, the year of the launch of Elvis Presley's career, and the relaunch of Bill Haley's as a rock'n'roller rather than a country singer. Haley had his first top 10 hit with a cover version of a Joe Turner rhythm & blues recording, "Shake, Rattle and Roll", and the following year became really big news as a result of the phenomenal success of his follow-up single "Rock Around the Clock".

Early rock'n'roll sleeves do not have their own distinct iconography. Bill Haley's Decca sleeve for his album *Rock Around the Clock* (1956) features a playful illustration based on the word "rock" which would not have been out of place on the cover of an album of light jazz. There is an unembellished directness about the early Presley and Little Richard album sleeves which have become emblematic of the raw immediacy of early

rock'n'roll. Presley's first release on RCA Victor, the eponymously titled *Elvis Presley* (1956) has spawned many homages, not least The Clash's *London Calling* (1977) and *Soundgarden* (1989). And yet it is remarkable how swiftly the rebellious, badly behaved streak of rock'n'roll was brought under control by the major record labels. The raw spontaneous documentary style of Presley's early album sleeves was soon superseded by a bland studio look characteristic of much subsequent 1950s rock'n'roll sleeve design. The niche record companies, such as Chess, King and Atlantic, which were successfully riding the rhythm & blues and rock'n'rock wave, were beginning to seriously erode the domination of the American best sellers charts by the big four – Columbia, RCA Victor, Capitol and Decca – who fought back by buying the upstarts recording artists' contracts and then the companies. RCA Victor had started the trend by buying Elvis Presley's recording contract from Sam Phillips, owner of Sun Records, for $35,000 in November 1955. Increasingly the acceptable face of rock 'n' roll became the cherubic face and the pompadour. Anodyne white Hollywood types such as Ricky Nelson, Fabian, Pat Boone and The Everly

Brothers came to the fore and rock'n'roll album sleeve design settled into a fixed idiom to accompany their watered-down version of the rock impulse. The early death of one of the big rock 'n' roll names, Buddy Holly, didn't help, nor did the fact that three of the other big personalities – Little Richard, Fats Domino and Chuck Berry – were black, and their record company's were anxious not to reinforce their "dangerous" reputations through the design of their album covers.

A similar pattern can be seen in other record markets. The British promoter Larry Parnes with his rosters of clean-cut rock stars like Billy Fury and Marti Wilde, and Joe Meek who produced the Tornados, can be seen as part of the same phenomenon, confirming with what ease the big record companies corralled and then tamed the first wild wave of rock'n'rollers. However, lame as some of this subsequent rock 'n' roll may have been, the highly standardized studio portraits of its stars have subsequently become an iconic representation of the rock star persona.

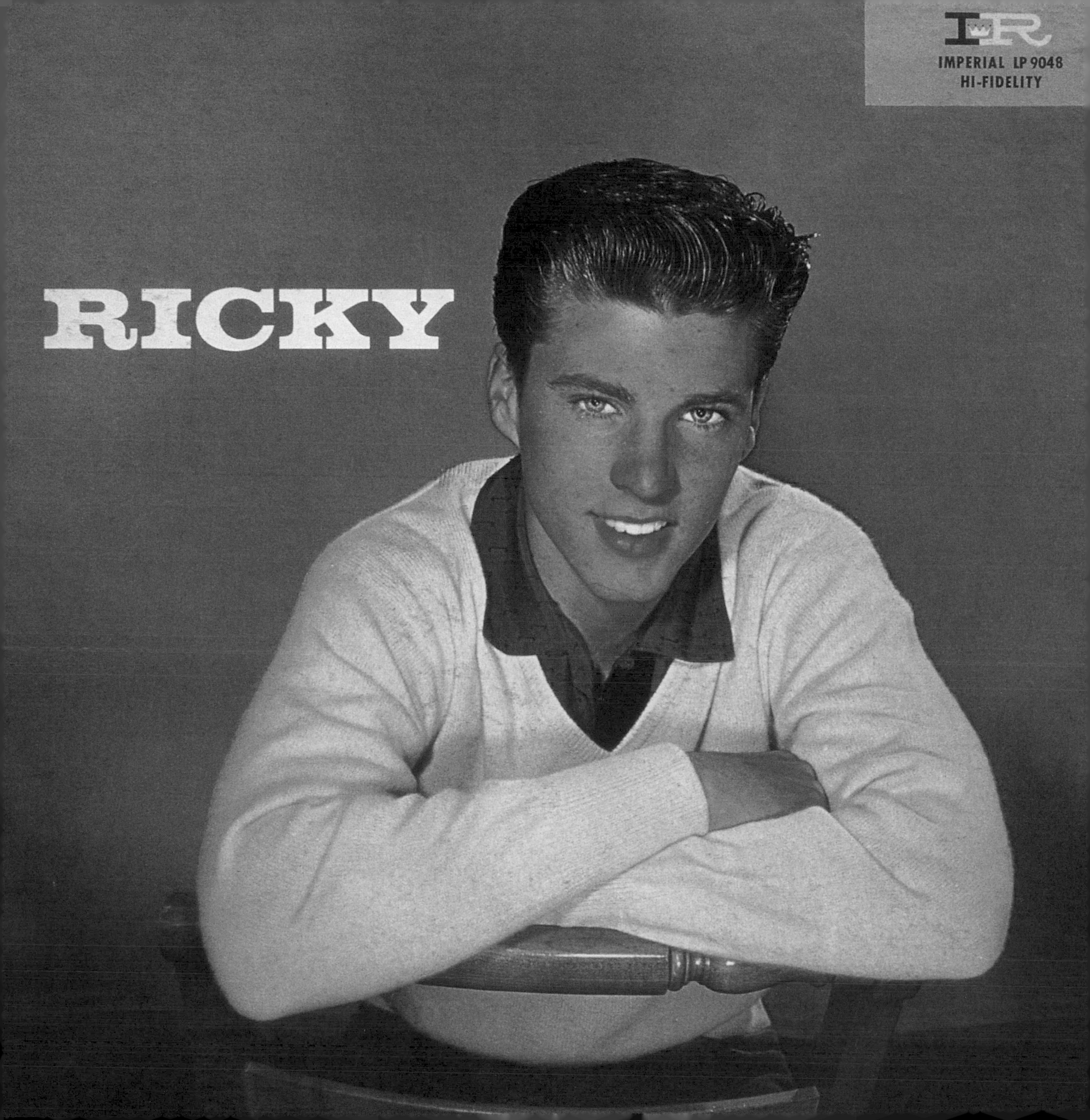

RICKY

IMPERIAL LP 9048
HI-FIDELITY

JOHN COLTRANE  GIANT STEPS
FULL *dynamics-frequency* SPECTRUM ATLANTIC 1311

1

1 **Giant Steps**, JOHN COLTRANE, Atlantic, 1960.
   Design: Marvin Israel. Photography: Lee Friedlander.
2 **Blues and Roots**, CHARLIE MINGUS, Atlantic, 1959.
   Design: Marvin Israel. Photography: Lee Friedlander.
3 **Soul Brothers**, MILT JACKSON & RAY CHARLES,
   Atlantic, 1959.
   Design: Marvin Israel. Photography: Lee Friedlander.

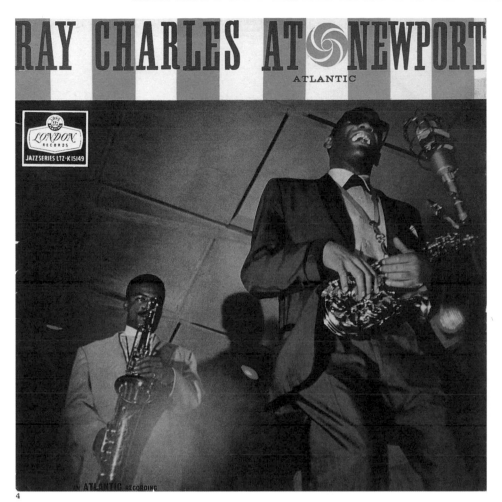

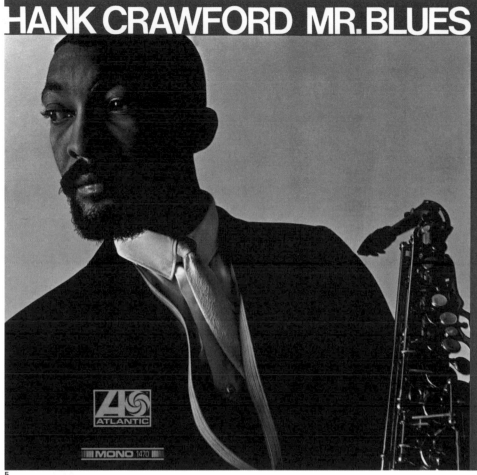

4 **Ray Charles at Newport**, RAY CHARLES, Atlantic, 1958.
Design: Loring Eutemey. Photography: Lee Friedlander.

5 **Mr Blues**, HANK CRAWFORD, Atlantic, 1967.
Design: Loring Eutemey. Photography: Lee Friedlander.

Marvin Israel and Loring Eutemey were friends and colleagues who created the look of Atlantic Records, album sleeves in the late 1950s and early 1960s. Atlantic was launched by the Ertegun brothers, sons of the Turkish ambassador in the late 1940s, and became a highly successful second-tier record company during the '50s. It was eventually bought by Warner Bros. in 1967. Although Atlantic had a diverse roster of stars, the presence of the Modern Jazz Quartet, John Coltrane, Shorty Rogers, Mel Tormé and Ray Charles is indicative of the fact that jazz and rhythm and blues were a speciality. Israel joined Atlantic as art director in the mid-'50s following a spell at the fashion magazine *Seventeen*. Along with Art Kane he is considered to have been one of the magazine's most influential art directors, taking care always to maintain supportive relationships with the various photographers he employed. In the words of fashion photographer Frank Horvat, Israel "was a small, not very healthy person, who dressed like a bum and furnished his studio with rejected objects he found in the streets. He made it a point to appear unfriendly, imitated in this by his ugly little dog, also called Marvin, about whom he would warn visitors 'be careful, Marvin bites'. In fact, both master and dog were as gentle and warm-hearted as can be."

At the time of Marvin Israel's move to Atlantic his friend Loring Eutemey was at Columbia, working as an art director with Neil Fujita. It was not long before he too was working for Atlantic.

Atlantic had been in the habit of commissioning album sleeve designs from a variety of designers, including Burt Goldblatt and Robert Guidi, but on his arrival Israel began to assert a more coherent design policy, with himself and Eutemey undertaking most of the design. Their approach at Atlantic is best described by Eutemey in a letter he wrote to jazz critic Jorge Garcia: "Marvin and I shared a desire to employ graphic design in a way that would elevate the status of jazz and rhythm and blues artists. Commercial considerations interfered, but I tried to give those mostly black artists a graphic package that had the dignity and gravitas usually given to classical musicians." The abiding impression of Atlantic album sleeves of this period is their restrained elegance and deceptive simplicity. In pursuit of a sense of class Israel and Eutemey were not averse, for example, to pairing the music of the Modern Jazz Quartet with cover images by J.M.W. Turner and Rousseau.

Given Israel's background as an art director, it is not surprising that the quality of Atlantic's album sleeves of this period owe much to the skills of the photographers he commissioned. Lee Friedlander's is perhaps the most outstanding contribution. Although he made a specialism of photography for LP sleeves at this time he subsequently had far wider a reputation than that of jazz and album sleeves. His photographic work for Atlantic was published as *American Musicians* in 1998, and he has exhibited different aspects of his photographic oeuvre several times at the Museum of Modern Art, New York.

Israel handed over responsibility for design at Atlantic to Eutemey when he decided to move on from Atlantic in 1963. He took over Henry Wolf's job as art director at Hearst Corporation's *Harper's Bazaar* but was fired fairly soon. From then on he concentrated on photographic book design, dying while organizing a Richard Avedon show. Eutemey continued to work for Atlantic until the mid-1970s, long after the Ertegun brothers had sold the company to Warner Bros. He continued to design thereafter, with many clients in the magazine and book publishing world.

The Jimi Hendrix Experience

reprise 6261

are you experienced

1960–69
Teen Culture, Pop, and Psychedelia

Are You Experienced.
THE JIMI HENDRIX
EXPERIENCE, Reprise, 1967.
Art direction: Ed Thrasher.
Photography: Karl Ferris.
[previous pages]

Cliff Sings.
CLIFF RICHARD AND THE
SHADOWS, Paramount, 1960.
Design: unknown.

Dream with Dean.
DEAN MARTIN, Reprise, 1964.
Photography: Phil Stern.

If anything summed up the state of the music business at the turn of the decade it was Frank Sinatra's "Rat Pack" movie *Ocean's Eleven*. The movie was an eloquent testament to the "establishment" mentality that prevailed at the crowning heights of the American entertainment business. The film portrayed the Rat Packers as the perfect personification of contemporary masculine ease and elegance, led by Sinatra and fellow crooner Dean Martin. They were also boozy, macho, and brazenly sloppy. This was old-time show business at its most glamorous and self-indulgent. The year of the release of the movie also marked the arrival at the threshold of adulthood of the generation born post-1940. They were too young to have been much affected by the War itself, but had been brought up under the post-war settlement which envisaged a benign, conformist society within which lurked the wartime expectations of mass conscription, directed labour, and communities of endeavour. By 1960 it was a model ripe for dissent. Within a few years the showbiz that *Ocean's Eleven* represented would be the antithesis of cool and, for society at large, teenagers would have usurped a whole generation of established stars as arbiters of hipness. The emergence of mass culture, the development of counter-cultures, and protest movements are all aspects of the decade's social effervescence. This was not just generation- changeover but a fundamental restatement of modernity in which youthfulness became a guarantee of principle, creativity, and radicality, with music central to self-expression. It caused a revolution in record companies, in the market for recorded music, and in design for music.

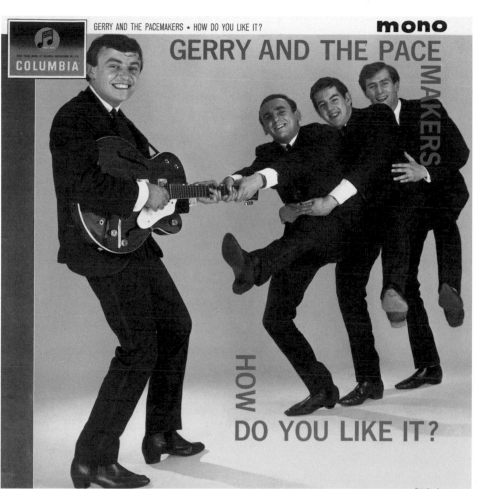

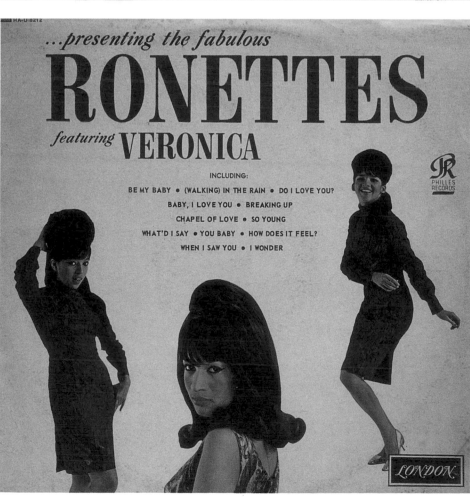

How Do You Like It?
GERRY AND THE
PACEMAKERS,
Columbia, 1963.
Photography: Edgar Brind.

**Presenting the Fabulous
Ronettes Featuring Veronica.**
THE RONETTES, Philles
Records, 1964.
Photography: Three Lions Studio.

Record sales grew very quickly during the 1960s, although the 45 rpm singles market which was by far the most important part of recorded music sales in 1960, registered a slight decline during the following decade. In Britain, for example, the market for singles in 1960 was 47 million and had scarcely changed by 1970. The British LP market, on the other hand, showed significant growth throughout the decade, doubling from 32 to 65 million between 1967 and 1970 alone. This remarkable growth was launched by the emergence of the "Liverpool sound" and the burgeoning number of pop groups brought to an eager teenage audience by Radio Caroline. This and other pirate radio stations became a symbol of a new, freewheeling popular culture, unregulated by government policy and approved playlists. Initially the album sleeves of the new generation of pop groups driving this increase in sales conformed to the model developed by the anonymous designers of American rock groups in the previous decade. They featured the standard group photograph: jovial, jokey or casual, and certainly never sullen. The slapdash cover of the Beatles' first album, photographed in the stairwell of EMI's headquarters, is a characteristic enough example. But as pop began to mutate into a whole range of rock genres over the next few years, the design of album sleeves began to matter to a new degree. The look of an album sleeve became an increasingly nuanced expression of the recording artist's musical and cultural allegiances, and his/her claims to what was ambiguously referred to – given the fortunes that were beginning to be made – as "street credibility".

mono

SURFER GIRL
THE BEACH BOYS

LITTLE DEUCE COUPE · SURFER GIRL · CATCH A WAVE · THE SURFER MOON · SOUTH BAY SURFER · HAWAII
IN MY ROOM · THE ROCKING SURFER · SURFER'S RULE · OUR CAR CLUB · YOUR SUMMER DREAM · BOOGIE WOODIE

SWINGING LONDON

RUSS SAINTY   THE FIRST IMPRESSION   BOULEVARD

Surfer Girl.
THE BEACH BOYS,
Capitol, 1963.
Photography: Ken Veeder at
the Capitol Photo Studio.

Swinging London.
RUSS SAINTY AND THE
FIRST IMPRESSION,
Boulevard, 1972.
Design: unknown.

Record company executives found themselves with new, fast-expanding markets driven by the rising purchasing power of an audience which was increasingly youthful. This audience not only had different values to them but also a taste for constant change. Over time the uncertainty this created would give more and more power to recording artists to dictate terms in their contractual negotiations with the record companies, including the artistic licence to commission their own designs for album sleeves. From here on, designers with a permanent allegiance to a single record company are almost entirely superseded by maverick independents. By the beginning of the '60s a large record company was no longer the place for a designer with an extraordinary singular vision. Over the next couple of decades this would be borne out by the increasingly clear distinction between in-house record company design and the work of outsiders hired job by job. Record companies like Columbia were already huge rule-bound corporations. Accordingly, the Bob Cato and John Berg spread in this section is the last devoted to the art directors of a major record company. Increasingly, art directors like Cato and Berg, who were quite often expected to oversee a record company's entire output, left the conception of individual designs to others. For the art directors of the major record companies, there were more important skills than being a brilliant designer. To survive and be successful they had to articulate and guide company policy; they ought, too, to have their finger on the pulse of the moment, ensuring the currency of that policy; they had to be gifted commissioners of designers,

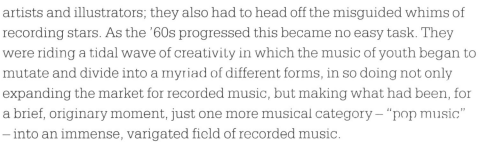

Poster: "Zig-zag".
BIG BROTHER AND THE
HOLDING COMPANY,
Avalon Ballroom, 1966.
Design: Mouse/Kelley.

Hair.
ORIGINAL BROADWAY
CAST, RCA Victor, 1969.
Design: unknown.

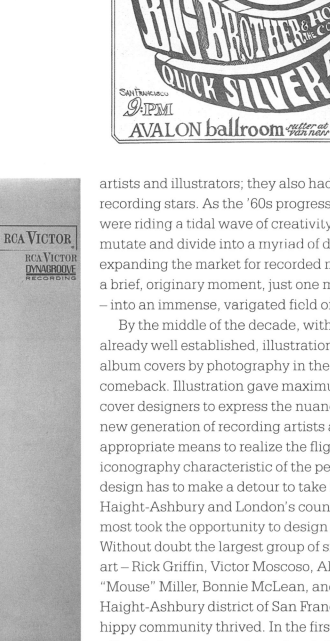

artists and illustrators; they also had to head off the misguided whims of recording stars. As the '60s progressed this became no easy task. They were riding a tidal wave of creativity in which the music of youth began to mutate and divide into a myriad of different forms, in so doing not only expanding the market for recorded music, but making what had been, for a brief, originary moment, just one more musical category – "pop music" – into an immense, variegated field of recorded music.

By the middle of the decade, with the counter-culture movement already well established, illustration, which gradually had been eased off album covers by photography in the previous decade, began to make a comeback. Illustration gave maximum freedom to the imagination of cover designers to express the nuances of meaning and association that a new generation of recording artists aspired to. It was also the most appropriate means to realize the flights of fancy and complex psychedelic iconography characteristic of the period. Here the story of album sleeve design has to make a detour to take in the mid-'60s poster designers of Haight-Ashbury and London's counter-culture underground (although most took the opportunity to design album sleeves at some point). Without doubt the largest group of significant exponents of psychedelic art – Rick Griffin, Victor Moscoso, Alton Kelley, Wes Wilson, Stanley "Mouse" Miller, Bonnie McLean, and Lee Conklin – were resident in the Haight-Ashbury district of San Francisco where, for a brief while, a large hippy community thrived. In the first half of 1967, the year of the "summer of love", the area experienced an influx of over 100,000 aspiring hippies.

Crown of Creation.
JEFFERSON AIRPLANE, RCA
Victor, 1968.
Art direction: John
Van Hamersveld.
Photography: Hiro.

Concerts and events staged at venues such as the Avalon Ballroom and the Fillmore Auditorium were a focus for the alternative communities being established across the whole Bay area. Almost immediately the concert posters, produced in a style which was originally known as "organic modern", became highly sought after, and some of the rarer examples are now amongst the most collected and valuable of pop memorabilia. The story is told of a bill-poster putting up posters for a weekend's concert at the Fillmore, only to realize that he was being followed by someone who was taking them down to keep as fast as he was posting them. The venue's promoter, Bill Graham, bowed to the inevitable and began to print enough posters to give them away free at his concerts, even using the strapline "this poster free to all in attendance" on some.

Although they were originally designed in anticipation of a brief moment of significance, advertising concerts and other "tribal" gatherings, these posters have become a long-lasting influence on illustration for music. Psychedelia, the visual style they developed to capture the mystical, drug-induced optical excitation experienced at the confluence of recreational drugs and rock – the closest most fans were likely to get to a visionary experience – was a highly original, all-over visual style quite without precedent, despite its acknowledged indebtedness to a variety of sources. It was a style which was to reverberate down the decades, its motifs reoccurring whenever moodshifters met dance music.

**Cruising with Ruben &
the Jets.**
FRANK ZAPPA AND THE
MOTHERS OF INVENTION,
Ryko, 1968.
Design: Cal Schenkel.

Ogdens' Nut Gone Flake.
THE SMALL FACES,
Immediate, 1968.
Illustration: P. Brown.

It has already been noted that the technical and aesthetic considerations that had shaped the direction of album sleeve design during the previous decade meant that, far from being taken seriously as a specific specialized area, it was almost entirely estranged from the graphic design mainstream by the beginning of the 1960s. The developments which were to occur as the decade progressed would only intensify that estrangement.

In fact, hardly any survey of contemporary graphic design published during the next twenty years would devote a section or chapter to album sleeve design, although adjacent categories such as book cover design were always more than adequately represented. Generally speaking, as far as the design establishment was concerned, album cover artwork would be synonymous with (what was considered) bad taste right up until the early years of the 1980s.

During the latter half of the '60s, album sleeve design became dominated by the self-indulgent experimentation of rock bands and their appointed designers. There was much amateurism, bad photography, and the use of a half-digested mish-mash of styles, more often than not overlaid with psychedelic motifs. The Who's *Magic Bus* album sleeve (1968) has many of the faults that horrified serious designers. But there was in this an adventurous and ambitious spirit trying to find new ways to express, in visual terms, the growth of the new music. And, in time, a degree of self-confidence emerged from this ferment which would mean that the best were truly memorable.

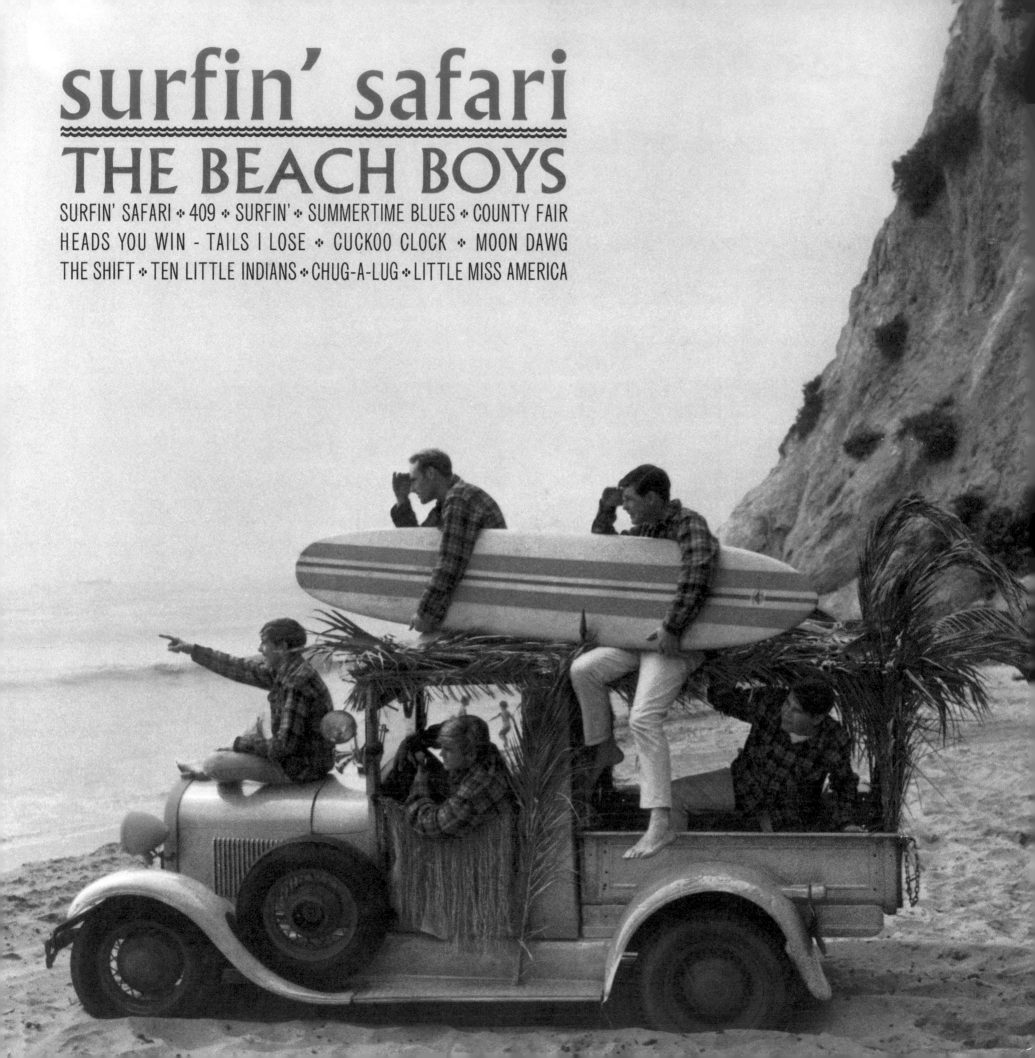

1 **Surfin' Safari**, THE BEACH BOYS, Capitol, 1962. [opposite]
Photography: Ken Veeder at the Capitol Photo Studio.
2 **Jan & Dean take Linda Surfin'**, JAN & DEAN, Liberty, 1963.
Design: Studio Five.
3 **Bustin' Surfboards**, THE TORNADOES, Josie, 1963.
Design: unknown.
4 **Summer Days**, THE BEACH BOYS, Capitol, 1965.
Photography: Ken Veeder at the Capitol Photo Studio.
5 **Surfin' Bird**, THE TRASHMEN, Garrett, 1964.
Design: unknown. Photography: Ted Volante.

Californian surfers were amongst the earliest self-identifying communities to develop a comprehensive alternative lifestyle with its own distinct mores and aspirations. Although the surfer lifestyle had values in common with mainstream society, not least its fascination with specialist equipment and apparel (a characteristic it shared with the contemporaneous biker subculture), its materialist impulses were deliberately limited as it sought to turn mainstream society's expectations of vacation into a permanent state of being. In America surfing became a big craze in the late '50s and early '60s spawning for a brief moment its own distinctive form of rock'n'roll. The chief exponents of surfer music were the Beach Boys, the Trashmen, the Astronauts, Dick Dale and the Deltones, The Ventures, the duo Jan & Dean, and the Tornadoes – the latter not to be confused with the UK instrumental group the Tornados of *Telstar* fame. The characteristics of surfer music were largely set out by the Beach Boys in the early to mid '60s. Their a cappella intros, driving rhythms, rich harmonies, and falsetto choruses were combined with lyrics about the surfing lifestyle (*Girls On The Beach*), fast cars (*I Get Around*) and other teen-oriented preoccupations of the day.

Typically the covers of surfer albums were designed to give passing credibility to the group's surfer credentials by photographing them in the surfer milieu of beach, surf and blue skies, surrounded by surfing accoutrements: boards, vehicles and clothing. The surf board is often a prominent motif, carried or standing upright. A common composition is the beach party with band members surrounded by girls in bathing costumes. Such images are a continuation of the "open-air camaraderie" theme developed by William Claxton for '50s West Coast jazz. The informal sailing group shot for the cover of the Beach Boys' *Summer Days* (1965) is highly reminiscent of Claxton's photograph for the cover of *Chet Baker & Crew* (1956). Surfer covers, notably the Beach Boys', mark an important stage in the development of rock group iconography. Black singing groups of the '50s of the kind that were to become a mainstay of Talma Motown's catalogue during the '60s, regularly appeared in matching stage costumes to accentuate their sense of group identity. This became accepted show biz style and initially the convention was generally adopted by white rock'n'roll groups. But in the case of surfer album sleeves a number of subtle new indicators of group identity are introduced. Take the covers of *Surfin' Safari* (1962) and *Surfer Girl* (1963) where the Beach Boys are photographed in a way which emphasizes the sense of group belonging, and carefully avoids privileging the status of any one member. A matching dress code is adopted, although deliberately undercut by being overtly informal. The group's casual approach to the photographic session projects its self-reliant nature, offering its audience a compelling representation of teenage independence, cohesion and singularity of purpose (Beach Boys sleeves of the early '60s are notoriously banal). Rather than dressing up for the occasion, the group presents itself with the informal assurance of a jazz combo, confident in its ability to provide its own vocals and music and, most importantly, its independence from Tin Pan Alley for the composition of its repertoire. Surfer album sleeves, then, are amongst the earliest attempts to picture that archetypal rock entity, the self-initiated, self-sufficient, self-sustaining group.

The Southern California lifestyle became one of the '60's most potent cultural commodities. Beach fantasies prospered in landlocked cities far from California's sunny shores. Surfer music (and music that had little to do with surfing which was packaged to appeal to the surfer bandwagon) became increasingly commercialized. Surfers were outraged at the commercialization of their subculture. Micki "Da Cat" Dora, Malibu's leading surfer bemoaned "Wall Street flesh merchants [who] desire to unify surfing only to extract the wealth". When Jan & Dean were approached by Columbia Pictures to star in a movie project to be called *Ride the Wild Surf*, he was rumoured to have taken a contract out on the duo.

By 1967 the Beach Boys had released *Pet Sounds* and demonstrated they had well and truly transcended their surfing roots. The following year, the Trashmen, who had started out playing surf music for a landlocked Minnesota audience (and were the only American group which could claim that the Rolling Stones had opened for them) had disbanded.

2

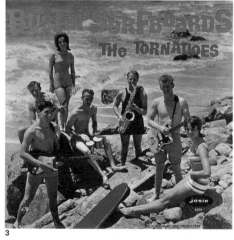

3

5

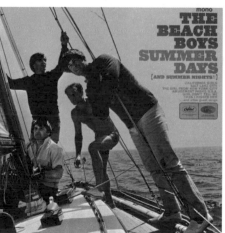

4

1

2

1   **The One Who Really Loves You**, MARY WELLS,
Tamla Motown, 1962.
Design: Barni Wright.

2   **The Marvelettes**, THE MARVELETTES,
Tamla Motown, 1965.
Design: unknown.

Berry Gordy Junior, who was a successful composer during the latter half of the 1950s with hits such as "Reet Petite" and "Money", launched Motown records in 1959 with his friend the singer Smokey Robinson. Motown grew to become America's most successful black independent record company. Despite its phenomenal success, the company was run like a family business – many of the recording stars it created were friends, acquaintances and members of the extended Gordy family. Motown was an unashamed hit-making factory and, as such, was intent on bringing black music into the American mainstream at a time when segregation was still a fact and discrimination overt. (Segregation was not finally outlawed by federal law until 1964). As a consequence, the album sleeves of early 1960s Motown records demonstrate the iconographic delicacies of representing black-ness to American white society at that time.

In the '50s black musicians were supplying a disproportionately large part of the market for popular music and undoubtedly were the source of a great many of its innovations. Clean-cut white crooners like Pat Boone produced cover versions of black musicians' recordings, often selling more copies than the genuine article. Motown was bent on establishing its own distinctive recording sound which was not so easy to replicate. It also sought to make black-ness acceptable, not just in the traditional niche markets, but across the whole face of America. At the time, Harry Belefonte, he of the mild demeanour and self-effacing dignity, was

the acceptable face of the black man. Nothing could have been further from the black stars of bebop who often projected an aggressive and confrontational attitude to their audiences. Motown sought to strike a conciliatory balance, although some early covers ducked the issue of black representation entirely by resorting to generalized illustration. Many of Motown's greatest successes in the early '60s were singing groups: the Temptations, Martha & the Vandellas, the Four Tops, and the Supremes. In this, Motown paralleled Phil Spector's success with girl groups – the Crystals and the Ronettes – where popular acceptability was likewise achieved by carefully subsuming the individuality of the members of the group to the group identity. Matching hair-dos and the strict observance of showbiz dress code, generally reinforced by light and playful drawn motifs and other graphic devices, were acceptable ways of portraying black recording artists in show business's gilded cage of emancipation and, at the same time, keeping them non-threatening. It is significant that in the case of the Supremes and the Miracles it was not until 1967 that their respective lead singers Diana Ross and Smokey Robinson were given featured status.

It was the subversion of this iconography of group identity by white groups (see pages 84–5), and particularly the invasion of British groups in the mid years of the decade, that made explicit the conservative nature of Motown's representations of black identity, even though, at the time, it served well the advancement of many black

recording stars into the mainstream of American popular music. There is an important sense in which the other bookend to the Motown sleeve look of the early '60s is the emergence of reggae a decade later, which proclaimed, both through its music and in the style of its album covers, the total repudiation by black musicians of such representational considerations.

Motown continued to be successful over many years, even surviving the move from its native Detroit to Hollywood. Finally the label was sold to MCA in 1986.

The Supremes ★ With Love From Us To You

mono

Tamla Motown
TRADE MARK OF MOTOWN RECORD CORPORATION

THE SUPREMES

WITH LOVE
(FROM US
TO YOU)

A HARD DAYS NIGHT
HOUSE OF THE RISING SUN
BITS AND PIECES
I WANT TO HOLD YOUR HAND
CAN'T BUY ME LOVE
YOU'VE REALLY GOT A HOLD ON ME
YOU CAN'T DO THAT
DO YOU LOVE ME
HOW DO YOU DO IT
WORLD WITHOUT LOVE
BECAUSE

3

4

5

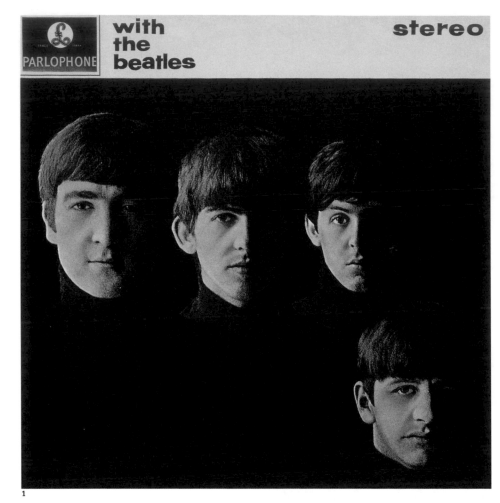

The Beatles, one of the pivotal phenomena in the development of popular culture in the 20th century, instigated fundamental changes in popular music, celebrity and the record industry. The group's comparatively short existence almost precisely spans the decade. Their album sleeves, many of which now appear deceptively simple, were groundbreaking and extraordinarily influential. Beatles' sleeves have produced more look-alikes, homages and pastiches than those of any other rock group. They set the pace in a revolution in record cover design, which led to the creation of an entirely new visual lexicon to symbolize the emerging rock genre.

The Beatles first breakthrough in album design was the darkly glamourous formalism of their second album *With The Beatles* (1963). The photographer, Robert Freeman, had previously used a similar composition to photograph the three partners of design group Pentagram – Bob Gill, Alan Fletcher and Colin Forbes – for *Vogue* soon after they started work together in 1962. In his subsequent version for the album sleeve the composition is transformed: the Beatles moody androgyny looming out of a uniformly black void making for an entirely different effect. Their image owed a good deal to Astrid Kirchherr who had had a powerful influence on their visual style through her association with their original bass guitarist Stuart Sutcliffe during the band's early sojourn in Hamburg. As George Melly put it in his 1970 book *Revolt Into Style*: "Among the vulgar fairground barking of the LP covers of its period, *With The*

Beatles had the dramatic impact of a bomb in a bouquet of multi-coloured gladioli."

With The Beatles was followed by a succession of album sleeves photographed by Robert Freeman, two of which were linked to films – *A Hard Day's Night* (1964) and *Help!* (1965) – which explored and extended the conventional group shot genre. The series culminated in *Rubber Soul* of 1965 where Freeman's use of a fish-eye lens effect and the biomorphic distortions of the title lettering gave the first intimations of the group's psychedelic phase. Their album of the following year, *Revolver*, was, in terms of its iconography, the full-blown thing, although perversely limited to black and white. The designer, Klaus Voorman, was an art student friend from the group's days in Hamburg, a boyfriend of Astrid Kirchherr before she met Stuart Sutcliffe, and at that time bass guitarist with the successful British band Manfred Mann. On first impression the cover's black and white drawing seems rather self-effacing, but its combination of sinuous organic linearity and the convolutions of secondary detail are classic hall-marks of the psychedelic style. It was a potent embodiment of the "Swinging London" tag, heralding the imminent arrival of "flower power" and "the beautiful people".

Sergeant Pepper's Lonely Hearts Club Band, released in June 1967 marks the highwater of London's hippy moment, an unstable mixture of LSD, the psyched-out music of the underground and an exuberant visual style which was a meld of stylistic sources. The Beatles were the undisputed

royalty of London's counter-culture scene and, for a while, they dispensed artistic patronage like renaissance princes (for a fuller account of this see "Psychedelia in London", pages 102–103). The complex tableau that Pop artist Peter Blake created for the front cover of *Sergeant Pepper's* speaks of the time and place in which it was made in a uniquely allegorical way. The Beatles, dressed in the satin uniforms of Sergeant Pepper's band – the pretext for the album's narrative structure – are surrounded by a galaxy of the heroes of popular culture of the type celebrated in Blake's paintings of the time. Close examination of the photograph reveals many telling details. The flower bed spelling out the Beatles' name conceals marijuana plants. In the detail of the image can be found a buddha, a doll bearing a sign saying "Welcome Rolling Stones", an image of the fifth Beatle, Stuart Sutcliffe, and effigies of the band from their "mop-top" period, borrowed from Madame Tussaud's waxworks museum.

The phenomenal success of *Sergeant Pepper's* made the task of producing a follow-up an extremely daunting one. In the event, the double album's profusion of songs was something of a curate's egg, but the sleeve, designed by another eminent pop artist, Richard Hamilton, avoided comparison by being *Sergeant Pepper's*' absolute antithesis. Instead of Blake's rumbustious space-filling detail there was only an outer gatefold of pure white stamped with "The Beatles" and a serial number, slightly askew. The "white album", as it subsequently became known, marked the

1 **With the Beatles**, THE BEATLES, Parlophone, 1963.
Photography: Robert Freeman.

2 **No 2**, THE ROLLING STONES, Decca, 1964.
Photography: David Bailey.

3 **A Hard Day's Night**, THE BEATLES, Parlophone, 1964.
Photography: Robert Freeman.

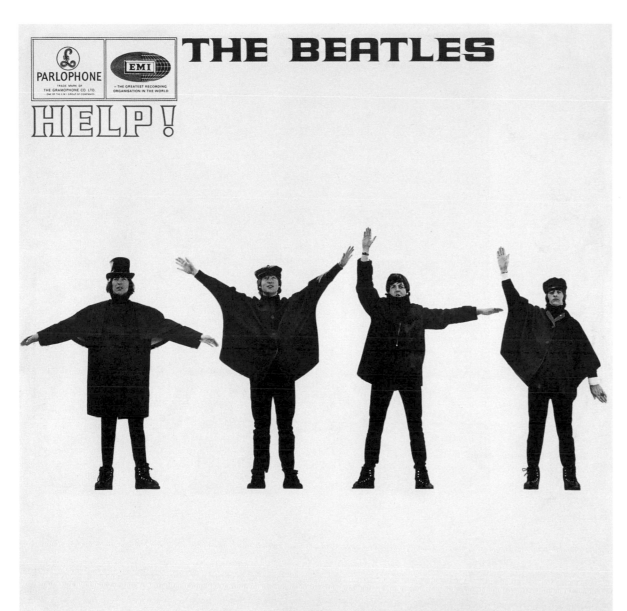

4

5

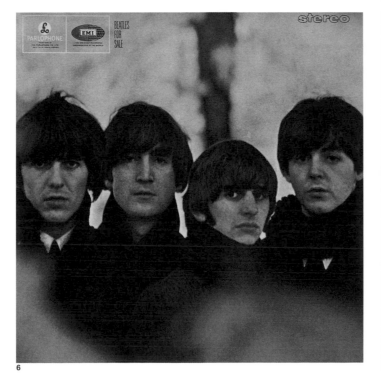

6

7

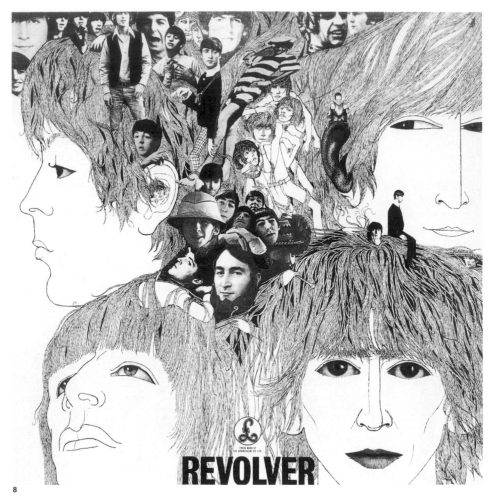

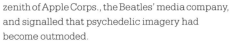

8

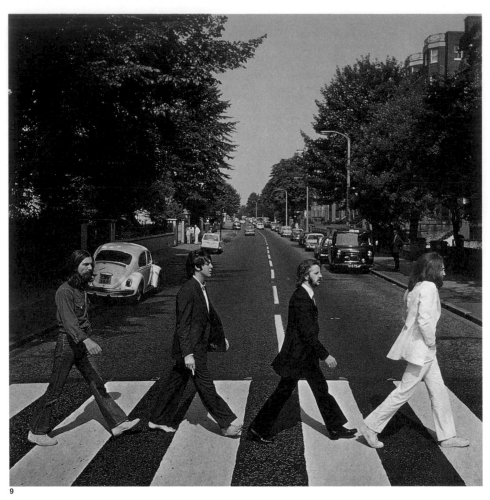

9

zenith of Apple Corps., the Beatles' media company, and signalled that psychedelic imagery had become outmoded.

Abbey Road (1969) was not the final Beatles album, Let It Be limped out after it with a make-do cover of individual portrait photographs, but it was the last before Lennon finally broke the spell of the collaboration by announcing his intention of leaving the group. The apparently ordinary idea for the cover of a photograph of the Beatles crossing the Abbey Road pedestrian crossing directly outside the EMI recording Studio in St John's Wood, London, where they were then recording, took on tremendous symbolic significance. Fans felt a sense of disquiet at the Beatles' lock-step gait and interpreted it as indicating an uncertain future for the band. The pedestrian crossing shot is one of the most repeated photographic exploits in the history of popular music, even parodied by Paul McCartney who replaced John, George and Ringo with an English sheepdog for the cover of Paul Is Live (1993).

The Beatles' judgement was not always infallible, as the notorious "butcher sleeve" for the American album release Yesterday And Today (1966) demonstrates. The album, compiled from three previously released UK albums, was a fairly cynical piece of marketing by Capitol to capitalize on the Beatles' 1966 American tour. The cover featured a photograph taken by Robert Whittaker, a well-known photographer of the London hippy scene who had pretensions to radicality through his connection to performance artists like Stuart

Brisley and Mark Boyle. Whittaker photographed the group garlanded with meat and decapitated dolls. The photograph was originally intended to be part of an allegorical triptych devised by Whittaker and the Beatles entitled Somnambulant Adventure. Dressed in their white coats the Beatles look as charismatic as butcher's boys. Three quarters of a million copies of the album were produced before the first complaints came in. Capitol's president, Alan W. Livingstone, using an excuse often employed to justify visual effrontery, claimed it was intended as "a pop art satire". Aided by an aside by Lennon about the cover being "as relevant as Vietnam", the photograph was attacked as an anti-war statement about American involvement in Vietnam and the album was hastily recalled. Some of the original covers were subsequently pasted over with a replacement photograph which fans could peel off. Pristine copies of the sleeve are now highly valued collectors' items.

8 **Revolver**, THE BEATLES, Parlophone, 1966. Design: Klaus Voorman.

9 **Abbey Road**, THE BEATLES, Apple, 1969. Photography: Iain MacMillan.

10 **Sgt. Pepper's Lonely Hearts Club Band**, THE BEATLES, Parlophone, 1967. [opposite] Design: MC Productions and Apple, Staged by Peter Blake and Jan Haworth.

1   Poster: Yellow Submarine, 1968.
United Artists, British Quad.

The hippy counter-culture of the mid-1960s produced its own distinctive visual style, psychedelia. Undoubtedly, the style's most ambitious and talented exponents were allied to the drug and rock communities that took root in the Haight-Ashbury district of San Francisco and in Notting Hill in London. Most notable were Rick Griffin, Victor Moscoso, the Mouse & Kelley studios and Wes Wilson in San Francisco; and in London Hapshash And The Coloured Coat, The Fool, Michael McInnerney and Martin Sharp.

Rock musicians were major figureheads of the hippy movement – espousing its experimentation with mind-altering drugs and the withdrawal to retreats such as the ashram of Maharishi Mahesh Yogi – and many commissioned album sleeves in the psychedelic style. For most major rock groups, such as the Beatles and the Rolling Stones, adherence to the style was comparatively brief, both having moved on by the end of the decade. For others psychedelia was a defining moment in the development of their identities, such as the quintessentially Californian band the Grateful Dead, which evolved out of the Warlocks, Ken Kesey and the Merry Pranksters' house band.

The psychedelic style achieved extraordinary popularity for several years before becoming rapidly outmoded. In its heyday many graphic artists in all parts of the world adopted the style. Even design veteran Milton Glaser produced a popular, if cliched, psychedelic profile portrait image of Bob Dylan. And Peter Max, also New York-based, helped develop a cartoon version of psychedelic iconography which was subsequently adopted by Heinz Edelmann for the Beatles' *Yellow Submarine* feature-length cartoon (1968).

The style incorporated graphic elements from a wide ranged of sources. As Richard Neville, founder of London underground publication *Oz*, put it: "…the whole world can be plundered for decoration – from food labels, oriental comic books, Tibetan scrolls and Encyclopedia Britannica. Copyright is ignored." More specifically, psychedelic imagery was bent on simulating hallucinogenic disorientation through optical excitation. The hallmark of the style was the combining of convoluted, lysergic illustrative material – sometimes multilayered – and excessive biomorphic typographical forms into a seamless amalgam. The best designers gave such

free rein to the distortion of typography forms, which were sometimes reminiscent of Art Nouveau motifs, that textual meaning became indecipherable to all but the initiated. This amalgam of letter and image forms was often enhanced by the use of brilliant colour combinations and newly available Day-Glo inks.

As Neville's recipe suggests, the style is an extraordinary confluence of visual references: the graphic simplifications of Pop and the optical excitation of op art, the Pre-Raphaelites, the Art Nouveau of Alphonse Mucha and Aubrey Beardsley, the work of visionary artists such as William Blake, the children's fantasy illustrations of Edmund DuLac and Arthur Rackham, Tolkein and Celtic decoration are all assimilated, as is the influence of the late 19th century Symbolists such as Gustave Moreau. Subtle differences can be discerned in the mix of sources employed by individual practitioners, and there are marked differences in the way the style developed on the West Coast and in London. Despite the catalogue of sources that can be cited, psychedelia is a highly original and distinctive style which is extraordinarily evocative of the period.

2 **Abraxas**, SANTANA, CBS, 1970.
Illustrator: Abdul Mati Klarwein. Graphics: Robert Venosa.

3 **Turn On, Tune In, Drop Out**, Various Artists, Mercury, 1967.
Design: unknown

4 **The Psychedelic Sounds of the 13th Floor Elevators**,
13TH FLOOR ELEVATORS, International Artists, 1967.
Design and illustration: John Cleveland.

5 **Poster: Bob Dylan**, 1966.
Design: Milton Glaser.

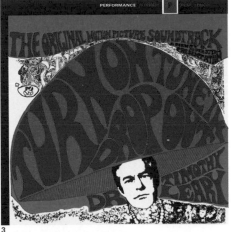

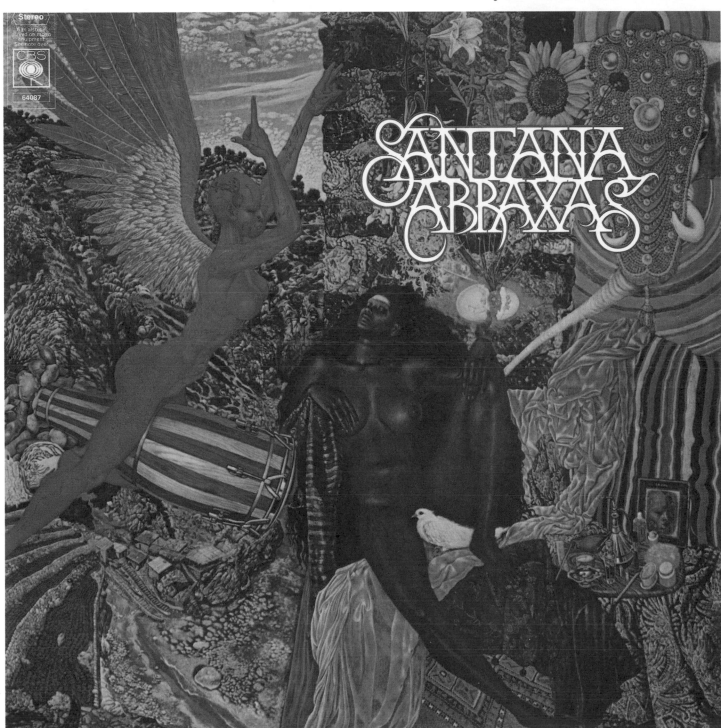

1960–69 **Teen Culture, Pop, and Psychedelia** **MOUSE & KELLEY**

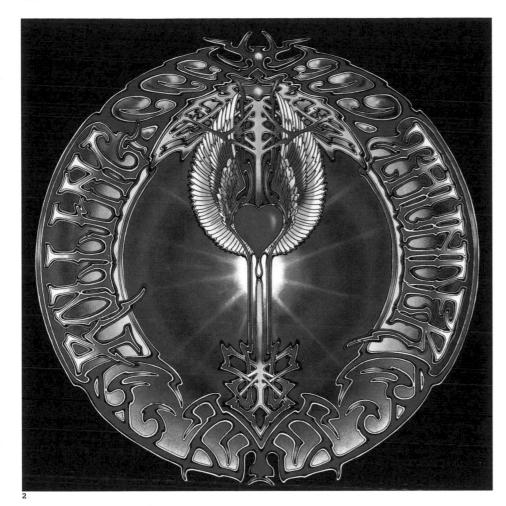

2

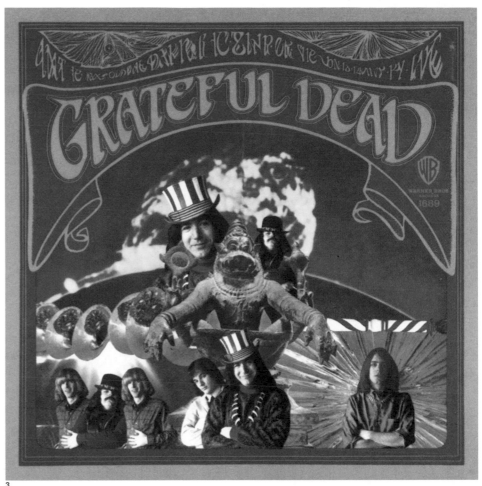

3

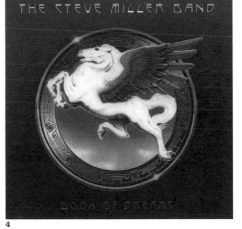

4

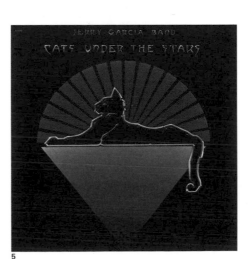

5

Although Haight-Ashbury's designer/ illustrators worked for many clients during psychedelia's heyday, psychedelic iconography was initially developed to advertise concerts at local venues, most notably the Fillmore Auditorium and the Avalon Ballroom, where famous promoters Bill Graham and Family Dog introduced many of the progressive bands of the West Coast scene.

Under the direction of Chet Helms, Family Dog produced concerts, dances and other events at the Avalon Ballroom at the rate of two to five a week from February 1966 until the end of 1968, resulting in the production of some 150 posters. The designers most frequently used to produce posters for the Family Dog promotions at the Avalon were the Mouse & Kelley Studios and Victor Moscoso.

Bill Graham was once moved to declare that "Stanley Mouse put the face on rock and roll music." Stanley Miller, born in 1940, son of a one-time Disney animator, began designing in his home town of Detroit under the *nom de plume* of Mouse Studios. Before arriving in San Francisco he was already a legend for the custom airbrush teeshirts designs which he produced to order at events such as the Michigan State Fair. A meeting with Alton Kelley in 1965, soon after his arrival in the Bay Area of San Francisco, led to the establishing of the Mouse & Kelley Studios.

Kelley was one or the original members of the Family Dog and had designed posters for the early psychedelic happenings staged by Bill Graham and the Family Dog at San Francisco's Longshoreman's Hall. When Helms took control of

the Family Dog organization and began to make plans to promote concerts at the Avalon Ballroom, he was not convinced that Kelley had sufficient expertise to supply poster designs of the quality he required. Instead he commissioned Wes Wilson whose proficiency was already well-known. Teaming up with "Mouse" Miller quickly satisfied Helm's reservations since Miller had a comprehensive command of printing know-how, and they began to produce posters for the Avalon on a regular basis.

The Mouse & Kelley Studios was the most prolific and long-lived design studio founded during San Francisco's hippy heyday. Besides their output of concert posters, singly or together, for the Avalon and many other venues, they designed album covers for artists on the West Coast scene through the 1970s and into the 1980s. Many were exquisite examples of psychedelic decoration, most notably the album sleeve for Grateful Dead's *American Beauty* (1970). As the decade turned, Stanley Mouse in particular was prepared to adopt a more eclectic approach to design. His sleeve for the Grateful Dead's *Workingman's Dead* released the same year as *American Beauty* has the appearance of a Victorian book frontispiece. Elements of his pre-Haight-Ashbury cartoon style of drawing figure on the Grateful Dead's *Europe '72* album cover. And yet it is Mouse & Kelley's psychedelic illustration which is always most notable: the sleeves of *Rolling Thunder* for Mickey Hart (1972), *Book Of Dreams* for The Steve Miller

Band (1977) and Journey's *Captured* (1981) are all accomplished examples of the style. Mouse & Kelley Studios was still producing posters for Bill Graham when he closed his follow-up venue to the Fillmore, the Winterland Arena, in 1978.

1 **American Beauty**, GRATEFUL DEAD, Warner Bros, 1971. Design: Mouse & Kelley Studios. [opposite]
2 **Rolling Thunder**, MICKEY HART, Warner Bros, 1972. Design: Mouse & Kelley Studios.
3 **Grateful Dead**, GRATEFUL DEAD, Warner Bros, 1967. Design: Mouse Studios. Photography: Herb Greene. Illustration: Kelley.
4 **Book of Dreams**, THE STEVE MILLER BAND, Capitol, 1977. Design: Mouse & Kelley Studios. Art Direction: Roy Kohara.
5 **Cats Under the Stars**, JERRY GARCIA BAND, Arista, 1978. Design: Mouse & Kelley Studios.

1

Victor Moscoco, who sometimes worked under the pseudonym Vincent, was born in 1936 in La Coruña, Spain. He studied art at Yale University and the Cooper Union in New York before arriving in San Francisco. Although the output of his Haight-Ashbury period shares many characteristics with the other exponents of the psychedelic style, Moscoso's version is marked by the extreme degree of optical excitation it produced due to his use of colour and form. This attribute of his work is often ascribed to the influence of one of his teachers at Yale, the abstract painter Josef Albers, who made the study of colour, and its affects, a central concern of both his teaching, and his own practice.

Moscoso arrived in San Francisco in October of 1959 to continue his art training by enrolling on the Masters programme at the San Francisco Art Institute. He subsequently obtained a teaching post at the Institute and also established a freelance practice working as a graphic artist. By the mid-1960s he was involved in the developing psychedelic scene in the Bay area, and by late 1966 had begun to produce posters for Family Dog promotions at the Avalon Ballroom. At about the same time he began to produce posters for the Matrix Club, a blues and rock venue which Jefferson Airplane co-founder, Marty Balin, had launched the previous year. Aware of the growing after-market for posters, Moscoso's agreement with the Matrix allowed him to publish the Matrix posters under his own imprint, "Neon Rose". The Neon Rose series mark the apex of his optical

period. His combinations of intense, saturated colours of an almost identical tone caused an optical vibration of the posters' images in a way which was reminiscent of the then-fashionable op-art painting of artists Victor Vaserely and Bridget Riley. Moscoso was very active as a poster designer through 1967 and 1968, designing for a variety of venues in San Francisco and Los Angeles, although most regularly for the Matrix and the Avalon. He continued to produce posters for the Avalon, even after a change of management at the venue caused by complaints from local residents about the Family Dog flouting the closing time agreement. The Matrix flourished throughout the '60s, only the Fillmore and the Avalon exceeded the number of posters produced to advertise events at the venue.

Moscoso went on to design several album sleeves in a semi-psychedelic style, mostly notably for the Steve Miller Band's *Book Of Dreams* (1968), Herbie Hancock's *Headhunters* (1973), and Jerry Garcia's *Garcia* (1974). He worked as a staff artist at *Rolling Stone* magazine for a period in the late '60s and, besides Robert Crumb, he was perhaps the most memorable contributor to the West Coast comix scene, producing work for publications such as *Zap*, *El Perfecto*, *Snatch*, and *Yellow Dog*. His strips were also published in London underground publications *Oz* and *International Times*.

2

3

4

5

4 **Garcia**, JERRY GARCIA, Warner Bros/Round, 1974.
Design: Victor Moscoso.
5 **Poster: "Flower Pot"/Blue Cheer,** Avalon Ballroom, 1967.
Design: Victor Moscoso.

1 **Children of the Future**, STEVE MILLER BAND, Capitol, 1968.
Design: Victor Moscoso. Photography: Elaine Mayes.
2 **Headhunters**, HERBIE HANCOCK, Columbia, 1974.
Design: Victor Moscoso. Photography: Waldo Bascom.
3 **Poster: Oxford Circle, Big Brother & the Holding Co,
Lee Michaels**, Avalon Ballroom, 1966.
Design: Victor Moscoso.

1 **Poster: Quicksilver Messenger Service**, Fillmore
  Auditorium, 1966.
  Design: Wes Wilson.
2 **Poster: The Byrds**, Winterland & Fillmore Auditorium, 1967.
  Design: Wes Wilson.
3 **Poster: Captain Beefheart**, Fillmore Auditorium, 1966.
  Design: Wes Wilson.

The posters of Wes Wilson, born 1937, are a perfect expression of the morphology of San Francisco's psychedelic art. Although actively producing in a full-blown psychedelic style for only a comparative short time, from February 1966 until May 1967, he produced an enormous number of posters for the two legendary San Francisco concert venues of the '60s, the Avalon Ballroom and the Fillmore Auditorium.

After attending San Francisco State University, Wilson went to work for a small San Francisco press called Contact Printing where he learned how to design the multiplate layouts necessary to print colour posters. Contact's proprietor, Bob Carr, largely produced posters and handbills for San Francisco's jazz, art and poetry scene. Wilson's

work for the company brought him into contact with the hippy scene's two most important concert promoters, Family Dog's Chet Helms and Bill Graham. Both started regular concerts at, respectively, the Avalon Theatre and the Fillmore Auditorium in February 1966. Initially, Wilson produced nearly all the posters for both venues, but pressure of work forced him to concentrate on designing for only one of them. In the end he chose to work for Bill Graham, whom he considered was less likely to interfere in the design process than Chet Helms.

Wilson's approach to poster design was rooted in his instinctive understanding of the accumulative effect of building up a design by overlaying different colours. He acknowledged not

only selecting colours through his professional experience as a printer, but through visual experiences with LSD. Graphically speaking, American poster designers William H. Bradley (1868–1962), Claude Fayette Bragdon (1866–1946) and Maxfield Parrish (1870–1966) were influences, as were European designers Jan Toorop and Alfred Roller. Wilson particularly acknowledged Alfred Roller – designer and founding member of the Viennese Secessionist movement for which he designed many exhibition posters – as being a particular source of inspiration for his letter forms.

Over an eighteen-month period Wilson produced numerous posters for the Fillmore, undeterred by Graham's occasional complaints about the illegibility of his designs. Disputes about

WES WILSON, BONNIE McLEAN, AND LEE CONKLIN

4

5

money finally brought his association with Graham's organization to an end in May 1967. By then so many artists had adopted his style that Graham was able to replace him with relative ease. The mainstream's brief and ill-advised flirtation with psychedelic imagery is best summed up by Wilson being commissioned to produce a programme cover for the 1968 convention of the Operational Research Society of America's Technical Institute of Military Science. He gave them an image of a woman crucified.

Wilson disappeared from the San Francisco scene in the early 1970s, disillusioned with his career and financial prospects as a poster designer. He moved to the Ozark mountains in Missouri where he has sinced lived a life of rural

seclusion. In addition to Wilson, two other designers, Bonnie McLean and Lee Conklin, produced significant bodies of work for the Fillmore in the full-blown psychedelic style. McLean, who took over from Wilson, produced designs very much in the Wilson mould during the second half of 1967, before she too left. She was succeeded by Lee Conklin who produced about forty posters for the Fillmore, most of them in 1968. His style was somewhat different from his two predecessors, featuring almost caricature-like imagery. He produced the line-drawing double image for Santana's first album in 1969.

4 **Santana**, SANTANA, CBS/Columbia, 1969.
   Design: Lee Conklin.
5 **Poster: Eric Burdon & The Animals**, Fillmore
   Auditorium, 1967.
   Design: Bonnie McLean.

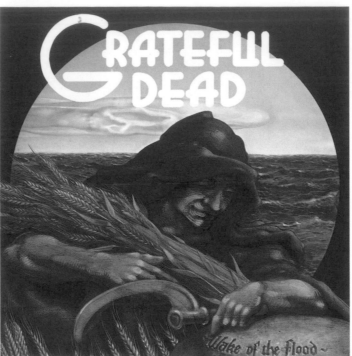

Rick Griffin's designs of the period 1967–69 are some of the most highly developed expression of the Haight-Ashbury psychedelic style. Griffin, born 1944, a one-time illustrator for Southern California surfer magazines and member of a proto-hippy commune called the Jook Savages, moved to San Francisco in 1966. Initially he produced designs for Stanley "Mouse" Miller in the 19th-century Wild West revivalist look originally favoured by the Family Dog organization. In this style he designed the poster for the Gathering Of The Tribes Human Be-in in Golden Gate Park featuring – among others – Timothy Leary, Allen Ginsberg, Lawrence Ferlinghetti and Jerry Rubin. In 1967 he also began to design for San Francisco music venues the Fillmore Auditorium and Avalon Ballroom. His revivalist style gradually morphed into his more innovative psychedelic style. Here he combined bold colour and heraldic-cum-druggy pictorial elements to compliment his highly individual typographic inventions. He retained an attachment to the over-elaborate typefaces which were such a feature of the Wild West revivalist look, although in his hands their serif letter forms became strangely transmogrified into almost indecipherable freizelike patterns and biomorphic motifs. The reader's bafflement was further intensified by Griffin's habit of slipping into his designs meaningless extra bits of calligraphy. These impenetrable typographical codes which prevented the uninitiated from getting the message were a perfect representation of the counter culture's desire for meaning that dropped out of conventional understanding. He was soon in demand for numerous commissions. One of the most notable was to design the sleeve for the third album by the Grateful Dead, based on a poster he had produced for a concert they had given at the Avalon. Originally the title of the album was to be "Earthquake Country" or "Upwind Of Disaster, Downwind Of Atonement" but the final title arose out of Griffin's habit of working his doodles of linked letters such as "OA" into acid-inspired forms. Robert Hunter, the Grateful Dead's lyricist, asked Griffin to link some of his palindromic doodles such as "OXO" and "MOM" together to make a title for the album. The result was *Aoxomoxoa*, widely considered to be the most perfect embodiment of West Coast psychedelia.

Griffin, like his friend and sometime collaborator Victor Moscoso, went on to produce work for underground comic publications. He had produced a comic-striplike poster for the Quicksilver Messenger Service for their 1967 appearance at the Avalon Ballroom. "There was no story line or meaning to the sequence of panels. I just thought they looked good together and worked as a piece of graphics." In 1968 Robert Crumb, the most famous figure of the underground comic movement, had just published the first issue of his underground comic *Zap Comix* and was looking for artists to contribute to the second issue. He remembered Griffin's poster and searched him out, instigating Griffin's involvement in the underground comix scene. His contributions were full of mystic psychedelic imagery, often a series of conventional storyboard frames with little discernible narrative and sometimes consisted of an entire page occupied by a single convoluted image of intertwined elements. He contributed a strip to Alan Aldridge's *Beatles Illustrated Song Book* (published in 1969) to accompany the lyrics of *Why Don't We Do It In The Road?*.

Griffin also made a key contribution to the early days of the other long-lived publication to come out of the San Francisco hippy milieu, the music scene paper *Rolling Stone*. According to publisher Jann Wenner, he had to grab the "unfinished design" of the *Rolling Stone* logo from Griffin's drawing board in order to meet the deadline for the first edition published on November 9, 1967. Edition 17 of *Rolling Stone*, of September 14, 1968, contained a spread on *Zap Comix* and featured a Rick Griffin drawing on the cover.

By 1970 Griffin had largely abandoned his psychedelic style, although he still continued to produce the occasional spread for comix publications. Perhaps this abandonment owes something to the religious conversion to Christianity which he underwent at the time. He resurrected his early cartoon figure Murphy for *Tales From The Tube* which initially appeared as an insert in *Surfer* magazine, but it became so popular that it went on to be distributed as a stand-alone publication. Like many illustrators of his generation he flirted with airbrush techniques for a while, particularly for surfing posters. He began to produce historical seafaring subjects painted in a traditional, almost old-masterly, style, one of which became the cover of the Grateful Dead's 1973 album *Wake Of The Flood*, renewing his association with the band. The album was the first to be issued on the band's own record label, and Griffin not only designed the unusually sombre sleeve with its reaper on the front and cackling crow on the reverse, but also a skull-head clown logo for the label. He also produced a significant body of biblical imagery based on the Gospel According to St John. Griffin died in a motorbike accident in 1991.

3

4

3   Poster, **"Morning Paper"**, Quicksilver Messenger Service, Avalon Ballroom, 1967.
Design: Rick Griffin.

4   Poster: **"The Flying Eyeball"**, Jimi Hendrix at the Fillmore & Winterland, 1968.
Design: Rick Griffin.

1 **Bee Gees 1st**, THE BEE GEES, Atco, 1967.
Designer: Klaus Voorman.

2 **The 5000 Spirits or The Layers of the Onion**, THE
INCREDIBLE STRING BAND, Elektra, 1967.
Design: Simon & Marijke (The Fool).

3 **Magic Bus, The Who on Tour**, THE WHO, Decca, 1968.
Design: unknown.

4 **Axis Bold as Love**, THE JIMI HENDRIX EXPERIENCE,
Polydor, 1967.
Design: David King, Roger Law.

5

6

5/6 Disraeli Gears, CREAM, Polydor, 1967.
Design: Martin Sharp. Photography: Bob Whitaker.

In the "Swinging London" ferment of the mid-1960s the watchwords were fashion, style and counter-culture. Many London-based rock musicians had studied at art school, John Lennon, Pete Townshend, Jimmy Page, Ray Davies, Keith Richards, and Eric Clapton among them, and they were developing an increasingly sophisticated understanding of how "image" – which included their album sleeves – could act in parallel with their music. Success gave them increasing power to bargain with their record companies. They began to demand that their album sleeves reflect the druggy-sexual liberation, utopianism, and disdain for bourgeois conventions which were rapidly gaining coherence as the counter-culture milieu. As 1966 drew to a close this counter culture began to take concrete form. Underground publication *IT* (*International Times*) was launched in October and *Oz* early in the following year. Underground venues such as UFO and Middle Earth were launched to stage multimedia happenings and concerts. As in San Francisco, they adopted psychedelia as their house style.

Perhaps the most celebrated psychedelic design team of the London hippy scene was Hapshash and the Coloured Coat, the prolific partnership of Michael English and Nigel Waymouth (see pages 104–105). Martin Sharp and Michael McInnerney were two other gifted exponents of the style. Sharp designed early issues of *Oz*, creating the paper's distinctive blend of images and text. He also designed posters for clubs such as UFO, and two album sleeves for Cream, most notably *Disraeli Gears* (1967). Sharp's posters were were predominantly printed on metallized paper. Sometimes they were related to specific events and sometimes ambitious attempts to visualize the mythological constellations of hippydom. Good examples include "Live Give Love" (1967) and "Legalise Cannabis, Speakers Corner, Hyde Park, 16th July" (1967).

Michael McInnerney was art director at *IT* until it was closed down by the Obscene Publications Squad. He produced numerous posters in the psychedelic style, most notably for the *IT* benefit event "14 Hour Technicolour Dream" staged at Alexandra Palace, London, in 1967.

As with most other developments in the London music scene during the '60s, The Beatles – by now well on their way from pop music to polymorphous psychedelic rock – played an important role in the promotion of psychedelic imagery. To the public at large, psychedelia announced its arrival in the summer of 1966 through their *Revolver* album sleeve designed by Klaus Voorman. Another benefactor of the Beatles' patronage was the Dutch design collective The Fool. The Fool's members were Simon Posthuma, Marijke Koger, Josje Leeger and Barrie Finch. They designed many of the Beatles' hippy period clothes. And during 1967–68 they created major internal and external decorations in the psychedelic style for the Beatles' short-lived Apple shop, on Baker Street, London. Their design philosophy was that design should reflect the possibilities inherent in small, self-sufficient communities. Design was all-over, do-it-yourself, based on handicrafts, low technology solutions and personal involvement: the perfect expression of hippy ideals.

Inevitably the visual excesses of the psychedelic style began to pall. In January 1968 the journal *Design* featured an article entitled "Are We Suffering From Psychedelic Fatigue?" Commentator Margaret Duckett described psychedelia as "the Parkinson's disease of the retina." It was time for psychedelia's practitioners to move on … or find themselves out of commissions.

1

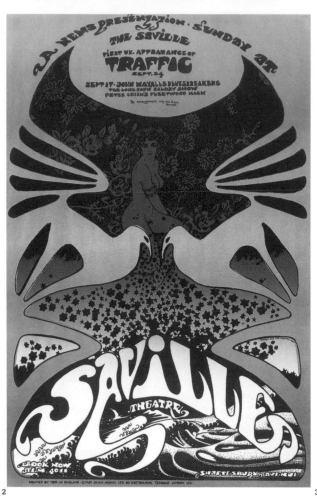

2

3

In March of 1967, Michael English and Nigel Waymouth (both born 1941) formed a prolific but short-lived partnership called Hapshash And The Coloured Coat to produce posters for the hippy underground scene. During the eighteen months of their collaboration they designed some of the most memorable psychedelic posters produced in London during the blooming of psychedelia.

In October, 1966, the Indica Bookshop began to publish a counter-culture newspaper called *IT* (*International Times*) and English, who had studied art at art schools in Hammersmith and Ealing, London, was one of the team producing it. He was introduced to Waymouth in early 1967 when the latter was painting the facade of King's Road boutique Granny Takes a Trip of which he was part owner. Having decided to collaborate on designing posters, they originally called themselves Cosmic Colours and then Jacob and the Coloured Coat before settling on Hapshash and the Coloured Coat. Their first client was UFO Club, a once-a-week underground venue in Tottenham Court Road. UFO stood for "Unlimited Freak-Out", besides its more usual meaning. In George Melly's words, "the aim of UFO was mind-expansion and hallucination at the service of the destruction of the non-hip and the substitution of 'love', in the special, rather nebulous meaning that the word holds for the underground."

Hapshash and the Coloured Coat quickly secured commissions from other venues on the underground scene, including a series of four for the Saville Theatre which Beatles manager Brian Epstein had taken on to promote new rock acts. Many of Hapshash's illustrative work was published in *IT*, and its underground rival *Oz* (launched early 1967). Their posters for concerts and events were subsequently reproduced in large quantities by poster companies, launched on the back of the fashion for psychedelic posters. The promoter of UFO, Elektra record executive Joe Boyd, launched a poster company called Osiris Visions which published many Hapshash posters. Both *International Times* and *Oz* also launched their own poster companies.

Hapshash designs shared the biomorphic convolutions of graphic and typographical element of their Haight-Ashbury counterparts, although with a specifically English flavour. Their iconography reflects the world of the Pre-Raphaelites, Tolkein and visionary English artists such as William Blake, although echoes of the exhibitions of Alphonse Mucha's paintings and Aubrey Beardsley drawings, both held at the Victoria and Albert Museum (1963 and 1966 respectively), can also be detected in the development of their psychedelic iconography. The celebrity of their partnership was such that English and Waymouth were invited to record an album as Hapshash and the Coloured Coat (featuring The Human Host and the Heavy Metal Kids) for which they designed the album sleeve. The sleeve is a perfect example of the symmetrical decorative mandala of the psychedelic style, and certainly a great deal more memorable than the recordings it contains.

After the amicable dissolution of Hapshash and the Coloured Coat, English went on to develop a widely influential form of airbrush illustration. In 1970 he published four posters called "Rubbish Prints" which were internationally successful. They were instrumental in creating the fashion for a pneumatic and vapid form of airbrush painting which became widely popular in the early 1970s. Waymouth too became an artist and has lived in Los Angeles since 1995.

1 **Poster: UFO Coming**, UFO club, 1967.
   Design: Michael English, Nigel Waymouth.
2 **Poster: Traffic**, Saville Theatre, 1967.
   Design: Michael English, Nigel Waymouth.
3 **Illustration: "Position 70"**, *Oz* magazine, 1967.
   Design: Hapshash and the Coloured Coat.
4 **Hapshash and the Coloured Coat**, VARIOUS ARTISTS,
   Minit/Liberty, 1967. [opposite]
   Design: Hapshash and the Coloured Coat.
   Photography: Ekim Adis.

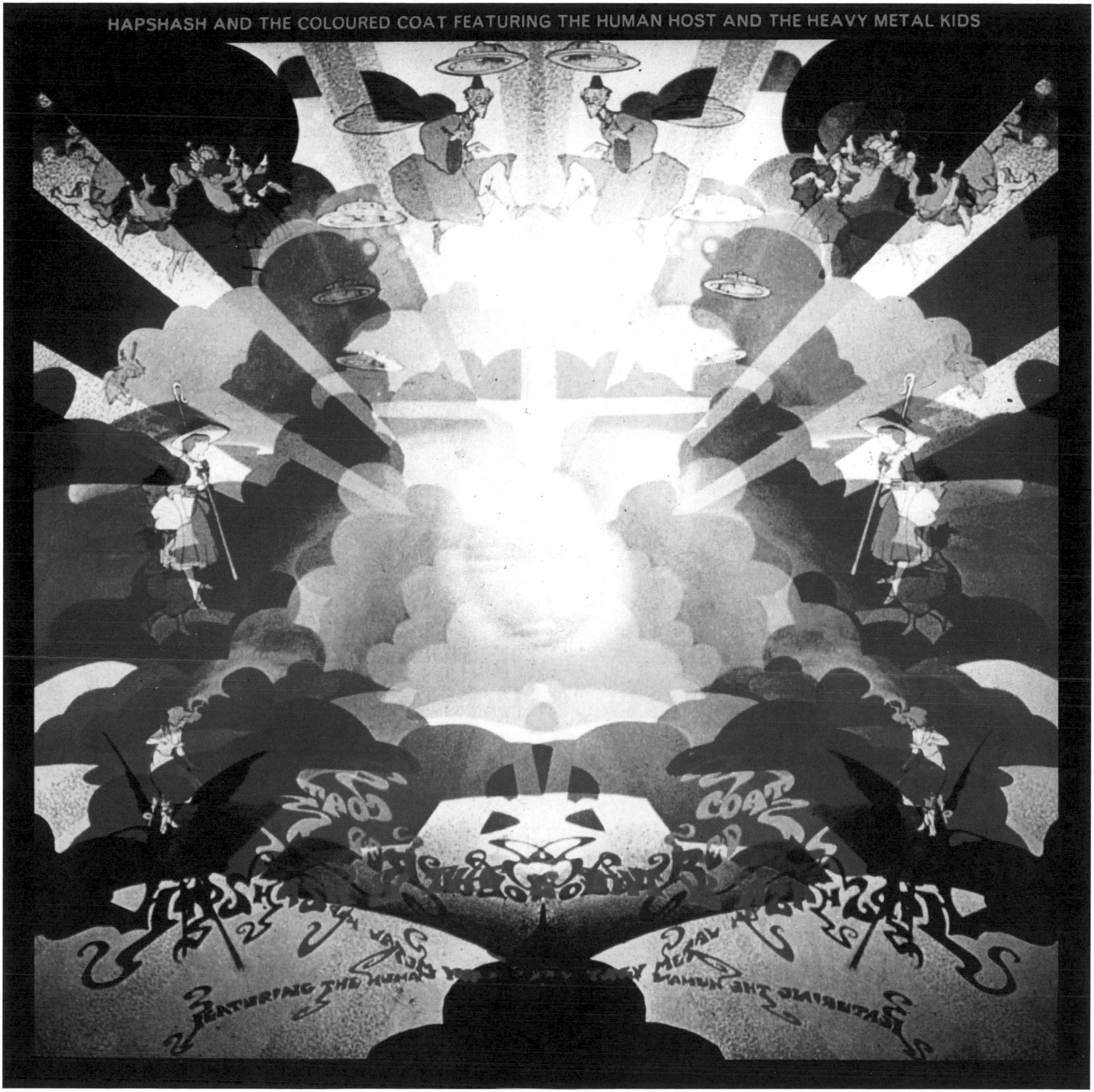

2

3

4

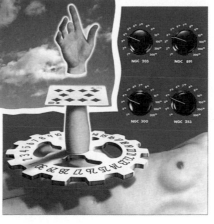

5

Bob Seidemann was born in 1942 in Northern California. He is best characterized as a people photographer, to make a nice distinction from the role of portrait photographer. During his career he has photographed all manner of people, architects, artists and pioneers of aviation, but he began photographing the bands and musicians of the hippy counter culture in the Haight-Ashbury district of San Francisco in the mid-1960s. He is particularly associated with the Grateful Dead and once famously photographed a nude Janis Joplin. He was a friend of many of the San Francisco poster artists and provided photographs for some of their posters. His first album sleeve was for the Eric Clapton super-group Blind Faith in 1969. Seidemann's photomontage of a barely pubescent naked girl was controversial and banned in America. Seidemann subsequently produced the Magritte-inspired cover for Jackson Brown's *Late For The Sky* (1974) and in the same year the equally surreal beach scene for Neil Young's *On The Beach*. He has been involved in the design of many Grateful Dead album sleeves and solo off-shoots. The quantity of his album sleeves has not been great, but the few he has produced, particularly the early ones, have inspired many myths and as many imitations.

In the mid-'60s Seidemann was producing photographic posters for a small San Francisco poster publisher called Berkeley Bonaparte run by Louis Rapoport, who specialized, in his own words, in "advertising to join the mutants and leave the world" (and later, incongruously, became

a well-known historian of the Jewish diaspora and news editor of the *Jerusalem Post*). Seidemann soon found himself immersed in Haight-Ashbury's burgeoning counter culture. In particular he struck up friendships with Rick Griffin and Stanley "Mouse" Miller, both of whom he would later collaborate with on album sleeve design. In 1967 Seidemann reputedly gave up photography after producing a portrait image of Christ for Berkeley Bonaparte which frightened him witless. He subsequently moved to London, where he had contacts in the underground scene, intent on escaping the souring of the Haight-Ashbury milieu. Meanwhile, according to "Mouse" Miller, who was still in San Francisco, Eric Clapton telephoned him from London and said: "Stanley, come and paint my Rolls Royce." To which Miller replied: "Sure, be right there." At the time Clapton was living at the notorious Pheasantry on King's Road, and when Miller arrived he discovered Seidemann was there too. Subsequently the two Americans were asked to collaborate on the design of an album sleeve for an as-yet unnamed new band that Clapton was forming. Seidemann's memory of his reaction was: "This was big time. It seems though the western world had, for lack of a more substantial icon, settled on the rock and roll star as the golden calf of the moment. The record cover had become the place to be seen as an artist."

Seidemann spent two weeks scouring London for exactly the type of model he had in mind for his cover image: "A girl who was in the twilight zone. A girl with innocence and yet approaching

womanhood…The virgin with no responsibility is the fruit of the tree of life, and the spaceship is the fruit of the tree of knowledge…What I had in mind was that the release of the record would coincide with the landing on the moon. As man steps into the galaxy, I wanted innocence to carry my spaceship…" Seidemann commissioned the silver aircraft the girl is holding from Mick Milligan, a jewellery student at the Royal College of Art, and made two trips to Dorset to find and photo-graph the background he required. Reputedly, Seidemann dubbed the photo "Blind Faith" and Clapton adopted the name for his band. Seidemann insisted the finished image should be left unadorned by any lettering. When executives at Polydor balked at the cover, not surprisingly, Clapton had to argue long and hard before they caved in. Inevitably it was banned in America which only added to its notoriety. Perhaps the miracle is that it got made at all.

1 **Blind Faith**, ATCO, 1969. [opposite]
Design and photography: Bob Seidemann.
Spaceship built by Mick Milligan.

2 **Even in the Quietest Moments**, SUPERTRAMP, A&M, 1979.
Photography: Bob Seidemann.

3 **On the Beach**, NEIL YOUNG, Reprise, 1974.
Design: Gary Burden for R Twerk & Co. Photography: Bob Seidemann. Lettering: Rick Griffin.

4 **Late for the Sky**, JACKSON BROWNE, Asylum, 1974.
Photography: Bob Seidemann. Lettering: Rick Griffin.

5 **Garcia**, JERRY GARCIA, Warner Bros, 1972.
Design and photography: Bob Seidemann.

PEEL SLOWLY AND SEE

Andy Warhol

2

3

5

4

Andy Warhol was born in 1927 in Pittsburgh. In the early 1960s he developed a means of making paintings based on the emerging technology of photo-silkscreen printing which brought him great fame. Drawn to celebrity, through both his life and work, he became the personification of a voyeuristic blankness which was greatly influential within the rock and pop worlds. His uncanny ability to select and re-form media images became his great hallmark, although he was also an impressive colourist. The proposition of endless repetition inherent within his images also struck a chord with late 20th century sensibility. Although he undertook comparatively few design commissions for album covers, at least two are seminal and he was, and remains, a fundamental influence on the pop sensibility of youth culture.

Warhol's parents were immigrants from Mikova in what is now the Slovak Republic. Warhol moved to New York at the age of 21 in 1949 and started his career as a commercial artist, making illustrations for greetings cards, fashion shoe illustrations and advertisements, and window displays. The elegant economy of his line drawing shows a distinct affinity with the work of Ben Shahn and the blotted-line drawing technique of David Stone Martin. Throughout the 1950s he worked tirelessly to reach the first rank of illustrators and commercial artists. He had numerous clients for his drawings of fashion accessories (often embellished with gold) including magazines such as *Vogue* and

stores such as Bonwit Teller. His widowed mother, Julia Warhola, lived with him in New York from 1952. She often contributed her decorative calligraphy to his drawings, including some of those commissioned for album covers by Reid Miles at Blue Note.

Warhol's first paintings of Dick Tracy (1961) were used as a window display by Lord & Taylor, Manhattan. In 1965, his career as an artist already established, Warhol met the members of the Velvet Underground at New York's Cafe Bizarre and before long he had become their promoter and manager. This arrangement lasted long enough for him to design the sleeve for their first album recorded in New York and Los Angeles in the spring of 1966. Their LP cover featuring the image of a banana with a peelable skin is one of the most memorable images in the history of album design, although arguably the image and typographical "Andy Warhol" over-emphasize the degree to which Warhol, in his role of producer and manager, contributed to the band's music, most of which had been composed well before their meeting with him. His association with the Velvet Underground occurred during a period when Warhol was much involved in performance events and film making. The Velvet Underground and Nico featured in Warhol's happening, "The Exploding Plastic Inevitable" at the Dom club and contributed to the soundtracks of his films, including *Chelsea Girls*. During this period Warhol's studio "the Factory" was open house to a stream of celebrities and

hangers-on, ending in 1968 when he was shot by Valerie Solanas, author of the revolutionary tract *SCUM Manifesto*. He spent the final decades of his life consolidating his career as a blue chip artist, and amassed a huge fortune by producing silkscreen portraits of the international glitterati. He created the *Sticky Fingers* album sleeve for the Rolling Stones in 1971 and *Love You Live* in 1977. He also produced album sleeves based on his portraits, notably Paul Anka's *The Painter* (1976), Diana Ross's *Silk Electric* (1982), John Lennon's *Menlove Ave.* (1986) and Aretha Franklin's *Aretha* (1986). Warhol died in 1987.

1   **The Velvet Underground and Nico**, THE VELVET UNDERGROUND, Verve, 1967. [opposite] Illustration: Andy Warhol.

2   **Kenny Burrell**, KENNY BURRELL, Blue Note, 1957. Illustration: Andy Warhol. Design: Reid Miles.

3   **Menlove Avenue**, JOHN LENNON, Capitol, 1986. Illustration: Andy Warhol. Art Direction: Roy Kohara, Mark Shoolery.

4   **Silk Electric**, DIANA ROSS, Capitol, 1982. Illustration: Andy Warhol.

5   **Sticky Fingers**, THE ROLLING STONES, Rolling Stones, 1971. Concept and photography: Andy Warhol. Design: Craig Braun, Inc.

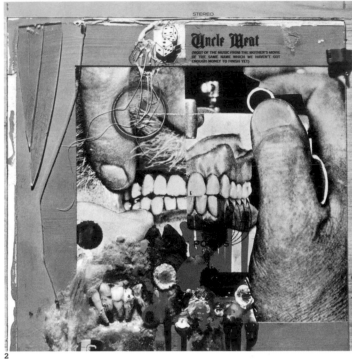

In the mid-1960s, at the beginning of his prolific recording career, Frank Zappa was looking for someone who could supply him with sleeve designs for his albums that would be as provocative as his music; which would reflect the melange of musical forms he so ruthlessly tortured; which would defy categorization and visualize fusion before fusion music had a name. Zappa chose Cal Schenkel, a painter, designer and illustrator from Philadelphia whom he met in New York in 1967. Schenkel was swiftly put to work. At the time, Zappa had an apartment in Charles Street and as Schenkel remembers it, "The art studio was in his apartment – but that was only for a brief period. I didn't actually live there, but I would commute to work at his place." Later in the year, Zappa moved to Los Angeles, taking Schenkel with him. Zappa rented a property known as the Log Cabin as a base for his operations there, and Schenkel set up an art studio in a wing of the building which had previously functioned as a dentist's office.

Zappa had recently signed a recording contract with Metro-Goldwyn-Mayer label Verve and his first release for them was *Lumpy Gravy* (1967). The following year he released two Mothers of Invention albums: *We're Only in It for the Money* and *Cruising with Ruben and the Jets*. The commercial and artistic success of Zappa's prodigious output gave him the clout to negotiate a fresh recording contract with the Warner Bros. label Reprise which enabled him to release material through his own label, Bizarre Records. His first Bizarre release was *Uncle Meat* (1969). That year also saw the release of *Hot Rats* and *Burnt Weeny Sandwich*. Cal Schenkel was entrusted with the design of sleeves for all these albums (although he had originally produced the assemblage used on *Burnt Weeny Sandwich* in early 1967 for an Eric Dolphy album that was never released.) His entirely unaccountable cover for *Hot Rats* features the strange succubus image of a member of a "groupie collective" called the GTOs emerging from the disused lilypond of a burned out Beverley Hills mansion. The photograph by Ed Caraeff is sandwiched between two uncompromising strips of black-on-white sans-serif lettering announcing the album's identity. For *We're Only In It For The Money* Schenkel organized an entirely disrespectful pastiche of the Beatles' *Sergeant Pepper* cover, photographed by Jerrold Schatzberg.

Not long after the launch of Bizarre, Zappa started a second label, Straight Records, to release the material of other musicians he was interested in. During the late 1960s and into the 1970s Straight released albums by Alice Cooper, Tim Buckley, Lord Buckley, Lenny Bruce, Jeff Simmons, Wild Man Fischer, the GTOs (featuring Pamela Des Barres) and Captain Beefheart. Schenkel produced sleeve designs for many of them, but perhaps the most memorable is his design for Captain Beefheart's album *Trout Mask Replica* (1969), for which Schenkel bought a species of giant carp in a local fish market to make the mask worn by Captain Beefheart.

The close association between Schenkel and Zappa was to continue until the latter's death in 1993. Over the years nearly all albums released by Zappa were designed by Schenkel, perhaps the most well-known exception being the sleeve of *Weasels Ripped My Flesh* (1970) which Neon Park was commissioned to paint.

1   **Trout Mask Replica**, CAPTAIN BEEFHEART, Straight, 1969. Design: Cal Schenkel. Photography: Cal Schenkel, Ed Caraeff.

2   **Uncle Meat**, THE MOTHERS OF INVENTION, Transatlantic/ Bizarre, 1969. Photography: Cal Schenkel, Ed Caraeff.

3

5

1

1 **The Best of the Doors**, THE DOORS, Elektra, 1985.
Design: unknown. Photography: Joel Brodsky.
2 **Strange Days**, THE DOORS, Elektra, 1967.
Concept and art direction: William S. Harvey.
Photography: Joel Brodsky.

2

WILLIAM S. HARVEY AND JOEL BRODSKY AT ELEKTRA

Elektra was launched by Jack Holzman in the mid-1950s and by the late 1960s it was one of America's most successful independent record companies. Being small, it was prepared to take risks and sign talent that many of the larger labels were slow to recognize. During the second half of the 1960s its roster included some of America's most innovative rock acts: Love, Nico, The Paul Butterfield Blues Band, the Incredible String Band (for America) and Tim Buckley. But its greatest signing was undoubtedly the Los Angeles group the Doors, and the group's greatest asset was Jim Morrison. He was the only home-grown rock group front man with the charisma and striking physical beauty to compete with the likes of Jagger and Lennon. Though a less talented songwriter than either, he carried off the wayward, West Bank existentialist poet-manqué to perfection.

The designer responsible for the look of the Doors' album sleeves was Elektra's art director, William S. Harvey. Harvey had been with the company since the beginning. He acted as manager of the company's offices as well as being the company's art director. He had oversight of the company's visual output down to Elektra's butterfly logo, and was responsible for designing most of the company's album releases. One of the photographers he enjoyed working with was Joel Brodsky who, for a while, effectively became Elektra's in-house photographer. Brodsky made a speciality of photographing musicians and had a natural eye for a controversial image. He and Harvey produced three Doors album sleeves of the late '60s and early 1970s and helped to define the Morrison look which was to become such an effective element in his posthumous cult.

Brodsky's first photographic session with the group was in 1967, prior to the release of their first album *The Doors*. In the end Harvey decided to create a montage group shot for the front cover from photographs by Guy Webster and one of Brodsky's

shots was used only for the back cover. Never the less, Brodsky's session came to be the source of some of Morrison's most iconic images, particularly what came to be known as the "young lion" shot. Both the photograph which appears on the interior gatefold of *Weird Scenes Inside The Gold Mine* (1972) and versions of the "young lion" shot of Jim Morrison with arms outstretched which appeared on the two *The Best Of The Doors* albums (1973 and 1985) date from this first session. After the success of *The Doors*, Brodsky and Harvey went on to collaborate on the sleeve for *Strange Days* (1967). Morrison did not want the band on the front cover, and they came up with a carnivalesque image of a performing troupe entertaining the young woman standing at the door of her mews house. The Fellinesque image was an enigma to rival the visual complexity of *Sergeant Pepper's* and, for the time, was startlingly original. Harvey and Brodsky subsequently produced the sleeve for the Doors' fourth album *Soft Parade* (1969), and Harvey photographed the band for the cover of live album *13* in the following year. But Elektra's days as an independent company were drawing to a close; in the same year it was bought by Warner Bros. Although Harvey stayed with Elektra, his freedom became increasingly proscribed, while Brodsky moved on to work for other labels. One of his most memorable images was the famous beach image of Isaac Hayes for the cover of *Black Moses* (1971). Hayes' previous album had been his soundtrack for "Shaft" which had won both an Oscar and a Grammy award. To ensure that Hayes' follow-up should build on its success, designer Ron Gordon was instructed to come up with a stunning package, irrespective of cost. He commissioned Brodsky to take the "Black Moses" picture of Hayes, which was made into a cruciform fold-out sleeve 90cm (3 feet) wide by 120cm (4 feet) long: a classic example of extravagant '70s album packaging.

3   **The Doors**, THE DOORS, Elektra/Asylum, 1967.
    Art direction and design: William S. Harvey.
    Photography: Guy Webster.
4   **13**, THE DOORS, Elektra, 1970.
    Art direction and design: Robert L. Heimall.
    Photography: William S. Harvey.
5   **Black Moses**, ISAAC HAYES, Enterprise 1971.
    Design: Ron Gordon. Art Direction: The Graffiteria/David
    Krieger. Photography: Joel Brodsky.

5

3

4

MONK.

1

2

1 **Monk**, THELONIUS MONK, Columbia, 1965.
Art direction: Bob Cato. Design: Gerald Smokler. Photography: W. Eugene Smith.
2 **Wow**, MOBY GRAPE, Columbia, 1968.
Design and illustration: Bob Cato.
3 **Born to Run**, BRUCE SPRINGSTEEN, CBS, 1975.
Design: John Berg, Andy Engel. Photography: Eric Meola.
4 **Greatest Hits**, SANTANA, CBS, 1974.
Design: John Berg. Photography: Joel Baldwin.
5 **Chicago**, CHICAGO, Columbia, 1970.
Design: John Berg. Photography: Nicholas Fasciano.

After an eventful decade during the 1950s, sleeve design at Columbia/CBS entered a settled period under Bob Cato and John Berg, who directed design at the company for twenty-five years.

Cato was born in 1923. He studied art in Mexico with José Clemente Orozco and David Alfaro Siqueiros, and then at Chicago School of Design with Moholy-Nagy, and became an accomplished photographer and artist. He was Alexy Brodovitch's assistant at *Harper's Bazaar* before becoming art director at various magazines. In 1960 he took over from S. Neil Fujita as head of design at Columbia. He appointed John Berg as his assistant in 1961. Cato was promoted to vice president of the creative department in 1965, and Berg filled his old post.

Cato commissioned and produced a succession of covers for a roster of recording artists as diverse as Johnny Mathis, Leonard Bernstein, and Lenny Bruce. His Columbia highlights include a surreal-ist collage in the style of Max Ernst for *Wow* by Moby Grape (1968) and art direction for the moody, minimalist *Monk* by Thelonius Monk (1965).

Berg was made creative director in 1969 and Cato left in 1970. Cato then worked for a number of large corporations, including as vice president for creative services at United Artists Records and Films, before launching his own design company Bob Cato & Associates (1977–89). "Retirement" was spent in book design, and assignments teaching at Rochester Institute of Technology and the School of Visual Arts. Cato died in 1999.

John Berg was born in Brooklyn in 1928. He has described himself as coming out of a "multi-discipline graphic background." Returning to New York from working for the Atlanta Paper Company he went to work in magazines, including *Esquire*, *Coronet*, and *GQ*, and then for a short while he designed an award-winning glamour magazine called *Escapade*. From there he went to American Heritage before finally landing a job at Columbia. During his long career at Columbia, which ran on until 1985, he was responsible for the design of in excess of 5000 album covers. During his time he not only oversaw design output from the East Coast design studio but also set up studios in Los Angeles and Nashville to service Columbia's increasing output of recordings.

Berg was an eclectic and adaptable designer, embracing the passing stylistic fashion with great skill. An adept collaborator, he worked with a bewildering range of musicians, photographers and designers during his years at Columbia. It was a career with many highlights, but his development of a consistent logo for the band Chicago's albums, in conjunction with illustrator Nick Fasciano, is particularly noteworthy, not least since his brief to Fasciano was, in Berg's own words, to "produce a Coca-Cola rip-off". Berg ensured that Chicago's logo-led cover design concept was coherently developed over a number of album sleeves, and in so doing he gave character and a sense of continuity to a recording act that was otherwise visually anonymous.

THUNDER ROAD
Bruce Springsteen: guitar, vocals, harmonica
Garry Tallent: bass guitar
Max M. Weinberg: drums
Roy Bittan: Fender Rhodes, glockenspiel
Clarence Clemons: saxophones
Background vocals: Roy Bittan,
Mike Appel, Steve Van Zandt

TENTH AVENUE FREEZE-OUT
Bruce Springsteen: guitar, vocals
Garry Tallent: bass guitar
Max M. Weinberg: drums
Roy Bittan: piano
Clarence Clemons: tenor saxophone
†Randy Brecker: trumpet, flugel horn
†Michael Brecker: tenor saxophone
**Dave Sanborn: baritone saxophone
Wayne Andre: trombone

NIGHT
Bruce Springsteen: guitar, vocals
Garry Tallent: bass guitar
Max M. Weinberg: drums
Roy Bittan: piano, harpsichord, glockenspiel
Clarence Clemons: saxophone

BACKSTREETS
Bruce Springsteen: guitar, vocals
Garry Tallent: bass guitar
Max M. Weinberg: drums
Roy Bittan: piano, organ

'BORN TO RUN
Bruce Springsteen: guitar, vocals
Garry Tallent: bass guitar
Ernest "Boom" Carter: drums
*David Sancious: keyboards
Danny Federici: organ
Clarence Clemons: saxophone

SHE'S THE ONE
Bruce Springsteen: guitar, vocals
Garry Tallent: bass guitar
Max M. Weinberg: drums
Roy Bittan: piano, harpsichord, organ
Clarence Clemons: saxophone

MEETING ACROSS THE RIVER
Bruce Springsteen: vocals
Roy Bittan: piano
Richard Davis: bass
†Randy Brecker: trumpet

JUNGLELAND
Bruce Springsteen: guitar, vocals
Garry Tallent: bass guitar
Max M. Weinberg: drums
Roy Bittan: piano, organ
Clarence Clemons: tenor saxophone
Strings arranged and conducted by Charles Calello

†Appear courtesy of Arista Records
*Appears courtesy of Epic Records
**Appears courtesy of Warner Reprise

PRODUCED BY BRUCE SPRINGSTEEN, JOHN LANDAU, AND MIKE APPEL
*PRODUCED BY BRUCE SPRINGSTEEN, AND MIKE APPEL

BRUCE SPRINGSTEEN
BORN TO RUN

3

4

5

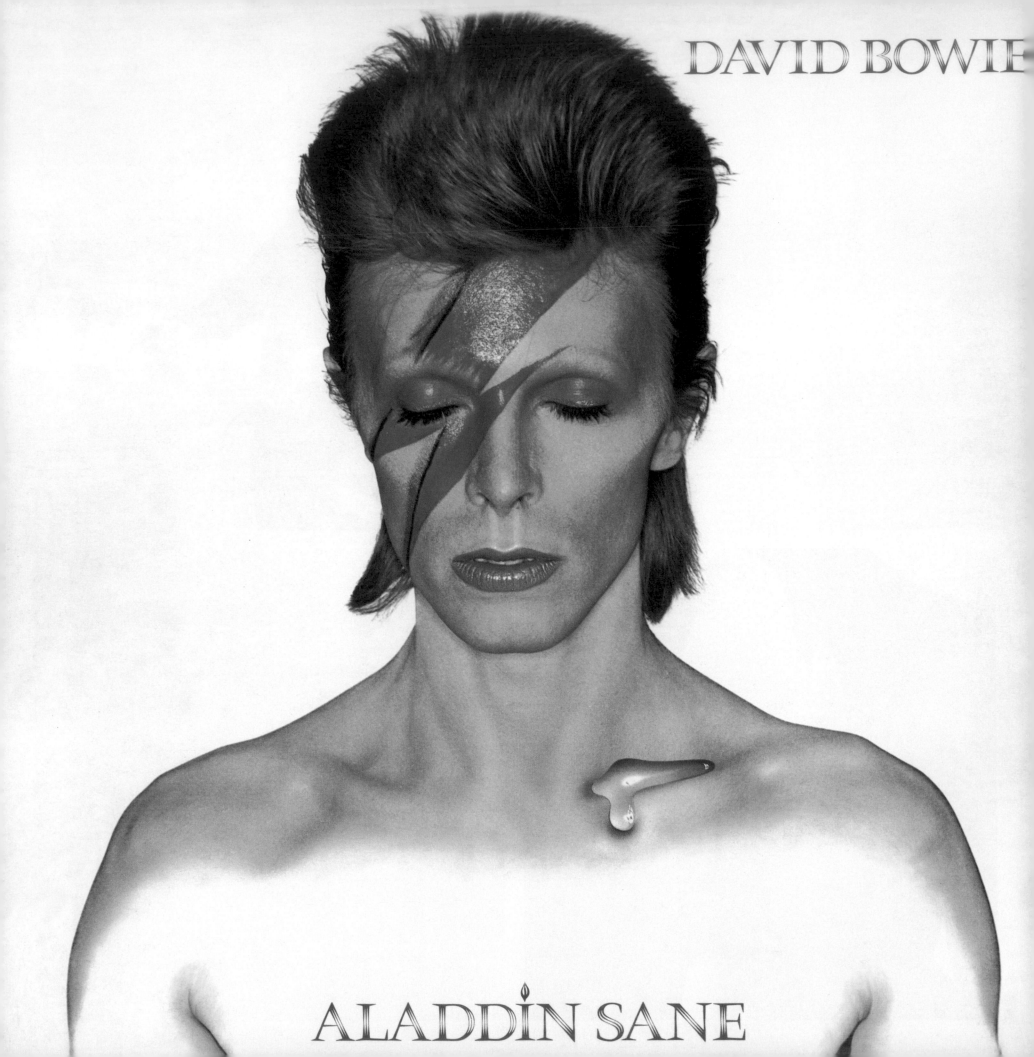

1970–79
From Progressive Rock to Punk

Aladdin Sane.
DAVID BOWIE, RCA, 1973.
Design: Duffy and Celia Philo
for Duffy Design Concepts.
Make up: Pierre Laroche.
[previous pages]

Blues for Allah.
GRATEFUL DEAD, United
Artists/Grateful Dead, 1975.
Illustration: Philip Garris.

Surf's Up.
THE BEACH BOYS,
Stateside/EMI, 1971.
Design: Ed Thrasher/
Jack Rieley.

By the beginning of the 1970s rock had been firmly established as the musical field in which innovation in design was most prevalent, even if crass vulgarity was equally common. During the second half of the 1960s illustration had become the dominant fashion in rock album sleeve design. Illustration gave maximum freedom to the imagination of sleeve designers and was the most appropriate medium for realizing the psychedelic iconography that musicians of the period demanded. As the '70s got underway the original biomorphic forms of acid-inspired imagery were already out of fashion, although West Coast illustrators like Peter Lloyd and Philip Garris skillfully combined psychedelic motifs with other styles: airbrush modern in Lloyd's case and sword'n'sorcery fantasy in Garris's. A range of illustrative styles appeared to replace psychedelia, some drawing on contemporary inspiration, others – explicitly nostalgic – harking back to earlier times through period images and typography. For many, Pop Art had been the big art news of the '60s and its influence on records sleeve design was increasingly noticeable by the beginning of the '70s. In Britain Richard Hamilton and Peter Blake had shown the way, in America, Andy Warhol. A new generation of illustrators began to use Pop Art as their inspiration for album sleeve images. In particular, a fashion grew for the slick effects of airbrush painting, especially on the West Coast where Los Angeles was now becoming the undisputed centre of the recording industry. The airbrush Pop style was inspired by local Los Angeles Pop artists such as Mel Ramos, and, from the East Coast, James Rosenquist and Tom Wesselmann. Photorealist painters who had also

Ooh La La.
THE FACES, Warners, 1973.
Design: Jim Ludwig.

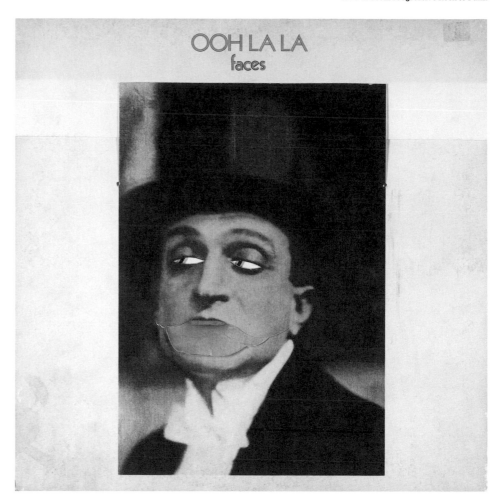

come to prominence in the '60s such as Chuck Close, Malcolm Morley, and Richard Estes were also highly influential. Many of them employed airbrush techniques in their paintings, and they help to set the fashion for an album sleeve style whose subject matter consisted, largely, of close-ups of everyday objects, pin-ups, and fast food in which detail consisted of smooth, glossy surfaces with exaggerated highlights.

As the '70s proceeded photography began to make a fight-back, particularly where the size of the sleeve origination budget was not a major consideration. Elaborate cover concepts began to appear which featured location photography, built sets, special effects and impressive production values. London-based design group Hipgnosis was the most inventive and ambitious exponent of this trend.

By the early '70s the gatefold album sleeve had become the industry standard. This gave designers a 24 x 12 inch (60x30cm) centre-spread as well as a wraparound outer cover of the same dimensions to work with. This enormous canvas has been seen by some commentators as marking the high-water mark of album cover design. What is unarguable is that enormous care and financial resources were lavished on record covers during this period. Not only was a gatefold *de rigueur*, a full-colour inner sleeve with additional graphic elements and lyrics was usual. This was also the heyday of novelty covers and all manner of complex visual jokes, inserts and shaped sleeves were produced. Origami insets, pop-ups, cut-outs, and moving parts graced albums cover such as The Faces' *Ooh La La* (1973) with its top-hatted man with a moveable jaw and eyes, The

School's Out.
ALICE COOPER, Warners, 1972.
Design: Wilkes & Braun, Inc.
Concept: Sound Packing Corp.

Blank Generation.
RICHARD HELL AND THE
VOIDOIDS, Sire, 1977.
Design: unknown.

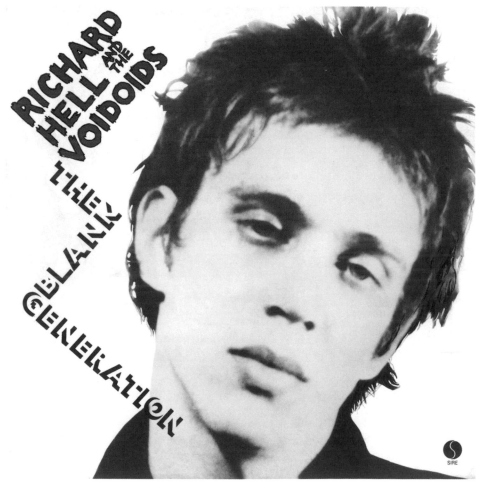

Wailers' Zippo lighter sleeve for *Catch A Fire* (1973) and, almost last of the breed, Led Zeppelin's *Physical Graffiti,* and the Rolling Stones' *Some Girls* (both 1978) with their complex cut-out windows. Even more excessive was the Rolling Stones album cover for *Sticky Fingers* by Andy Warhol (1971) which featured a real fly zipper. Thousands of copies were packed without interleaved protection and the records ruined in transit.

A late '70s innovation was the 12-inch (30cm) single. These large format 45s had superior sound quality to the standard 7-inch (18cm) single. They were deemed collectors items and often produced in limited editions. Invariably, unlike the 7-inch variety, they had specially designed sleeves, although they were commissioned on very restricted budgets. Nevertheless they offered designers another canvas for their work of the same dimensions as albums. On the other hand reggae music did not, in the main, benefit from the lavish packaging budgets which other forms of '70s rock enjoyed, special exceptions such as *Catch A Fire* apart. The same vitality that marked the Jamaican recording scene in the '70s characterizes reggae album sleeves. They made a virtue of directness, and the ready symbolism with which reggae abounded gives them a special place in the album sleeve iconography of the 1970s.

In London Roger Dean, much commissioned by British bands of the hippy wing of the progressive rock movement, was at his best when given a gatefold to realize his widescreen vision on. He spent the decade developing his own idiosyncratic, fairytale off-shoot of psychedelic imagery on a succession of album sleeves. His most long-lived collab-

Fragile.
YES, Atlantic, 1972.
Illustration and photography:
Roger Dean.

Brain Salad Surgery.
EMERSON LAKE & PALMER,
Manticore, 1973.
Design and art direction: Fabio
Nicoli Associates.
Illustration: H R Giger by
arrangement with the House
of Ideas, Zurich.

oration was with the band Yes who, although they had originated in the London underground of the '60s, were now becoming a significant international act, particularly in Europe and America. The flickering idealistic struggle within progressive rock between music and money which had much preoccupied rock stars in hippicdom's heyday was quietly decided in favour of money (and power). Led by Led Zeppelin and Emerson, Lake and Palmer, an endless stream of British acts began to be fed into the maw of the great American concert tour machine. An early result of the increasing power of successful rock musicians was the advent of the supergroup – groups formed by the elite of progressive rock's aristocracy. Inevitably, the marketing departments of record companies loved the idea. The archetypal supergroup was Blind Faith formed by Eric Clapton in 1969 out of the death throws of Cream. The band consisted of Eric Clapton, Ginger Baker, Ric Grech, and Steve Winwood. Unfortunately most supergroups were highly unstable due to the temperaments of their members, and Blind Faith was no exception. The group recorded only one album, but the cover by Bob Seidemann became as celebrated as the band. It featured the head and torso of a naked pubescent girl and was promptly banned in America. Its unequivocal subject matter and its photographic surrealism would be extremely influential during the '70s.

With success, progressive rock began to show increasing signs of pompous high-mindedness, for example when Yes produced an 80-minute mood piece entitled *Tales From Topographic Oceans*. A sense of

Teenage Depression.
EDDIE AND THE HOTRODS,
Island, 1977.
Design: Michael Beal.

Your Generation.
GENERATION X,
Chrysalis, 1977.
Design: unknown.

Go 2.
XTC, Virgin, 1978.
Design: Hipgnosis.
[opposite, top left]

Gorjanka.
MURACK KESHIAJEW,
Melodiya, 1970.
Design: unknown.
[opposite, top right]

The Man-Machine.
KRAFTWERK, Capitol, 1978.
Design: Florian Schneider
/Ralf Hutter/Studio Klefisch.
Photography: Gunter Frohling.
[opposite, bottom]

empty production values permeated everything. Supergroups came and went with amazing rapidity; elite bands declared "we don't do singles", instead they did concept albums. Album sleeves became increasingly complex exercises. The paucity of the music underpinning all this meant that audiences became increasingly cynical about the self-indulgence and megalomania of it all. Economic retrenchment due to the two '70s oil crises meant that most of this extravagance had been brought to a halt by the latter half of the decade. But, even more important was the ideological and artistic revolt against this climate of self-aggrandisement. The inevitable result was punk.

Punk was adopted as the standard-bearer for a mass of forces for change which erupted into popular consciousness in the mid-'70s. In Britain, at least, they included feminism, the increasingly strident disruption of modernist aesthetics in art practice, the beginnings of post-colonial discourse, the final sweeping away of the last vestiges of the post-War settlement, the popularization of semiotics, and the intensified scrutiny of popular culture by academic cultural studies. It was a time when even Hipgnosis – in atonement for past sins (seemingly), and momentarily under the influence of conceptual artist Joseph Kosuth – produced a cod-Marxist semiotic deconstruction of the album cover for XTC. Punk was folk music for a disaffected youth who watched the antics of established rock musicians in scornful disbelief (although, despite much high seriousness about punk, its coexistence with disco is a fact). Just as punk swept away a whole generation of rock stars, so too it swept

This is a RECORD COVER. This writing is the DESIGN upon the record cover. The DESIGN is to help SELL the record. We hope to draw your attention to it and encourage you to pick it up. When you have done that maybe you'll be persuaded to listen to the music – in this case XTC's Go 2 album. Then we want you to BUY it. The idea being that the more of you that buy this record the more money Virgin Records, the manager Ian Reid and XTC themselves will make. To the aforementioned this is known as PLEASURE. A good cover DESIGN is one that attracts more buyers and gives more pleasure. This writing is trying to pull you in much like an eye-catching picture. It is designed to get you to READ IT. This is called luring the VICTIM, and you are the VICTIM. But if you have a free mind you should STOP READING NOW! because all we are attempting to do is to get you to read on. Yet this is a DOUBLE BIND because if you indeed stop you'll be doing what we tell you, and if you read on you'll be doing what we've wanted all along. And the more you read on the more you're falling for this simple device of telling you exactly how a good commercial design works. They're TRICKS and this is the worst TRICK of all since it's describing the TRICK whilst trying to TRICK you, and if you've read this far then you're TRICKED but you wouldn't have known this unless you'd read this far. At least we're telling you directly instead of seducing you with a beautiful or haunting visual that may never tell you. We're letting you know that you ought to buy this record because in essence it's a PRODUCT and PRODUCTS are to be consumed and you are a consumer and this is a good PRODUCT. We could have written the band's name in special lettering so that it stood out and you'd see it before you'd read any of this writing and possibly have bought it anyway. What we are really suggesting is that you are FOOLISH to buy or not buy an album merely as a consequence of the design on its cover. This is a con because if you agree then you'll probably like this writing – which is the cover design – and hence the album inside. But we've just warned you against that. The con is a con. A good cover design could be considered as one that gets you to buy the record, but that never actually happens to YOU because YOU know it's just a design for the cover. And this is the RECORD COVER.

Murad Kashlajew
Gorjanka
Ballettsuite Nr. 2

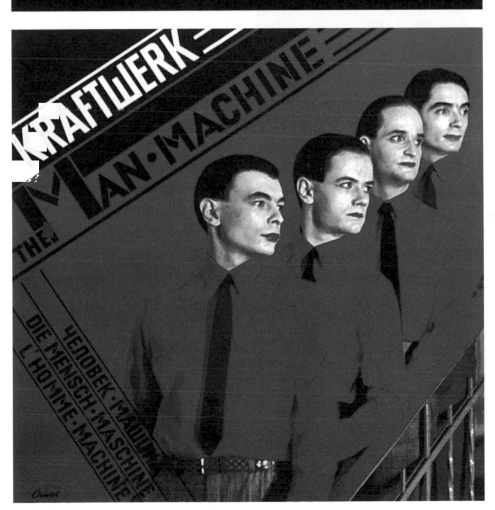

away a whole generation of album sleeve designers; the wise moving on to design pastures new. At root, punk was another glorious spit in the eye, and found its perfect visual representations in Jamie Reid's sleeve designs for the Sex Pistols.

In the context of British punk it is ironic that the punk catch-phrase that resounded most tellingly was "Never trust a hippy" since Ray Lowry, designer of The Clash's *London Calling* sleeve, had been the London hippy scene's favourite underground cartoonist. Another ex-hippy, Barney Bubbles, once Hawkwind's album sleeve designer, now rehabilitated at independent record label Stiff, became doyen of the post-punk design scene. In many respects punk seduced '70s urban youth for the same reasons the hippy underground collectives of the '60s had seduced a previous generation – and both fostered the same kinds of collaborative ventures. Given punk's nihilistic edge, it is surprising that its most long-lasting effect was an incredible burgeoning of small-scale record labels and distributors. *The International Discography of the New Wave* of 1982 listed 16,000 records on more than 3,000 labels. And big record labels too were thriving on the back of sales by all kinds of music. By '78, worldwide sales for CBS had reached $1.2 billion, the first US record company to cross the billion-dollar mark. Another of the world's biggest record companies, selling 200 million records a year during the decade, was Melodiya, the record production arm of the Soviet Ministry of Culture. Its vast output was unknown in the West, but collectors now prize Melodiya sleeves for their off-key colours and stolid, Soviet imagery.

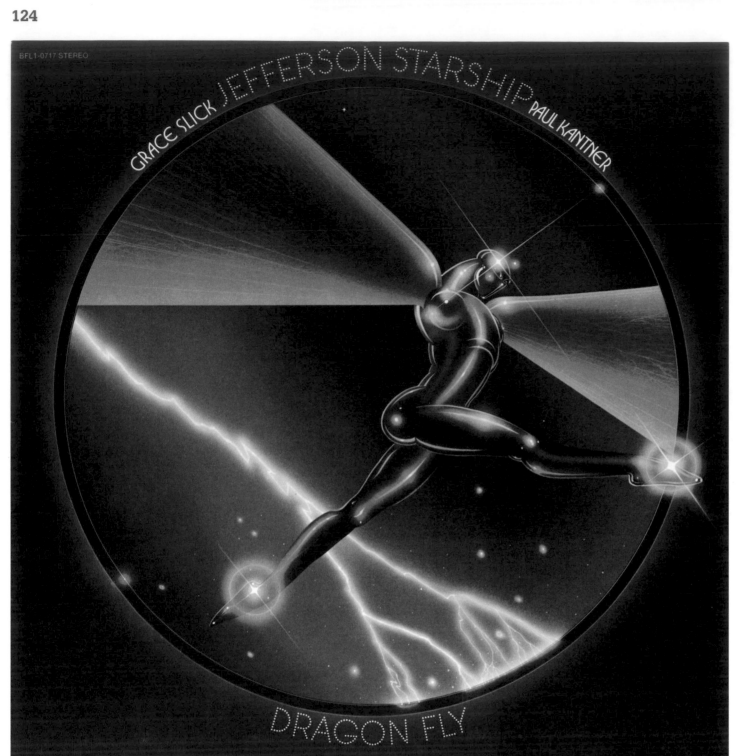

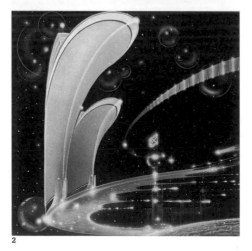

POST-PSYCHEDELIC ILLUSTRATION ON THE WEST COAST

3

By 1970 the American record industry, which traditionally had been concentrated on the East Coast, had gravitated very significantly to the West Coast. This reflected both the growing importance of West Coast companies such as Warner Bros., United Artists, and A&M, and the cluster effect resulting from the number of huge entertainment companies that saw Los Angeles as their natural home.

By the beginning of the '70s emerging West Coast recording acts no longer wanted album sleeves that smacked of the psychedelic iconography of the acid rock bands which had made their names in Haight-Ashbury's heyday. Illustration continued to be a fashionable choice for album sleeve design, but now a more favoured style was a re-casting of pop art imagery painted in a bland, glossy airbrush technique in which everything was equally air-filled, from junk food to pin-ups. Major exponents of this form of airbrush illustration were Peter Palombi, Charles White III and David Willardson, all of whom attracted a great many album sleeve commissions during the early years of the '70s. A more idiosyncratic exponent of airbrush techniques was Peter Lloyd, whose style occupies a transitional place in post-psychedelic illustration. The spectral distortions of his airbrush forms in his sleeves for Jefferson Starship's *Dragon Fly* (1974), *Kansas* (1974), and Rod Stewart's *Atlantic Crossing* (1975) suggest the final fling of the San Francisco acid style. Philip Garris created another sort of psychedelic hybrid for the Grateful Dead's *Blues for Allah* (1975),

combining acid letter forms with fantasy imagery in the shape of The Fiddler, precursor of Iron Maiden's living skeleton, Eddie.

Another popular form of illustration in the early '70s was derived from the invigoration of the comic book and cartoon style of drawing instigated by the underground comix publishing phenomenon of the late 1960s. Here Robert Crumb was the most influential figure, although his sleeve for *You Can't Get Enough Of That Stuff* by The Hokum Boys (1975) was one of the very few that he produced in the years following the success of his cover for Big Brother & The Holding Company's *Cheap Thrills* (1968). Neon Park produced a succession of illustrations for the sleeves of Little Feat albums which crossed the San Franciscan acid comix style with Disney. Both Victor Moscoso and Rick Griffin were also influential in their post-psychedelic comix styles. Even Stanley Mouse of the Mouse & Kelley Studios occasionally reverted to his pre-San Francisco cartoon style of illustration, as can be seen from his sleeve for the Grateful Dead's live album *Europe '72*.

Another designer/illustrator who adopted a cartoon style of illustration for a while in the early '70s was John Van Hamersveld. Notable examples of album sleeves by him in this vein are Jimmy McGriff's *Black Pearl* (1971), the Bonzo Dog Band's *Beast Of The Bonzos* (1971), and Beans' debut album (1972). Van Hamersveld is a good example of the young, adaptable designers who came to the fore on the West Coast in the early years of the '70s. Born in Los Angeles in 1943, he hung out

4

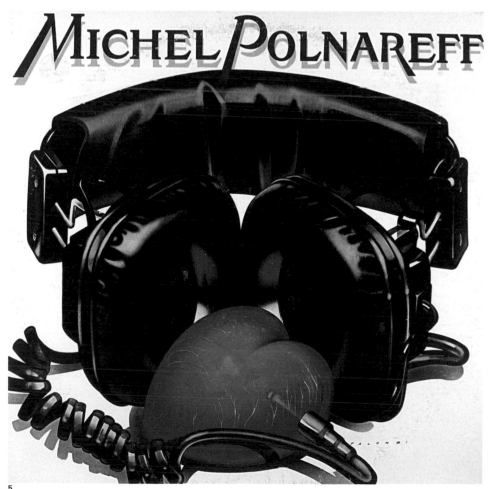

5

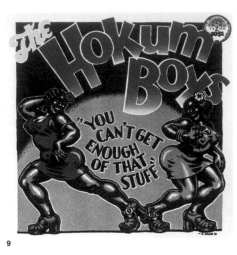

with fellow surfer Rick Griffin when young, and like him he studied at Los Angeles's Chouinard Art School, working for a number of clients, including *Surfer Magazine*, while still a student. He finished his studies in 1965 and landed an art director's job at Capitol Records where he worked on in-house designs for Beatles and Beach Boys releases. In 1967, inspired by the concert events pioneered in San Francisco by Family Dog and Bill Graham, he became a partner in a rock promotion organization called Pinnacle Rock Concerts which began to stage multimedia concerts at the Shrine Auditorium. Initially he designed the posters for the Shrine concerts himself but the following year, increasingly in demand as a designer, he began to commission posters from other designers including Neon Park, Rick Griffin and Victor Moscoso. He designed the atomic fireball sleeve for Jefferson Airplane's *Crown of Creation* (1968) in collaboration with photographer Hiro. Later in the year he was invited to London to work for Apple Records, where John Kosh was art director. Apple Records was part of the Beatles short-lived, anarchic conglomerate Apple Corps, where in the words of Philip Norman, the Beatles' biographer, "Several times each week, the call would come to Apple from Heathrow Airport's Immigration Department, announcing that yet another Beautiful Person had arrived from California with beads and bells, but without funds or definite accommodation, to look up his four brothers in Karma and Sergeant Pepper." Even Merry Prankster Ken Kesey was brought to London to

write a "street diary" although somehow the project never got off the ground and eventually he disappeared back to California, leaving the IBM typewriter specially purchased for his project at the front desk. Van Hamersveld did rather better, returning to Los Angeles in 1969 with an enviable range of music world contacts, and in the following years he enjoyed an incredibly prolific period designing for the music industry. As with many of his contemporaries, the keynote of his output was its versatility. He not only supplied illustrations and custom lettering but increasingly also undertook photograph-based assignments, most notably in collaboration with photographer Norman Seeff on sleeves for the Rolling Stones's *Exile On Main St.* (1972), Steve Miller Band's *The Joker* (1973), Kiss's *Hotter Than Hell* (1974), and Bill Withers' *'Justments* (1974). In his varied career as a designer and illustrator he has produced over three hundred album sleeves.

Two expatriate British designers, Mick Haggerty and John Kosh, also made considerable contributions to West Coast album sleeve design in the '70s. Both made something of a speciality of being a friendly face for British bands recording, or otherwise resident, on the West Coast. Haggerty's career has been marked by his considerable ability to adapt to the prevailing fashion, and in the album sleeve designs he undertook during the mid-'70s he showed himself to be a proficient exponent of a variety of styles of illustration. John Kosh served his apprenticeship in design for music working for a large printing company in London

before becoming a full-time designer. He ran the Beatles' design office in the short active existence of Apple Corps. During his association with Apple he designed sleeves for two Lennon side projects, The Plastic Ono Band's *Live Peace In Toronto* and *Wedding Album* (both in 1969) as well as the sleeve of the Beatles' last album *Let It Be* (1970). At the same time he also established a freelance design practice specializing in working for the record industry with offices in London and New York. In 1974 he began to work for design company Album Graphics and in the following year he moved his base to Los Angeles. Freelance commissions there soon allowed him to launch his own studio again, although he had a spell as art director at RSO starting in 1976. Among his most well-known album sleeves are the twilight shot of the Beverly Hills Hotel featured on the Eagles' *Hotel California* (1976), and the two Grammy award-winning albums he designed for Linda Ronstadt (1982 and 1985).

6 **Europe '72**, GRATEFUL DEAD, Warner Bros, 1972.
Illustration: Kelley/Mouse.

7 **Beast of the Bonzos**, BONZO DOG BAND,
United Artists, 1971.
Illustration: John van Hamersveld. Concept: Martin Cerf, John
Mendelsohn. Art direction: Norman Seef.

8 **Beans**, BEANS, United Artists, 1972.
Design and illustration: John van Hamersveld.

9 **You Can't Get Enough of That Stuff**, THE HOKUM BOYS,
Yazoo, 1975.
Design and illustration: Robert Crumb.

10 **Cheap Thrills**, BIG BROTHER & THE HOLDING COMPANY,
Columbia, 1967.
Illustration: Robert Crumb. [opposite]

THE MOTHERS OF INVENTION
WEASELS RIPPED MY FLESH
RZZZZZ!
NEON PARK

1 **Weasels Ripped My Flesh**, THE MOTHERS OF INVENTION, Warner Bros (Reprise), 1970. [opposite]
Illustration: Neon Park. Design: Ed Thrasher.

2 **Sailin' Shoes**, LITTLE FEAT, Warner Bros, 1972.
Illustration: Neon Park.

3 **The Last Record Album**, LITTLE FEAT, Warner Bros, 1975.
Illustration: Neon Park

4 **Images 1966 67**, DAVID BOWIE, Deram, 1973
Illustration: Neon Park. Design: Glenn Ross. Supervision and Concept: Vincent Biondi.

5 **Feats Don't Fail Me Now**, LITTLE FEAT, Warner Bros, 1974.
Illustration: Neon Park.

6 **Down On the Farm**, LITTLE FEAT, Warner Bros, 1975.
Illustration: Neon Park. Design: Eddy Herch.

Neon Park XIII, born Martin Muller in 1940, is most celebrated for the thirteen album sleeves he painted for Lowell George's band, Little Feat. His album sleeves are a perfect visual equivalent of the band's funky West Coast sound and surrealistic lyrics. Neon Park's own term for his style, "Zen Voodoo", ably captures the witty amalgam of folk art, pop, op, psychedelia, surrealism and magical realist imagery to be found in his work. The paintings are bold in colour and the drawing technique primitive in style, somewhat reminiscent of an updating of Le Douanier Rousseau. He is also known for the celebrated cover of *Weasels Ripped My Flesh* painted for Frank Zappa's Mothers Of Invention.

Neon Park came into contact with the San Francisco-based poster artists Victor Moscoso and Rick Griffin in 1968 while designing posters for the Shrine, a progressive rock venue in Los Angeles which they were also designing for. Subsequently he moved to San Francisco for a while and worked as a poster artist for the Family Dog organization. Frank Zappa had seen the drawings Park had made for a group called Dancing Food and asked him to visit him at his Log Cabin base in Los Angeles. The visit resulted in Park being commissioned to paint the sleeve for the 1969 Mothers of Invention album, *Weasels Ripped My Flesh*. At their meeting, Zappa showed Park a magazine with a cover story about a man in a barrel full of weasels. According to Park, Zappa said: "What can you do that's worse than this?"

While Neon Park was working for Zappa on *Weasels Ripped My Flesh* he met guitarist and songwriter Lowell George, whose playing on *Weasels Ripped My Flesh* is one of the rare recordings made of his contribution to the Mothers of Invention. George soon moved on to form his own band, Little Feat, but their meeting led George to commission Park to paint the cover for Little Feat's second album *Sailin' Shoes* (1972). The sleeve's image of an anthropomorphized cake with a slice missing between her legs and an approaching snail with phallus-like head is only slightly less provocative than the *Weasel* cover. Neon Park had recently been impressed by Mick Jagger in the film *Performance* and he put him lurking in the background of the picture dressed as Gainsborough's Blue Boy. Park's association with Little Feat lasted until it was disbanding in late 1978. George died the following year, shortly after his album *Thanks, I'll Eat It Here* came out. A collection of George's pre-Little Feat music titled *Lightning Rod Man* was released in 1993 with a Neon Park cover.

Neon Park's illustrations also appeared in many publications including *National Lampoon*, *Playboy*, *Glass Eye*, and *Dreamworks*. He and wife Chick Strand began to divide their time between Los Angles and San Miguel de Allende in Mexico. As time went by, the influence of Mexican art, especially that of the Huichol yarn paintings they collected, displaced the fantastical cartoon style of his earlier work. In the 1980s he devoted much of his time to works containing contrasting dual images, created in thin stripes by double painting over masking tape. Neon Park died of Lou Gehrig's Disease in 1993.

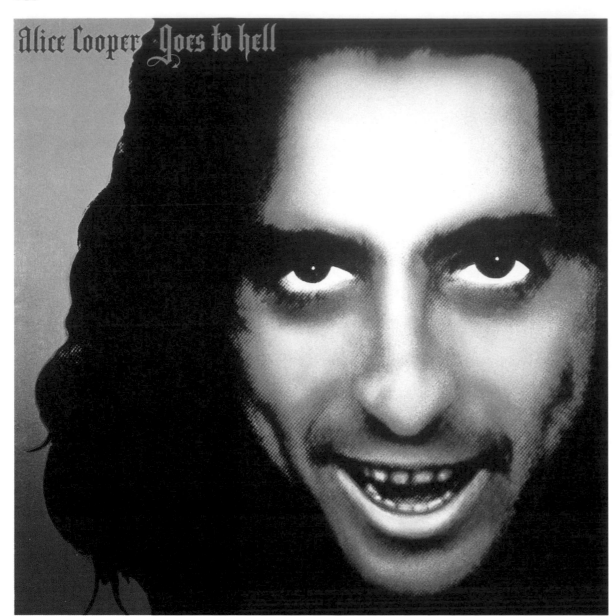

Alice Cooper Goes to hell

T O T O

(ī′so-lā′tion)

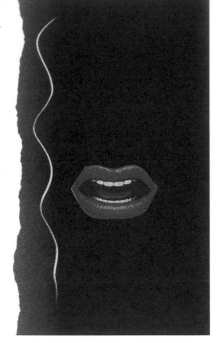

3

1   **Alice Cooper Goes to Hell**, ALICE COOPER,
Warner Bros, 1973.
Design: Rod Dyer, Brian Higiwara. Photography: Bret Lopez.

2   **The James Montgomery Band**, Island, 1976.
Design: Mike Fink at Rod Dyer, Inc. Illustration: Mick Haggerty.

3   **Isolation**, TOTO, Columbia/CBS, 1984.
Design: Bill Murphy at Dyer/Kahn Inc. Photography: Raul Vega.
Illustration: Robert Kopecky.

1

2

The founding of Rod Dyer Inc. marks the beginning of the reprofessionalization of design for the music industry on the West Coast. It signals a return to a more regulated relationship between independent designers and record companies' art directors after the free-wheeling late 1960s, with a number of specialist design companies becoming trusted suppliers of design solutions. Having previously worked in-house for Capitol, Dyer was in a good position to build such relationships: he understood LP sleeve design from the insider's angle and was also integrated into the California music design network.

Rod Dyer was born in 1935 in South Africa. He studied design at Johannesburg Technical College before emigrating to New York in 1956 where he worked for the design group Gore, Smith, Greenland for a year before going freelance. He moved to Los Angeles in 1960 and became an art director at Carson/Roberts in 1961. He moved on to became art director at Capitol Records in 1962, where he stayed for a year before a spell at the Charles Eames Office. He returned to Capitol in 1964 and remained art director there until 1967. In 1968 he founded the design company Rod Dyer Inc. The

company made a specialty of working for the Los Angeles-based entertainment industries and he became a doyen of the West Coast graphic design scene in the 1970s and 1980s, employing many designers and illustrators well-known for their work for record companies, including Bill Naegels, Richard Seireeni, Brian Hagiwara, Mick Haggerty and Norman Moore.

Rod Dyer Inc. was proficient at responding to its clients' demands for visual novelties which were a hallmark of the early '70s. As an example, Dyer's Zippo cigarette lighter sleeve for the Wailers' *Catch A Fire* (1973) is a period classic. *Catch a Fire*, which had top and bottom halves riveted together so that it hinge-opened, is now a collector's item. Only 20,000 copies were produced. Each cover was hand-assembled to get the two halves to fit, and were exorbitantly expensive to produce. A conventional sleeve with a photograph of Bob Marley smoking a spliff was substituted after the first shipment.

The output of Dyer's company is notable for its avoidance of a distinctive signature style, and his designers for their versatility. When commissions for sleeves for new recordings were unavailable

they would happily turn their hands to sleeves for compilations and back catalogue, as with Mick Haggerty's illustrations for the *Leonard Feather Presents Encyclopaedia Of Jazz* series (1974). This versatility was in clear counterdistinction to the policy of that other pioneer design group which specialized in design for music during the '70s, London-based Hipgnosis, which almost always stayed true to its obsession with special-effects photographic surrealism.

As Rod Dyer Inc. grew it inevitably became less engaged in album sleeve design. Clients such as Disney Channel, Paramount Pictures, 20th Century Fox, MCA, Gramercy Pictures, Surround Sound, and Guess Jeans offered a more stable fee income, but the Rod Dyer Inc. approach to album cover design was emulated by a number of other West Coast design studios during the 1970s, including Pacific Eye and Ear, Art Hotel, Art Attack, and Album Graphics Inc., where the accomplished British expatriate sleeve designer John Kosh was creative director in the mid-'70s. Also notable in sharing Rod Dyer Inc.'s catholic approach to design are the studios of two ex-Dyer designers, Mick Haggerty and Norman Moore.

4   **Catch A Fire**, THE WAILERS, Island Records, 1973.
    Design: Rod Dyer, Bob Weiner.
5   **Side 3**, RASPBERRIES, EMI/Capitol, 1973.
    Design: Rod Dyer. Art Direction: John Hoernle. Photography:
    Bob Gruen, Leandro Correa.
6   **Leonard Feather Presents Encyclopedia of Jazz On
    Records – Vol.5**, VARIOUS ARTISTS, MCA, 1974.
    Design: Rod Dyer. Illustration: Mick Haggerty.

5

6

4

Mick Haggerty was born in 1948 in London. He studied at Central School of Art and subsequently the Royal College of Art, reputedly dropping out before graduating in 1971. He has enjoyed a long and successful career as a designer to the music industry. He moved to California in 1973 where he established his design credentials by working at Rod Dyer Inc. He showed himself to be an accomplished, versatile illustrator able to produce, with equal facility, a variety of sub-pop art styles of illustration underpinned by a well-observed understanding of the distinctive Californian pop art of artists like Mel Ramos and Ed Ruscha. As with their work, most of his motifs were drawn from cinema, comics and other popular culture sources. A good example of his work of this period is the sleeve for Jambalaya's *High Rollers* (1973) and Hot Tuna's *Yellow Fever* (1975). In 1974 he went to work for Art Attack, another design studio specializing in design for record and show business companies. The following year he launched his own studio, Mick Haggerty Design, and quickly found himself with an extensive roster of clients. That year he designed the sleeve for Electric Light Orchestra's *Face The Music* in conjunction with John Kehe and photographers Norman Seeff and Fred Valentine. He was rapidly establishing himself as the designer of choice for British bands recording or otherwise resident in America. Perhaps his greatest success in this role was his collaboration with Mike Doud to design the album sleeve of Supertramp's *Breakfast in America* (1979), the

band's first LP, after moving to the USA. Although Doud is credited with having devised the various images combining breakfast and America that resulted in the matronly waitress impersonating the statue of Liberty and fronting a miniature Manhattan made out of breakfast implements, it was Haggerty who saw to the practical realization of the image, finding a model for the waitress and building the miniature Manhattan. In Haggerty's words: "It's New York seen through the eyes of someone that sees it not as a gateway to the east of America but as a gateway to Route 66. It was a West Coast treatment of an East Coast icon." The cover was enormously successful and won that year's Grammy for "Best Album Package".

The next year Haggerty was co-designer with Jeffery Ayeroff of the high-concept *Ghost In The Machine* for the Police which captured its theme with an inventive subversion of the LED display of digital watches which had recently begun to appear. At this time Haggerty's work began to undergo a change, perhaps influenced by the success of *Breakfast In America*. He began to design sleeves around photography rather than illustration, often combining photographic elements in a seamless whole in a manner which is to some extent reminiscent of the Hollywood surrealism that Hipgnosis is closely identified with. The sharks cleaving the lawn on the sleeve of Gamma 2's eponymous album (1980) and the Coconuts' cliff-top-at-sunset portrait on *Don't Take My Coconuts* (1983) are typical of this enlargement of his range of styles. His quest for

pictorial novelty has been constant. For example, for *The Pacific Age* by Orchestral Manoeuvers in the Dark (1986), he produced a five-colour block print in a primitive style, hand-chiselled from a block of wood after a trip to Baja in Mexico. Haggerty's credits read like a who's who of major recording artists of the last half century with David Bowie, the Beatles, Simple Minds, Talking Heads, and Roxy Music to be added to those already mentioned in this profile.

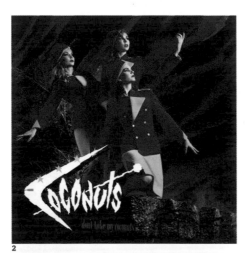

1 **Jerry Lee Lewis**, JERRY LEE LEWIS, Elektra, 1979.
Design: Mick Haggerty. Photography: Ethan A. Russell.
2 **Don't Take My Coconuts**, COCONUTS, EMI, 1983.
Design: Mick Haggerty. Photography: Larry Williams.
3 **Breakfast in America**, SUPERTRAMP, A&M, 1979.
Art direction: Mick Haggerty. Design: Mike Doud.
Photography: Aaron Rapoport.
4 **Gamma 2**, GAMMA, Elektra, 1980.
Design and art direction: Mick Haggerty. Photography:
Mick Haggerty, Jeffrey Scales.
5 **Let's Dance**, DAVID BOWIE, EMI, 1983.
Design: Mick Haggerty. Photography: Greg Gorman.
6 **Ghost in the Machine**, THE POLICE, A&M Records, 1980.
[opposite]
Design and art direction: Mick Haggerty, Jeffery Ayeroff.

THE POLICE

GHOST IN THE MACHINE

1

2

3

1   **The Magician's Birthday**, URIAH HEEP, Bronze/
    Mercury, 1972.
    Design and artwork: Roger Dean.
2   **Relayer**, YES, Atlantic, 1974.
    Design and artwork: Roger Dean.
3   **Tales from Topographic Oceans**, YES, Atlantic, 1973.
    Design and artwork: Roger Dean.
4   **Alpha**, ASIA, Geffen, 1982.
    Design and artwork: Roger Dean.
5   **Anderson Bruford Wakeman Howe**, ANDERSON BRUFORD
    WAKEMAN HOWE, Arista, 1989.
    Design and artwork: Roger Dean.

Roger Dean was born in 1944 in Kent, England. His father was an engineer in the British Army and most of Dean's childhood was spent on Army bases in Cyprus, Greece, and Hong Kong. He studied Industrial Design at Canterbury College of Art before going on to study on the MA Furniture Design programme at the Royal College of Art, graduating in 1968. Dean was commissioned to design his first album cover for a group called Gun while working on the interior design for the Upstairs room at Ronnie Scott's Jazz Club in London. In 1970 he was commissioned by Richard Branson to design a logo for his fledgling record label, Virgin Records. His wraparound sleeve illustration of flying mammoths for the Ghanian band Osibisa's first album (1972) led to him being commissioned to design the sleeve for the fourth Yes album release *Fragile* (1972). This was the beginning of a long association between Dean and Yes, during which he designed sleeves for *Close To The Edge* (1972), *Yessongs* (1973), *Tales From Topographical Oceans* (1974), *Relayer* (1974) and *Yesterdays* (1975).

Dean's series of sleeves for Yes was finally broken with *Going For The One* (1977) when Hipgnosis were commissioned as a consequence of a misguided aspiration to modernize the Yes visual persona. Even so, the Celtic knot logo Dean designed for Yes, which is a classic of psychedelic lettering, continued to be an unchanging feature of their album sleeves. The association with Dean as sleeve designer was subsequently reestablished, and his fantastical

widescreen landscapes have become the definitive Yes look.

The illustrative style, particularly as developed on the sleeves he produced for Yes, has been widely influential. His illustrations are a high fidelity reworking of fantasy themes, occasionally containing futuristic elements such as aliens, fabulous monsters and spaceships, but predominantly landscape vistas of a Tolkienesque, Middle Earth character. Childrens' illustrators of the Art Nouveau period such as Edmund Dulac and Arthur Rackham are an obvious source, although, as with many of his contemporaries, there is a definite visionary psychedelic flavour to the imagery.

Dean's association with Yes led to him receiving many commissions during the '70s (and into the 1980s) from Yes side projects, bands wanting to project themselves as belonging to the pomp rock wing of British progressive rock and others attracted by Dean's illustrative style. He was even commissioned to create a sleeve for a Motown compilation. Many of his illustrations were widely distributed as posters. He was almost entirely responsible for reviving the fortunes of the Big O Poster Company which had been set up by *Oz* magazine partner Peter Ledeboer with a retail outlet in Carnaby Street, originally to exploit the popularity of Martin Sharp's posters. The thriving market for posters which had developed in the late 1960s psychedelic period had suffered a great decline in popularity by the early '70s, a decline which, for a while,

poster-sized reproductions of Dean's illustrations help to reverse.

Dean subsequently launched his own publishing companies Dragons Dream and Paper Tiger and was responsible with Storm Thorgerson for the Album Cover Album (published in 1977) which is one of the earliest attempts to map out the story of album sleeve design. Several further volumes were subsequently published. He has continued to be interested in varied aspects of architecture and three dimensional design and with his brother Martyn launched a number of companies to exploit his ideas.

4

5

1

Tadanori Yokoo was born in 1936 in the rural Hyogo Prefecture of Japan where his family ran a kimono and fabric shop. He studied painting and illustration and achieved early success in his native Japan during the 1960s for his poster art, being crowned the king of Japanese Pop Art by the media. He is often associated with the post-war generation of Japanese intellectuals who rejected Japan's American-dominated, de-eroticized and rationalist society, a rejection which is often personified by cult novelist and right-wing activist Yukio Mishima who committed hara-kiri in 1970. Yokoo was a regular guest at Mishima's famous Christmas parties, where radical politics was a frequent topic. Others associated with this intellectual foment are film director Nagisa Oshima (*Merry Christmas, Mr Lawrence,* and *In the Realm of the Senses*), poet Matsuro Takahashi, writer Tatsuhiko Shibusawa and dancer Tatsumi Hijikata, founder of the legendary dance troupe, the Ankoku butô-ha.

Yokoo is both a maverick and a polymath. His varied career includes designing album covers for famous rock stars, making ceramics and installations, being an author, a stage director, designing belts for sumo wrestlers and playing the lead in Oshima's classic, *Diary of a Shinjuku Thief.* He came to international notice as an album sleeve designer in the 1970s while living in America. From a Western perspective, Yokoo's montages are classic post-psychedelic in style, sharing with psychedelia imagery the dense melange of visual sources, intense colour contrasts and optical excitation. His bold montages feature figures from both Eastern and Western popular culture, often mixing the banal and the highly loaded. He draws on sources as diverse as late 19th-century advertisements (Meiji bijinga), religious images of reclining Buddhas, flying angels and cut-outs from Michelangelo's Sistine Chapel frescos. Yokoo, however, is more knowingly eclectic and worldly in its choice of cross-cultural subject matter than Western psychedelic artist/designers. In this sense he is a paradox, being both distinctly Japanese, and standing in Japanese eyes for a resurgent independent Japanese sensibility and yet, at the same time, his designs are an important contribution to the

canon of Western post-psychedelic album sleeve illustration, albeit accented by a distinctive sensibility.

Yokoo was introduced to John Lennon at Jasper Johns' home in New York in 1972, a meeting which led to a commission to work on a Beatles compilation project. Album sleeve designs for Miles Davis, Santana, Cat Stevens and Earth Wind & Fire are highlights of his time in America. He designed two outstanding album sleeves for Santana, particularly notable being his design for their triple live album *Lotus*, recorded in Osaka in 1973 and released only on the Japanese market in an extraordinary sleeve which featured an extended essay in post-psychedelic imagery covering a bewildering array of foldout leaves with

a total size of 210cm by 90cm (7ft by 3ft) (1974). Such was the size of the export market in the album that CBS released it worldwide the following year. Yokoo is typically self-effacing about his time in America: "I was really happy to work for them as they were all so talented and gifted. It meant a lot to me that they were moved by my work and asked me to work with them directly."

Back in Japan, Yokoo reputedly gave up graphic design in 1981 to devote his energies to his painting, although he continues to produce designs from time to time, along with prints, ceramics and video art.

1 **Amigos**, SANTANA, Columbia, 1976.
   Design: Tadanori Yokoo.
2 **Agharta**, MILES DAVIS, CBS, 1975.
   Design: Tadanori Yokoo. Photography: Tadayuki Naitoh, Shigeo Anzai.
3 **Lotus**, SANTANA, Columbia, 1973.
   Concept: Tadanori Yokoo, Teruhisa Tagima, Hedeto Isoda. [artwork from inside album.]
4 **The Bermuda Triangle**, ISAO TOMITA, RCA, 1978.
   Design and photography: Tadanori Yokoo.

2

4

3

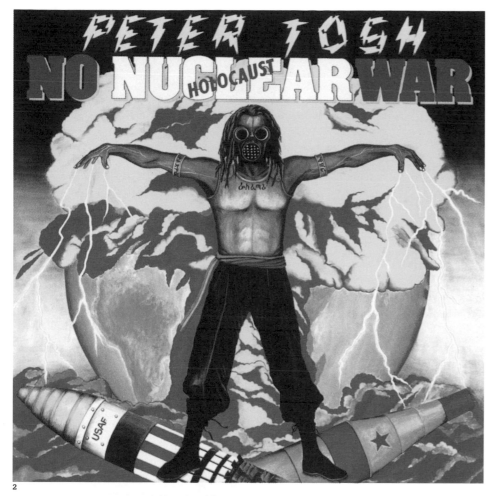

2

5

6

3

4

1 **Natty Dread**, BOB MARLEY & THE WAILERS, Island
  Records, 1975. [opposite]
  Design: Tony Wright.
2 **No Nuclear War**, PETER TOSH, CBS, 1987.
  Design: Neville Garrick.
3 **Blackheart Man**, BUNNY WAILER, Island Records, 1976.
  Design: Neville Garrick.
4 **Scientific Dub**, SCIENTIST, Clocktower, 1981.
  Design: Jamaal Pete.
5 **Don't Underestimate the Force, The Force Is Within You**,
  THE REVOLUTIONARIES, Channel One, 1981.
  Design: Jamaal Pete.
6 **Conquering Lion**, YABBY YU & THE PROPHETS, Micron
  Records, 1976.
  Design: Cogil Leghorn.

Reggae grew out of the informal, hand-to-mouth recording industry which developed in Jamaica during the 1960s. Initially album sleeves were often an afterthought to the music, resulting in sleeves which were perfunctory, haphazard and often derivative of existing formats, notably American black soul acts of the 1950s and early '60s. It was the connection to the well-established Jamaican communities in London that helped bring reggae to an international audience. Most particularly, Chris Blackwell was in a position to turn his enthusiasm for reggae into a specialty of his independent London-based record company Island Records which signed many of the big stars of reggae such as Bob Marley, Third World and Jimmy Cliff.

Musically, reggae grew out of ska and rock-steady, although by the end of the '60s it was becoming politically charged through its close identification with rastafarianism. The sleeves of roots albums began to reflect rasta's tumultuous blend of religious and political aspiration. It was a time when European powers were granting independence to many African states, and freedom from colonial rule raised hopes of a utopian Pan-Africanism. Although, as often reflected in reggae album sleeves, rastafarianism can be also anti-authority, anti-establishment and sometimes apocalyptic. Images of Marcus Garvey (1887–1940) and Haile Selassie (1892–1975) were two particularly important rasta symbols and appear in various guises on many reggae album sleeves. Jamaican Garvey was honoured for his

life spent in America articulating early expressions of black pride and solidarity, and for forging the movement to transport blacks back to the ancestral homelands in Africa. Haile Selassie, King of Ethiopia, was a political icon to many of those bent on resisting the enslavement of Africans by the West (he was deposed in a military coup in 1974). Hence the use of the lion on many album sleeves represented both Haile Selassie and Ethiopia. References to Babylon, the enslaved Israelites of Babylon and Zion were all used as parallels of the black modern experience – but where Africa, rather than Zion, was the promised land. Dreadlocks and spliffs were also enormously important symbols of the rasta ethos.

Many reggae album sleeves were created by the art departments of record companies or by freelance designers far from Jamaica, sometimes without any contact with the performers, who often simply accepted the record companies' decisions. London-based designers who specialized in reggae sleeves such as Tony Wright and Tony McDermott tended to produce a more sophisticated and style-conscious look than found on album sleeves produced in Jamaica. Wright, who for many years worked for Island Records, produced reggae album sleeves in a variety of styles, although some of the best, such as Ijahman Levi's *Are We A Warrior* (1979) or Bob Marley and the Wailers' *Natty Dread* (1975) are highly finished pieces of figurative painting.

Another prolific designer who worked for Bob Marley was Jamaica-based Neville Garrick, art

director of Tuff Gong from 1975, whose sleeves for Marley included *Rastaman Vibration* (1976), *Exodus* (1977), *Kaya* (1978), *Survival* (1979) and *Confrontation* (1983). He also designed for Burning Spear, Peter Tosh, The Upsetters, and Bunny Wailer. Educated in America, and with a background in advertising, Garrick saw himself as "adding some showbiz to the whole rasta thing" and brought an increased sophistication to locally sourced design.

There is a core of album sleeves in the reggae canon that employ a primitivist style of illustration halfway between graffiti and naïve art, accompanied by hand-drawn lettering. Many of the sleeves are by anonymous designers, but one of the most prolific designers to capture the unalloyed street side of reggae was New York-based Jamaal Pete. He uses a vigorous drawing style with hand lettering which gives the album sleeves he produced a particularly authentic and radical sense of difference, quite unlike the more conventional production values expected by the big record companies in London or New York.

1

2

1   **Their Satanic Majesties Request**, THE ROLLING STONES, Decca, 1967.
Design: Michael Cooper. Cover Photo: built by The Rolling Stones, Michael Cooper, and Artchie at Pictorial Productions, Mount Vernon, NY.

2   **Tongue Logo**, THE ROLLING STONES. Design: John Pasche.

3   **Exile On Main St.**, THE ROLLING STONES, Rolling Stones, 1972.
Design: John Van Hamersveld, Norman Seeff.
Photograph: Robert Frank.

4   **Let It Bleed**, THE ROLLING STONES, London, 1969.
Design: Robert Brownjohn. Photography: Don McAllester.

5   **Black and Blue**, THE ROLLING STONES, Rolling Stones, 1976.
Photography: Hiro.

The Rolling Stones are, without doubt, the premier surviving British rock band of the 20th century. Over a career spanning forty years they have been immensely influential, and in terms of sleeve design they have been always innovative and aspired to the highest standards.

Very much part of the same generation of British rock as the Beatles, the Rolling Stones album sleeves of the 1960s were mode-ish and largely derivative of Beatles' sleeves up to, and including, *Their Satanic Majesties Request* (1967). However from then on they set their own course and began to commission inventive and sometimes inspirational album sleeve design. In pursuit of their aims they have commissioned a galaxy of talent. They have, of course, always been able afford the best and they have employed celebrated designers from Robert Brownjohn to Stefan Sagmeister; famous photographers from David Bailey, through Hiro, to Annie Leibovitz; and blue-chip artists from Andy Warhol to Francesco Clemente. None the less, they have spent their money wisely and with sharp antennae for the changing style. And sometimes they have taken risks and commissioned young, untried designers in the early stages of their careers.

Their Satanic Majesties Request (1967) was the final album sleeve by the Rolling Stones to have more than a hint of a previous Beatles cover, in this case the elaborately staged tableau of *Sergeant Pepper's Lonely Hearts Club Band*. By their commissioning the same photographer, Michael Cooper, and by concealing miniature faces of the

Beatles in the flowers surrounding them for their fancy dress group shot, they contributed to the general perception that this was their riposte to the *Sergeant Pepper* sleeve, rather than being an original step of their own. However, from here on they began to develop an increasingly assured sense of how to project the band's distinctive persona, producing a string of sharp, innovative sleeves. Their first attempt was *Beggars Banquet* (1968) and then, the following year, *Let It Bleed* which featured a before-and-after record-changer/wedding cake assemblage devised by Robert Brownjohn (1925–70) who had been a partner in the design group Brownjohn, Chermayeff & Geismar in New York between 1957 and 1960. He had moved to London in the early '60s and established his reputation by producing the celebrated title sequences for the James Bond films *From Russia With Love* and *Goldfinger*.

John Pasche is a good example of a designer commissioned by the band early in his career. In the late '60s he was still studying graphic design at the Royal College of Art, London, when he was commissioned to produced posters, based on 1920s Art Deco travel posters, for a Rolling Stones concert tour. He went on to design poster campaigns for a further three of their tours. He also devised the famous lips and tongue logo for the Rolling Stones record label. It first appeared on the album *Sticky Fingers* (1971), with a notorious sleeve devised by Andy Warhol featuring a close-up of a jeans' crotch with a real fly zip. Pasche went on to form his own design studio, Gull

3

LET IT BLEED □ LOVE IN VAIN □ MIDNIGHT RAMBLER □ GIMMIE SHELTER □ YOU GOT THE SILVER
YOU CAN'T ALWAYS GET WHAT YOU WANT □ LIVE WITH ME □ MONKEY MAN □ COUNTRY HONK

London Records Inc. 539 West 25th Street, New York, N.Y. 10001   Printed in U.S.A.

4

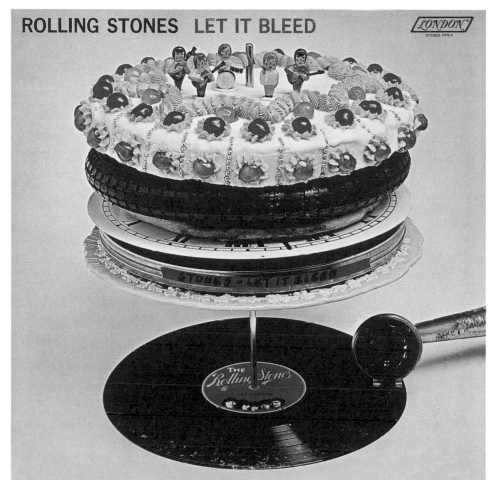

ROLLING STONES   LET IT BLEED

LONDON
STEREO NPS-4

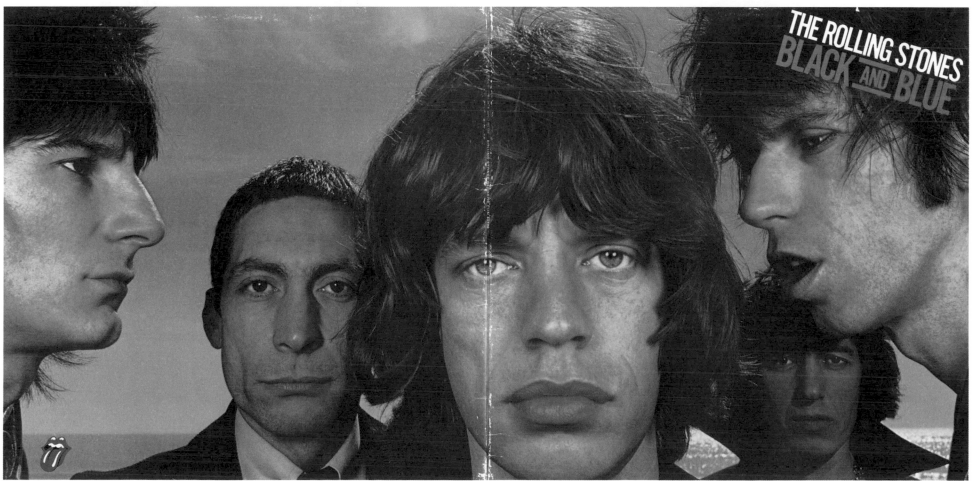

THE ROLLING STONES
BLACK AND BLUE

5

7

8

Graphics, with David Howells which was very active in album sleeve design during the 1970s. He later had a spell at United Artists Records as an art director and was creative director at Chrysalis Records for most of the 1980s where he designed covers for Ultavox, UFO and Jethro Tull, among many others.

John Van Hamersveld was commissioned to work on *Exile On Main St.* (1972) when working on a songbook for the band while they were staying in a hired mansion in Los Angeles. Robert Frank who was interested in making a documentary on the Stones (the unreleased *Cocksucker Blues*) was asked to provide a photograph for the front cover. Finally, one he had taken in 1950 of a collection of images tacked to the wall of a tattoo parlour somewhere on Route 66 was used.

The designer Peter Corriston had an extremely fruitful relationship with the Rolling Stones in the late '70s and early '80s. Corriston was a student at a variety of art schools in San Francisco, New York and Rome between 1967 and 1972. Back in New York he quickly established a reputation in the music business. Among his earliest clients were New York Dolls, Cheech and Chong, and Rod Stewart. In 1978 he worked with Mike Doud on the album sleeve for Led Zeppelin's *Physical Graffiti*, an elaborate package with cutout windows. The same year he was commissioned to design *Some Girls* for the Rolling Stones which employed similar window cut-outs. He subsequently designed *Emotional Rescue* (1980), *Tattoo You* (1982), and *Undercover* (1983) for the band.

Illustrator Christian Piper was brought in to produce the image of the tattooed head for *Tattoo You*. He had worked for the Rolling Stones before, painting the sunbather in the desert image for *Made In The Shade* (1976). Corriston went on to design album sleeves for many other recording acts, including Tom Waits, Sinead O'Connor and Pat Benatar. He worked for the Rolling Stones again in the 1990s, and was responsible for creating the corporate identity of MCA's new subsidiary Infinity.

After a prolonged fallow period in the late '80s, marked by solo projects and disagreements about the direction of the band, the Rolling Stones picked up pace again in the early 1990s with the *Voodoo Lounge* album and tour. Throughout the '90s they continued to commission quality designs and designers. Annie Leibovitz, who had photographed the band for the cover of *Dirty Work* in 1986, photographed Mick Jagger for the his solo album *Wandering Spirit* (1993). Jagger also commissioned a satyrlike drawing of himself by Italian artist Francesco Clemente for *Primitive Cool*. The Rolling Stones last studio album of the decade *Bridges to Babylon* (1997) was designed by one of the most inventive of '90s sleeve designers, Stefan Sagmeister.

6 **Under Cover**, THE ROLLING STONES, Atlantic, 1984.
[opposite]
Design: Peter Corriston. Photography: Hubert Kretzschman.
7 **Some Girls**, THE ROLLING STONES, Atlantic, 1978.
Design: Peter Corriston.
8 **Physical Graffiti**, LED ZEPPELIN, Swan Song, 1978.
Design: Mike Doud, Peter Corriston. Photography: Elliot Erwitt,
B P Fallen, Roy Harper. Tinting: Maurice Tate. Window
illustration: Dave Hefferman.
9 **Tattoo You**, THE ROLLING STONES, Rolling Stones, 1982.
Design: Peter Corriston. Illustration: Christian Piper.

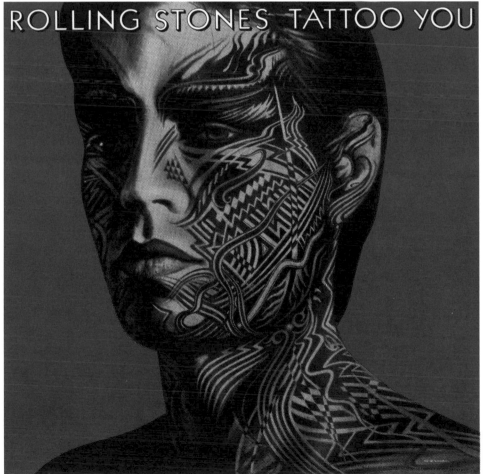

9

1

2

Bryan Ferry was born in 1945 in County Durham, England. His long career in the first rank of British rock stars a most unlikely thing for that vocation: an exercise in studied elegance. He has always paid the closest attention to the visual projection of himself and his band, Roxy Music, over the thirty years of his career, although one episode in particular stands out. It demonstrates that he understood, as early as 1970, that there was an increasingly apparent sense in which the rock star was a pose; a deliberately projected, self-conscious persona surrounded by an already delineated constellation of signification. Ferry explored this idea in a series of album covers which he masterminded for Roxy Music during the first phase of their career, between 1972 and 1976, during which both he and the band became established as international stars.

Art students are notorious for their acute sense of generation identification. This was as true of mid-1960s art students as it is now. Then a new generation of art students recently arrived at art school perceived their elders – barely a few years older than themselves – adopting the mantle of the counterculture: hippiedom, love-ins and flower power. The response of the sharpest of this new generation was to seek inspiration elsewhere. Thus a young Bryan Ferry, lucky enough to find himself being taught by pop artist Richard Hamilton in Newcastle University's Department of Fine Art, directed his thoughts not to the counterculture's visual style statements of psychedelia and kaftans, but to a rock'n'roll full

of allusions to old Hollywood, to haute couture, to arch style, all to be filtered through art's lens of knowingness.

1971 saw the launch of Ferry's idea of a modern rock vehicle: Roxy Music, a name which suggested both cinema architecture, with its fake grandeur and art deco interiors, and the movies screened there. He arrived in London to find post-psychedelic progressive rock, at its most precious, in full-spate. His desire to strike out in a very different direction was given special piquancy by the fact that Roxy Music's management, EG, also managed King Crimson, which at that time was definitely of the whimsical wing of British progressive rock. The first Roxy Music album sleeve, the eponymous *Roxy Music* (1972), explores the binary which Ferry saw as central to the mythic in rock music. This is the binary of rock star and fan. The primary image – the cover – is not to be misunderstood as some decorative anonymous model, she is the idealized fan, personification of feminine desir-ability. The greater the fan's status – the more glamorous her persona – the more exalted is the band of which she is the fan. The cover photograph, then, is of the Roxy fan who, by a kind of symbiotic magic, gives status to the band. She is the foil through which the band, represented in the gatefold (to the same degree of irony, campery and kitsch as the fan) is elevated to its place in rock's hallowed hall of fame. On subsequent album sleeves the fan as the phantasmagorical figure of glamour – formidable, intimidating, unattainable – is given flesh by *Playboy*'s 1972 Playmate of the

Year Marilyn Coles (*Stranded*), celebrated models of the likes of Amanda Lear (*For Your Pleasure*), and Jerry Hall (*Siren*) as well as Kari-Ann (*Roxy Music*). Whether dominatrix, vamp, lost-in-the-jungle waif, siren, victims of the paparazzi or extras in a Leni Riefenstahl film (with their little tunics and touches of ancient Greece), these figures of filmic glamour are material representations of the rock star's fantastical other.

1 **Roxy Music**, ROXY MUSIC, Island Records, 1972. Design: Bryan Ferry, Nick de Ville, Anthony Price. Photography: Karl Stoecker. [Left: outside gatefold. Right: inside gatefold.]

2 **For Your Pleasure**, ROXY MUSIC, Island Records, 1973. Design: Bryan Ferry, Nick de Ville, Anthony Price. Photography: Karl Stoecker. [Left: outside gatefold. Right: inside gatefold.]

3 **Country Life**, ROXY MUSIC, Island Records, 1974. [opposite] Design: Bryan Ferry, Nick de Ville, Anthony Price. Cover Design: Nick de Ville. Art Direction: Bryan Ferry. Photography: Eric Boman. Artwork: Bob Bowkett at CCS. Fashion: Anthony Price. [opposite]

ROXY MUSIC

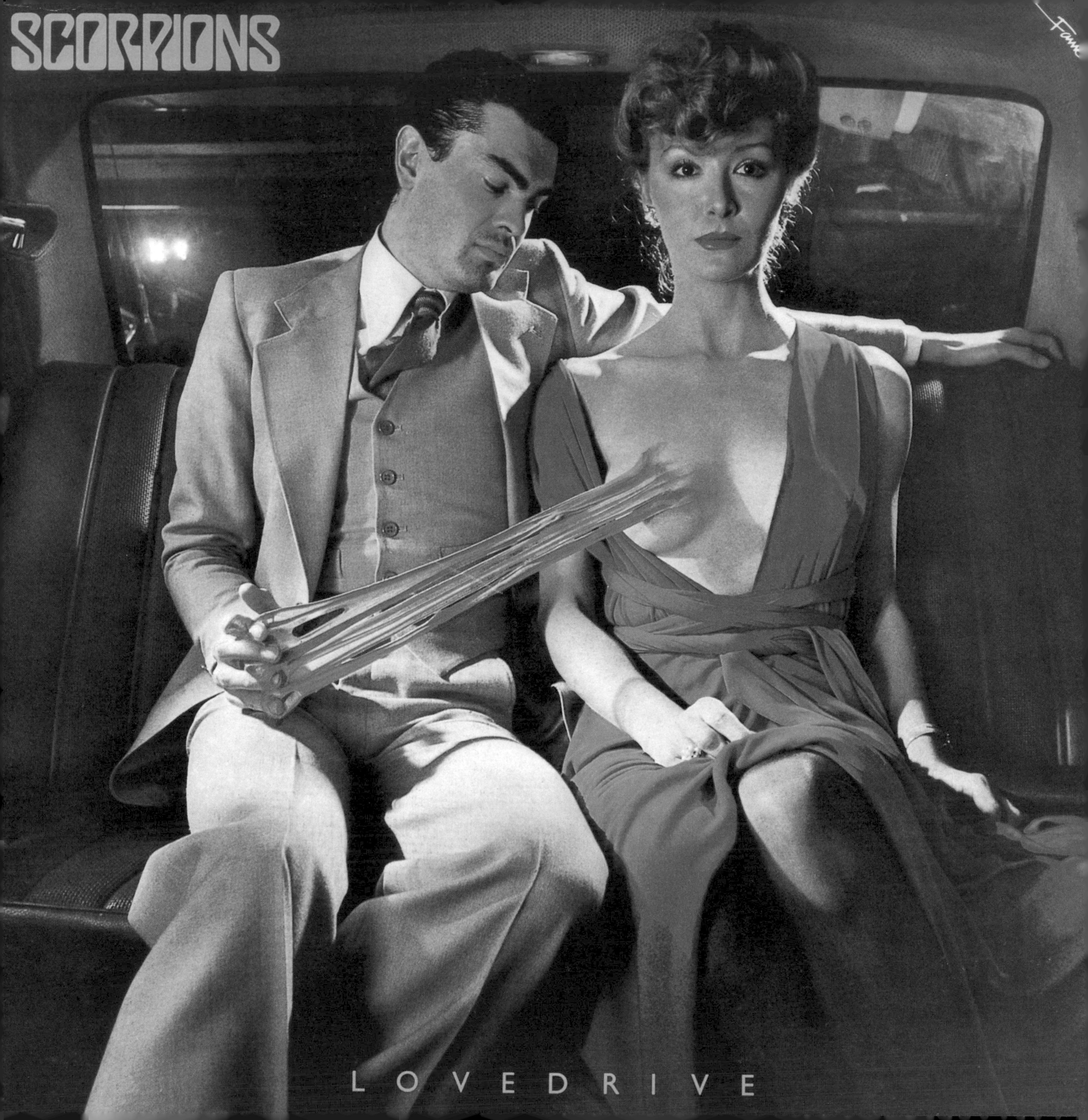
SCORPIONS
LOVEDRIVE

2

3

1 **Lovedrive**, SCORPIONS, Mercury Records, 1979. [opposite]
Design and photography: Hipgnosis.

2 **Atom Heart Mother**, PINK FLOYD, EMI, 1970.
Design: Hipgnosis, John Blake. Photograpy: Hipgnosis.

3 **Ummagumma**, PINK FLOYD, EMI, 1969.
Design: Hipgnosis, E. January. Photograpy: Hipgnosis.

Storm Thorgerson met Aubrey Powell while he was studying for his MA in Film and Television at the Royal College of Art. They launched design group Hipgnosis in 1968. During the design group's heyday in the 1970s, their brand of surreal cinematic narratives was practically *de rigueur* for British rock bands of a progressive persuasion. Their style which skillfully blended large-format photography with George Hardie's illustrational graphic overlays was, in many ways, a modernist recasting of the '60s fantastical illustrative style.

Their choice of imagery was very much part of the post-hippy mentality still in evidence in the early '70s: psychedelia by other means. The hallucinogenic imagery was often of surrealist derivation, echoing motifs from Dali, Magritte and the like, but its transformation into pin-sharp photographs gave Hipgnosis's images a unique presence. In a time before digital photography and image manipulation software such as Photoshop, photographic retouching was an absolute requisite of their work, and their retoucher Richard Manning was consummately skilled, ensuring their surreal visions were given the veneer of photographic veracity.

Illustrator George Hardie often contributed embellished logos and graphic overlays of a type which later found favour in the 1980s with design groups such as Assorted Images and Stylorouge. Such was the lure of Hipgnosis's style that they even stole Yes away from their long association with illustrator Roger Dean for the album *Going for the One* (1977).

In the early '70s Hipgnosis was a rarity in Britain: an independent design group specifically focused on designing for the record industry. Although the evolution of independent designers into groups specifically aiming to provide design services for the music world was imperceptibly gathering pace, it was the scale of the entertainment industry focused on Los Angeles that first encouraged this development, and where design studios, such as Rod Dyer Inc., were being established to service such needs. Thorgerson and Powell's partnership prospered and they were joined by Peter Christopherson in 1974. They also collaborated regularly with designer/illustrator George Hardie. Storm Thorgerson was in many ways the lynchpin of the company. As Peter Gabriel said of him: "It's always fun when you start meeting with him. He's got this box of slightly used ideas that he tries to palm you off with. Only the difficult sods get the original creative things, and everyone else gets the stuff that's been rejected. But that's part of the game and I used to enjoy it as well." Thorgerson was born in Middlesex, England, in 1944. His childhood had included a spell at A.S. Neill's "progressive" school Summerhill, and he had studied for a degree in English and Philosophy at Leicester University before going to the Royal College of Art.

Hipgnosis's first album sleeve design was for Pink Floyd's second album *A Saucerful of Secrets* (1968). Pink Floyd was formed by Syd Barrett, an art student at Camberwell School of Art, with Regent Street Polytechnic students Roger Waters,

4 **Going for the One**, YES, Atlantic Records, 1977.
Design: Hipgnosis.

5 **Technical Ecstasy**, BLACK SABBATH, Vertigo/
Warners Bros, 1976.
Design: Hipgnosis, George Hardie.

6 **How Dare You**, 10CC, Phonogram (Mercury) 1976.
Design: Hipgnosis, George Hardie. Photography: Hipgnosis,
Howard Bartrop.

7 **Presence**, LED ZEPPELIN, Swan Song/Atlantic Records, 1977.
Design: Hipgnosis, George Hardie. Photography: Aubrey Powell,
Peter Christopherson.

8 **Dark Side of the Moon**, PINK FLOYD, EMI, 1973.
Design: Hipgnosis, George Hardie.

4

5

Nick Mason and Rick Wright. The band (its name coined by Barrett as a homage to bluesmen Pink Anderson and Floyd Council) quickly established itself as one of the most prominent on the underground scene, playing venues such as the newly opened UFO and Middle Earth clubs. Their long association with design group Hipgnosis allowed them to develop a visual identity which, with its widescreen surrealist motifs, was the perfect compliment to their music.

Designing Pink Floyd's *A Saucerful of Secrets* album sleeve was the beginning of the design group's long and fruitful association with the band, although the partnership did not begin to strike an entirely consistent note until their eighth album *Dark Side Of The Moon* which launched them into the international mainstream in 1973. The album is still among the best-selling albums of all time, and the gatefold sleeve features George Hardie's famous prism image, splitting a beam of white light into its constituent colours only to recombine them in an endless cycle. Succeeding albums *Wish You Were Here* (1975) and *Animals* (1977) consolidated their reputation as one of the biggest progressive rock acts on the international circuit. Pink Floyd's sleeve art is amongst the most coherent and successful campaigns using album covers as a means of projecting a band's musical identity. The consistency of Pink Floyd's approach to sleeve design, despite considerable personnel changes, allowed Hipgnosis to develop a complex and innovative signature style for the band which can perhaps best be described as "Hollywood

Surrealism". Success in America allowed the band to extend its visual style to the staging of its stadium concerts which aimed for sensory overload, using blimps, huge props, pyrotechnics and state-of-the-art lighting to compliment the music. Roger Waters brought in political caricaturist Gerald Scarfe to work on animations and stage designs for the "The Wall" tour, a collaboration that culminated in Alan Parker's feature-length animated film. Waters left the band in 1981 and the visual thread developed with Hipgnosis was subsequently re-established.

Although most closely associated with Pink Floyd, Hipgnosis designed record covers for many important rock bands, including Led Zeppelin, Genesis, 10cc and Wishbone Ash. Particularly celebrated are Led Zeppelin's *Houses Of The Holy* (1977) and *Presence* (1976) and 10cc's *How Dare You* (1976) and *Bloody Tourists* (1978).

In 1983, the writing on the wall for big budget album sleeves, Thorgerson, Powell and Christopherson decided to follow the money and formed Green Back Films with the intention of entering the increasingly important market for the promotional films and videos which were being tied in to album releases. The company was disbanded in 1985 due to financial difficulties and artistic differences. Thorgerson continued to make videos for EMI and commercials for Hang Films until 1991, when he began to write art and science documentaries. He continues to be actively involved in album sleeve and book design.

6

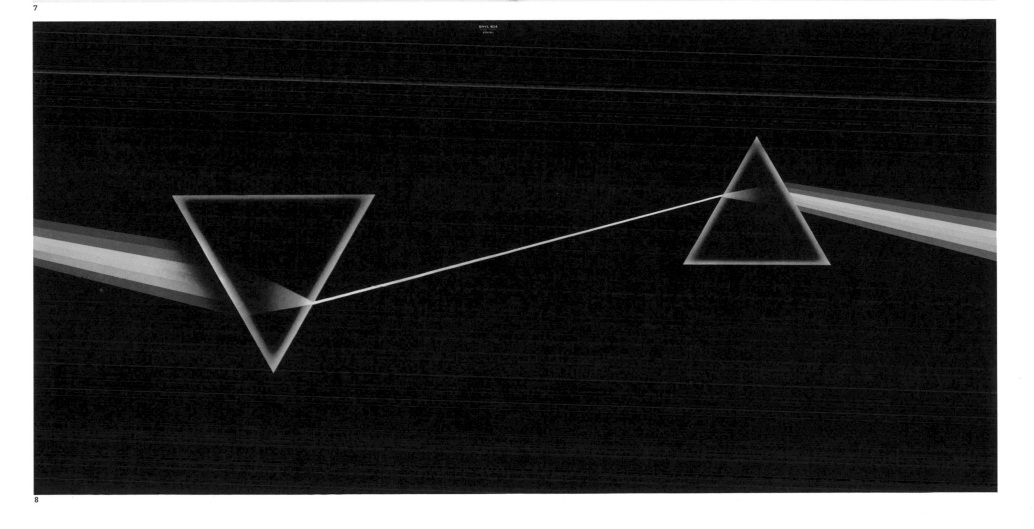

1

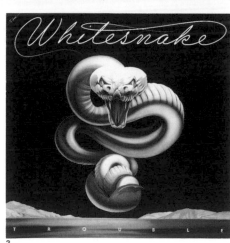

2

3

4

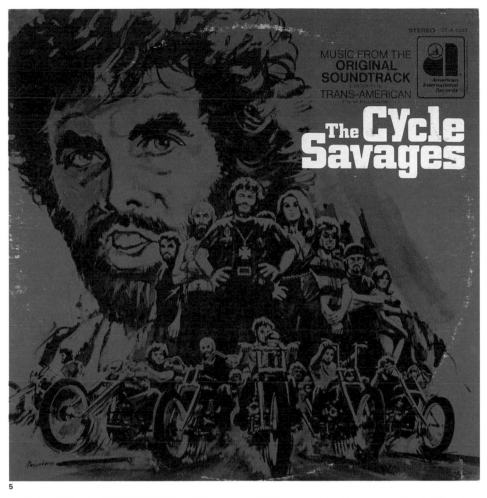

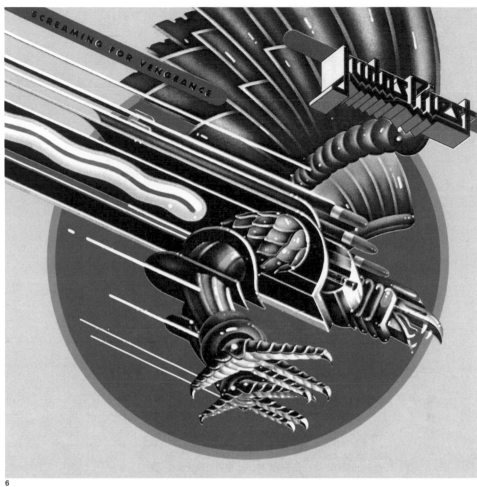

5

6

1 **Flirtin' with Disaster**, MOLLY HATCHET, Epic, 1979.
Design: Smay Vision. Art direction: Howard Fritzon.
Illustration: Frank Frazetta.
2 **Trouble**, WHITESNAKE, Sunburst/Fame, 1978.
Design and art direction: Bill Burks. Illustration: Bill Imhoff.
3 **Bat Out of Hell**, MEAT LOAF, Sony/Epic, 1977.
Design: Ed Lee. Illustration: Richard Corben.
4 **Killers**, IRON MAIDEN, EMI, 1981.
Illustration: Derek Rigg.
5 **The Cycle Savages**, American International, 1970.
Design: Bill Pate. Illustration: Robert Tanenbaum.
6 **Screaming for Vengeance**, JUDAS PRIEST, CBS, 1984.
Design: John Berg. Illustration: Doug Johnson.

Heavy metal art is an international style with its roots in the biker culture of the immediate post war period, the notoriety of which Hollywood first celebrated in the 1954 film *The Wild One* starring Marlon Brando and Lee Marvin. The characteristic attributes of biker culture – outlaw status, insistence on archetypal gender distinctions, the fetishization of black leathers and the motorbike, preferably the iconic Harley-Davidson – passed through numerous mutations during the rest of the century: rockers, Hell's Angels, greasers, Goths. Bikers first entered the public consciousness in a big way in the 1960s when the Hell's Angels identity was brought into stark contrast to the pacific nature of the hippies.

They gained particular notoriety for their "policing" of the Rolling Stones' free concert staged at Altamont in 1969 at the end of the band's "Let It Bleed" tour of America. Against a background of increasing menace and anarchy, a Hell's Angel laid out cold Jefferson Airplane's lead singer Marty Balin, and a member of the audience, Meredith Hunter, was fatally stabbed during the Stones' rendition of *Under My Thumb*, the Angels claiming that he had pulled a gun on "sissy" Mick Jagger.

The type of music that has come to be most closely associated with the biker culture and its diverse clans is heavy metal. This is a long tradition going back to Vanilla Fudge in America and Led Zeppelin and Deep Purple in Britain. The style was further defined by bands such as Van Halen (USA), Judas Priest and Def Leppard (UK)

and Rose Tattoo and AC/DC (Australia). Heavy metal music is famous for its relentless drive, repetitious music format and the reactionary (not to mention white supremacist) sentiments of its lyrics. Heavy metal split into many sub-genres during the 1990s, hybridizing with other musical genres. Industrial metal is a crossover with house/techno and grunge with punk, etc. The style of heavy metal album covers is, at its most archetypal, a form of Gonzo Gothic illustration which can also be found in fantasy comics and on the covers of sci-fi books which espouse similar lifestyle values. The preoccupations of classic heavy metal art are: the supernatural, sword and sorcery heroes, voluptuous but seriously psychotic heroines, Roswellian alien fantasies, and visions of a post-apocalyptic world of damnation and cruelty with heavy camp overtones. One of the most accomplished pioneers of the style is Frank Frazetta, born in New York in 1928 and a graduate of the New York Academy of Fine Arts, who covers the field from comic books, movie posters and book covers to album sleeves. His influence on heavy metal album sleeve illustration is far greater than his actual album sleeve output, although his Molly Hatchett sleeve for *Flirtin' With Disaster* (1979), with its rampant Viking warlord, is an archetypal example of sword 'n' sorcery subject matter. Melvyn is a good example of an illustrator in the Frazetta mould, and his sleeve for Judas Priest's *Hero, Hero* (1981) is highly reminiscent of Frazetta's *Flirtin' with Disaster* image. Doug Johnson supplied Judas Priest with two excellent

examples of heavy metal's heraldic bestiary: a heraldic missile-carrying eagle for *Screaming For Vengeance* (1982) and a jurassic tankasaurus for *Defenders Of The Faith* (1984). The self-parody implicit in a lot of this is made plain by Iron Maiden's mascot Eddie, the skeleton ghoul created by Derek Riggs in a cartoon fantasy style, who has featured, in numerous guises, on at least eighteen different Iron Maiden album sleeves. Finally, mention must be made of Richard Corben's contributions to Meat Loaf sleeves for *Bat Out Of Hell* (1977) and *Bat Out Of Hell II* (1993) which, appreciated in conjunction with Berni Wrightson's sleeve for Meat Loaf's *Dead Ringer* (1981), have elevated the motorbike as mythical steed to glorious heights of absurdity.

1

In terms of visual style the most appropriate way to think of disco is as the DIY appropriation of glam rock by nightclubbers. What is most fascinating about disco is that its highpoint, epitomized by *Saturday Night Fever*, was precisely contemporaneous with punk, but seemingly occupied an entirely unconnected parallel universe. Disco was in every conceivable way punk's antithesis. It was glitzy, escapist and kitsch. Abba, Boney M. and Chic were all part of disco's insistency on frivolity, the mass-vacation sophistication of booze and discoing till dawn, with a smidgen of cross-dressing gender-bending thrown in. John Travolta as Tony Mandero in the film *Saturday Night Fever* (1978) was the archetypal disco male, although, on the whole, disco males came a very poor second to their female counterparts who were, without exception, divas. The queen of divas was Donna Summer, and her greatest disco anthem was "I Feel Love".

Had disco royalty permitted males to its ranks then the Bee Gees would undoubtedly have been closest to the throne. Their soundtrack of *Saturday Night Fever* is the best-selling soundtrack album ever. Travolta in his Tony Mandero persona in characteristic disco pose, clad in his archetypal outfit of white suit and black shirt, is central to the cover designed by RSO's Susan Herr and Tom Nickosey. The design of the sleeve was a diplomatic compromise hammered out by the Bee Gees' and Travolta's managements. Central to the agreement was the understanding that the faces of Travolta and the Bee Gees would all be of precisely the same size. Herr's solution to this requirement was to montage Francesco Scavullo's photograph of the Bee Gees above a dancefloor publicity shot of Travolta. Herr was not overly impressed with the design at the time and she has admitted that "It's not one of my proudest moments of design. I didn't even give myself a design credit. It just says 'art prepared by...' There's just too much happening for it to be a very good design." As things have turned out the cover, from the lettering to the Bee Gees' notorious coiffures to Travolta's pose, has become one of the defining images of disco. As Herr concludes: "I thought it was too busy; twenty four years later, it's an icon."

As far as album cover design was concerned, being a disco diva was principally about dressing up and big hair. Disco album sleeves did not deal in subtleties (although, in fulfillment of weird Scandinavian design principles, Abba covers are memorably disconnected from disco logic). What disco diva sleeves required was the epitome of disco glam with as much verticality and glitter as possible. Amii Stewart got disco's dress-sense absolutely right for her 1979 *Knock On Wood* sleeve.

If Donna Summer was the butter-wouldn't-melt-in-her-mouth diva of disco, floating above the clouds for *A Love Trilogy* (1976), Grace Jones was the menacing ball-breaking diva from disco's inferno. She produced a number of stylish covers with Jean-Paul Goude, including *Nightclubbing* (1981). Perhaps the group to explore the furthest territories of disco excess in terms of dress sense was Boney M. Whether they were exploring outer space or surfing tsunami on their album sleeves, they were sure to be dressed in costumes that combined the maximum exposure of flesh with an outlandish style that looked as if it had been purloined from some operatic extravaganza of concubines, despots and chivalrous baritones.

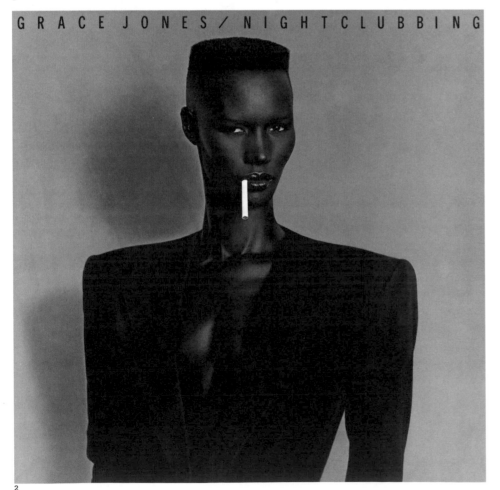

2

3

4

1   **Saturday Night Fever**, VARIOUS ARTISTS, RSO, 1978.
     Design: Susan Herr, Tim Nickosey.
2   **Nightclubbing**, GRACE JONES, Island Records, 1981.
     Design and photography: Jean Paul Goude.

3   **A Love Trilogy**, DONNA SUMMER, Casablanca, 1976.
     Design and art direction: Henry Vizcarra/Gribbitt!
     Photography: Jochen Harder.
4   **Oceans of Fantasy**, BONEY M., Atlantic, 1979.
     Design: unknown.
5   **Knock on Wood**, AMII STEWART, Ariola, 1979.
     Design: Cooke-Key. Photography: Brian Aris. [opposite]

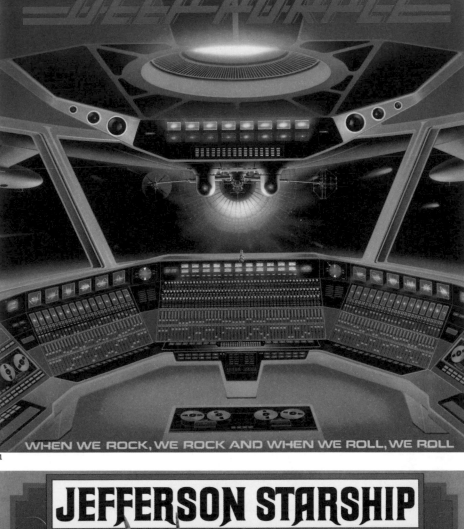

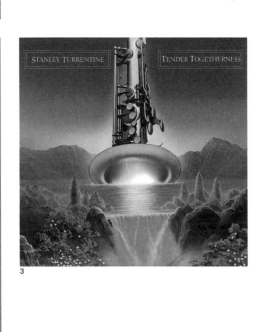

1. **When We Rock, We Rock and When We Roll, We Roll,** DEEP PURPLE, Warner Bros, 1978. Design: Gribbitt! Art direction: John Cabalka. Illustration: Shusei Nagaoka.

2. **Spitfire**, JEFFERSON STARSHIP, Grunt, 1976. Illustration: Shusei Nagaoka.

3. **Tender Togetherness**, STANLEY TURRENTINE, Elektra, 1981. Art Direction: Ron Coro, Art Sims for 11.24 Design. Illustration: Shusei Nagaoka.

4. **All'n'All**, EARTH, WIND AND FIRE, CBS, 1977. Illustration: Shusei Nagaoka.

5. **Out of the Blue**, ELECTRIC LIGHT ORCHESTRA, United Artists, 1977. Design Supervision: John Kosh and Ria Lewerke. Illustration: Shusei Nagaoka.

Shusei Nagaoka was born in 1936 in Japan. Most of his working life has been spent living in America, most recently in New York. An accomplished illustrator, his work can be found on posters, book covers and album sleeves. He is perhaps most closely identified with the pictorial style of the most successful soul dance band of the late 1970s, Earth, Wind & Fire with whom he has had a long and close association, not only designing a succession of album covers for them, but also tour programme covers and other illustrative material.

The album sleeve which first brought Nagaoka notice, and for which he was awarded *Rolling Stone*'s best album cover of the year award in 1976, was Jefferson Starship's *Spitfire*. The album's spectral landscape with a female rider atop a dragon creature which balefully snarls at the viewer, sums up many of the characteristics that are typical and lasting features of his work. In some ways his style is reminiscent of Roger Dean's (compare the dragon here with the one on Dean's sleeve for Asia's eponymous first album of 1985), but Nagaoka's work strives for the more obvious effects of a fantastical sublime, and his images are often organized more symmetrically in the vertical axis in a way which is reminiscent of psychedelic imagery of the previous decade.

His success with Jefferson Starship brought him two notable follow-up commissions which did much to cement his reputation. Under the design supervision of John Kosh and Ria Lewerke, he turned the flying saucer-shaped logo of Electric Light Orchestra's previous album, *A New World Record* (1976) into a fully realized space station with the ELO insignia at its centre for *Out Of The Blue* (1977). For Earth, Wind & Fire's *All 'n' All* (1977) he produced a cabalistic Cheops-style pyramid whose tip intersects the rays of the sun, atop a light-drenched pharoic, Valley of the Kings architectural folly. For some inexplicable reason Nagaoka's style chimed with the funky disco sensibility of the time, and besides further commissions for Earth, Wind & Fire, starting with their follow-up *I Am* (1979), he also designed several sleeves for Giorgio Moroder's Munich Machine, most notably the disco dancing robots of their eponymous first album (1977), and the debut album for Parlet (pronounced "par-lette"), one of P-Funk's short-lived girl groups. The album was called *Pleasure Principle* (1978) and for the cover Nagaoka produced an image of the group's singers, Debbie, Mallia, and Jeannette, in a Mothership setting.

During the final years of the 1970s and the early years of the 1980s Nagaoka continued illustrating album sleeves, and not just for funk acts. His repertoire of images, spanning archaic architectural sites, apocalyptic landscapes and sci-fi hardware, all rendered in a colour-drenched detail owing more to airbrush technique than observational drawing, enjoyed wide popularity. He used the same approach to book cover illustration, most notably for Jeffrey A. Carver's *Novels of the Starstream*, although he adopted a more sober approach when required, as, for example, in his memorable design for the poster of the "Shogun" exhibition at the Dallas Museum of Art in 1984.

EARTH WIND & FIRE

4

Electric Light Orchestra
Out of the Blue

TURN TO STONE
IT'S OVER
SWEET TALKIN' WOMAN
ACROSS THE BORDER

NIGHT IN THE CITY
STARLIGHT
JUNGLE
BELIEVE ME NOW
STEPPIN' OUT

CONCERTO FOR A RAINY DAY
STANDIN' IN THE RAIN
BIG WHEELS
SUMMER AND LIGHTNING
MR. BLUE SKY

SWEET IS THE NIGHT
THE WHALE
BIRMINGHAM BLUES
WILD WEST HERO

ALL MUSIC AND LYRICS
BY JEFF LYNNE.
PRODUCED BY JEFF LYNNE.

© ℗ 1977 United Artists Music & Records Group Inc.

® Trademarks owned by United Artists
Music and Records Group Inc. and used
by United Artists Records Limited under
authorisation.

MARKETED BY UNITED ARTISTS RECORDS

WARNING: Copyright exists in all records
issued by United Artists Records Limited.
Any unauthorised broadcasting, public
performance, copying or re-recording of
such records in any manner will consti-
tute an infringement of such copyright.
Application for public performance
licences should be addressed to Phono-
graphic Performance Limited, Ganton
House, 14-22 Ganton Street, London
W1V 1LB.

5

Patti Smith Horses

2

3

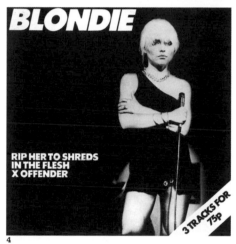

4

5

1 **Ramones**, THE RAMONES, Sire, 1976. [opposite]
Design: unknown. Photography: Roberta Bayley.

2 **Horses**, PATTI SMITH, Arista, 1975.
Design: Bob Heimall. Photography: Robert Mapplethorpe

3 **Easter**, PATTI SMITH, Arista, 1978
Photography: Lynn Goldsmith. Design: unknown

4 **Rip Her to Shreds** (single) BLONDIE, Chrysalis, 1977.
Design: unknown.

5 **Oh Bondage Up Yours!**, X-RAY SPEX, Virgin, 1977.
Design: unknown.

Nothing divides pop sociology as much as punk. Some see punk as inextricably linked to the consciousness of working-class youth. Others see punk not as proletarian or even about protest but as being all about style. The latter have tended to see the trends in music and design for music that followed punk as punk-by-other-means. Punk's moment of consequence for music and design was glorious and timely, but its inherent nihilism meant that stylistically speaking it was ultimately reductive, although its attendant hands-on, DIY attitude was immensely liberating. It suffered from a fashionable adherence to Maoist ideas of cultural revolution, even then being worked through to their logical conclusion by the Khmer Rouge, whose disdain for education, people with glasses and organized thought of any kind were striking characteristics. It was fortunate that in the West these consequence of this cultural impulse were vented in the direction of fashionability, not least Malcolm McLaren's Couture Situationniste. In Britain the most important designer of the punk moment was Jamie Reid. His graphic work with the Sex Pistols was the perfect manifestation of punk's bedsit smash'n'grab aesthetic. His repertoire of cut-outs, torn edges, photocopied photographs and ransom-note lettering quickly became central to punk's visual idiom. With respect to the photographic image, post-Warhol techniques of simplification (posterization) knocking out the mid tones to either black or white, making for a high-contrast, low-detail

version of the original, was a look that the then-current generation of photocopiers was excellent at producing. This low-overhead, corner shop means of reproduction was accessible and instant and is used on numerous punk album and single sleeves. Punk lettering was best handmade, stencilled, slapped together from cut-outs, tapped out on a clapped-out portable typewriter or produced by some other labelling system of the period such as Dynotape.

As far as imagery is concerned, punk design relied on a number of distinctive sub-tropes, most of which would be more fully explored in the eclectic style wars which followed punk. The apocalyptic was central to the punk repertoire, not only scenes recorded from the punk underworld such as the histrionic suicide image from Eddie and the Hotrods' *Teenage Depression* (1977) or the blindfolded heroin user on Chelsea's *Alternative Hits* (1980), but also the kind of apocalyptic menace of burning cars (actually police cars set on fire during a riot in protest at the murder of gay politician, Harvey Milk) to be found on the Dead Kennedy's *Fresh Fruit for Rotting Vegetables* (1980). More sophisticated ways of creating violent and politically offensive images were also popular. Some adopted the cut-and-paste montage techniques reminiscent of John Heartfield's anti-Nazi political cartoons (although, confusingly, some punks also adopted Nazi regalia). The extravagant cover of the Crass's *Penis Envy* (1980) is a good example of ambitious montage in the punk idiom.

It is a curious fact that although the British punk movement was much more orientated to fashion and self-conscious style statements than was American punk, Jamie Reid's somewhat austere high-mindedness meant that he did not go on to extend punk's visual subculture. The design work for which he is remembered remains specifically tied to the 1977 moment of the Sex Pistol's heyday, a moment which the British establishment intended to be devoted to the celebration of the British monarchy. The final split of the Sex Pistols was announced on the front page of the *Sun* newspaper on January 19, 1978. Sid Vicious lay in a New York hospital following a drug-induced coma. It could as well have been the announcement of the end of punk as a musical movement. Punk's creed of "learn three chords and form a group" inevitably led to a restricted musical palette, and all but the most dedicated diehards soon concluded that they had sufficient punk records. By 1978 the end of punk's moment of blazing glory was signalled by the portrait photography of Johnny Rotten, weirdly metamorphosed into a psychotic optician, on the cover of Public Image's *First Issue*.

The punk impulse in design was rather a different matter. Here punk demonstrated rather more staying power and, although some of the best punk design belongs to 1977, the punk argot continued to be explored for a long time afterwards. The Clash's *London Calling* was released in 1979, the Dead Kennedys' *Fresh Fruit for Rotting Vegetables* in 1980.

American punk always had a more grown-up quality than British punk. Many of its musicians were more heavyweight and their subsequent careers more enduring. Visually it tended to be more dour and Spartan than the British version, being less pronouncedly connected to metropolitan fashionability, and album sleeve design reflects this. Two of the most notable American album sleeves associated with the arrival of the punk aesthetic are the Patti Smith covers *Horses* (1975) and *Easter* (1978). Her image on these two albums offered a radical portrayal of the uncompromising, surly, tough woman of punk. Although she was not sexy and glamorous in the conventional way, there was something provocatively erotic in the androgynous challenge

she offered those conventions. Not only did she shock executives at Arista with her visual persona, she extended the repertoire of musical identities available to other women performers. Even so, it is noticeable that by 1979's *Wave* she had appreciably toned down the punk look, appearing in the cover photograph sheepishly acting as a perch for two white doves.

What punk did successfully propagate was the idea that individuals should take control of both the means of production and the channels of distribution. In this sense of engagement with mainstream business it differed markedly from the "drop-out" mentality inherent to hippiedom. One of the most notable features of the British punk scene was the rise of numerous independent record

companies such as Stiff, Rough Trade, Illegal, Raw, and the Buzzcockss label, New Hormones.

As with psychedelia a decade before, mainstream design flirted with the punk argot for a short time before retreating to its polite, serviceable Swiss post-constructivist idiom. It was the post-punk exuberance of Neville Brody, Peter Saville, Malcolm Garrett and Barney Bubbles which were to shake up mainstream design. A last irony of the punk moment, given the plainer visual character of American punk, is that if the summer of 1977 has an heir in the field of graphic design it is Seattle-based Art Chantry, whose work throughout the 1980s and 1990s has shown that the idea of subculture design can be sustained and developed into a complex visual vocabulary.

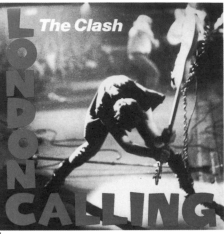

7

6   **The Clash**, THE CLASH, CBS, 1977.
Design: J.Guttner. Photography: Kate Simon.
Art direction: Roslav Szaybo.
7   **London Calling**, THE CLASH, CBS, 1979.
Design: Ray Lowry. Photography: Pennie Smith.

6

8

9

10

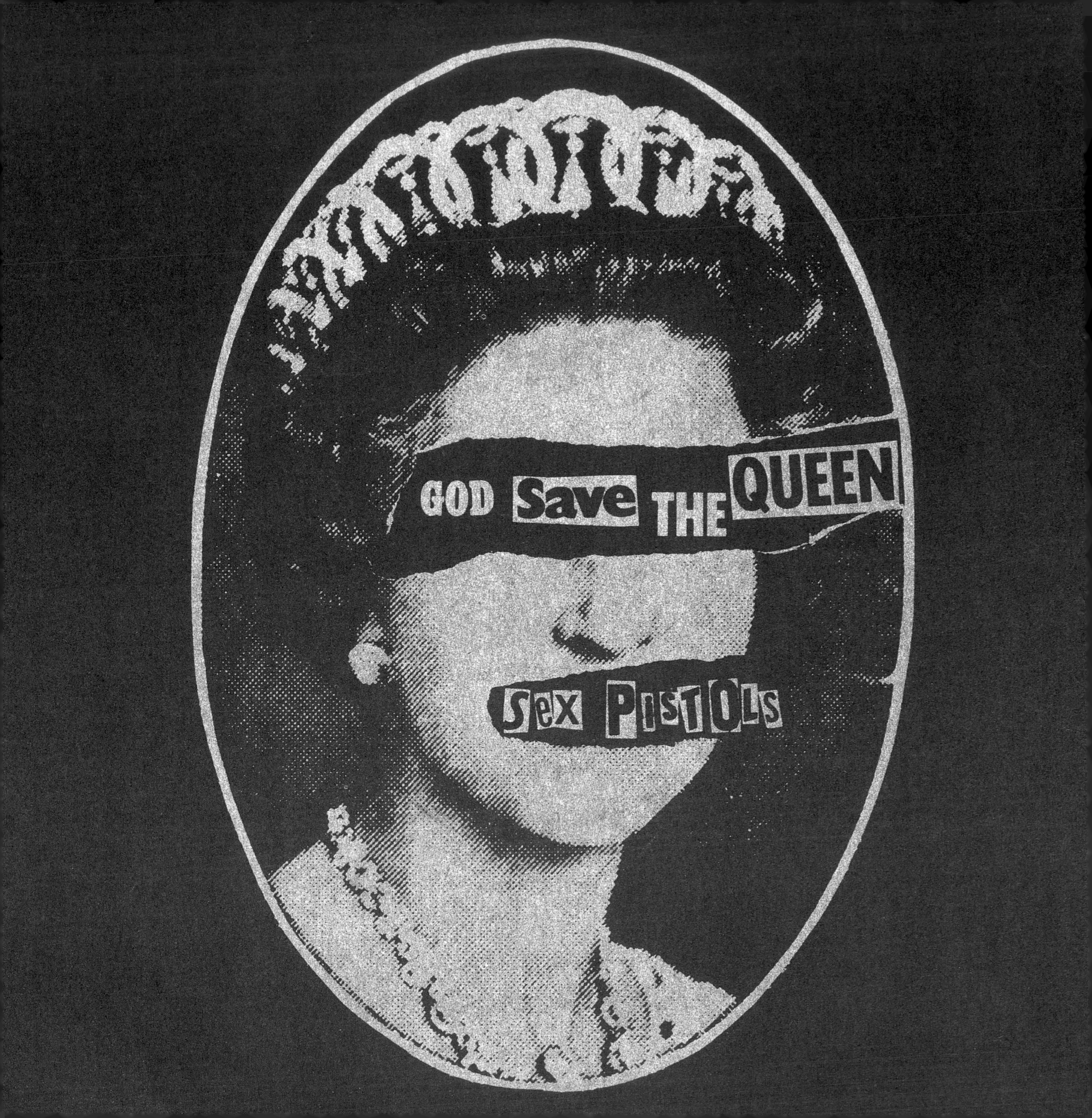
GOD Save THE QUEEN
SEX PISTOLS

Jamie Reid was born in 1947 in Shirley, a suburb of Croydon, England, and his childhood was spent in a politically active household. His father, John MacGregor-Reid, was the left-wing City editor of *The Daily Sketch*, a national daily newspaper since defunct. His brother Bruce served as a press officer for the nuclear disarmament activists Committee of 100 in the early 1960s. On the advice of his secondary school art teacher he enrolled at Wimbledon Art School as a foundation course student in 1962 when still only 16. In 1964 he moved to Croydon Art School where the future punk entrepreneur Malcolm McLaren was also studying, although the two did not meet until April 1968. They were both student radicals in the then current Maoist vein, attacking institutional authority within the college and instigating student sit-ins. A pivotal influence on Reid's development as a designer was the Situationist International movement which advocated social interventions through a combination of radical artistic and political action. The Situationist International was founded by artists from several European counties in 1957 at a conference in Italy, but by the early '60s the charismatic but misanthropic Guy Debord had come to dominate the movement. His seminal work was *The Society Of The Spectacle* (1962). The Situationists' heyday was the civil insurrection in France of May 1968. Although the SI played an important part in inspiring and instigating the uprising, it was unable to channel the civil strife towards Debord's cultural and political revolution. However, during the insurrection student leaders produced posters in support of their cause employing silkscreen printing, a primitive version of the technique already adopted by Andy Warhol in New York. Their posters where restricted to bold images and simple lettering made with hand-cut and simple photographic stencils. The authorities' attempts to shut off the source of these posters failed because the police did not recognize stacked silkscreens as their possible source. The do-it-yourself immediacy which was characteristic of these posters, as well as the ideological cause they espoused, was to be a fundamental influence on the vocabulary of punk a decade later.

The events of 1968 led Reid, together with Nigel Edwards and Jeremy Brook, to found in 1970 a "shit stirring" community paper in Croydon called *The Suburban Press* as a vehicle for his Anglicized version of Situationist interventions focused on local politics and council corruption. Six issues of *Suburban Press* were published. During this period Reid also edited, designed and printed the first English-language anthology of Situationist writings published under the title *Leaving the Twentieth Century*.

In 1976, McLaren sent Reid a telegram: "Got these guys; interested in working with you again." At this time McLaren and Vivienne Westwood were running London's definitive punk shop Sex. McLaren wanted to broaden the basis of their activities beyond retailing, and had become manager to punk rock band the Sex Pistols fronted by Johnny Rotten (John Lydon). McLaren's plan was that, with Westwood dressing them and Reid acting as their in-house graphic designer, they had

a perfect vehicle to take on the world with their subversive anarchic mischief. In the autumn of 1976 Reid helped McLaren to set up the Sex Pistols' management company, Glitterbest. Reid not only designed the group's record covers but also adverts, posters and stickers. Glitterbest produced a single-issue fanzine titled *Anarchy in the UK* to coincide with the Sex Pistols' "Anarchy in the UK" tour designed by Jamie Reid, Sophia Richmond and Vivienne Westward. Reid acted as general factotum to the group, organizing their live appearances. He was not greatly interested in the pop phenomenon as an expression of youthful rebelliousness. For him: "I saw punk as part of an art movement that's gone over the last hundred years, with roots in Russian agitprop, surrealism, dada and Situationism." He regarded his posters and record sleeves as designed "to articulate ideas, many of which were anti-establishment and quite theoretical and complicated." Reid often appropriated and subverted familiar images; the poster for the Pistols' second single, "God Save the Queen", was based on the official jubilee portrait taken of the Queen by Cecil Beaton which Reid had seen in the *Daily Express* newspaper. His designs for the Sex Pistols flaunted what he called "cheap hype". He had to revise his designs for *Never Mind the Bollocks Here's the Sex Pistols* continually because of changes in the album's title and contents. "It caused me enormous aggravation", says Reid. His repertoire of torn edges, cut-outs and ransom-note lettering was imitated by hundreds of punk bands. In 1987 he published *Up They Rise – The Incomplete Works of Jamie Reid*, co-designed by Malcolm Garrett.

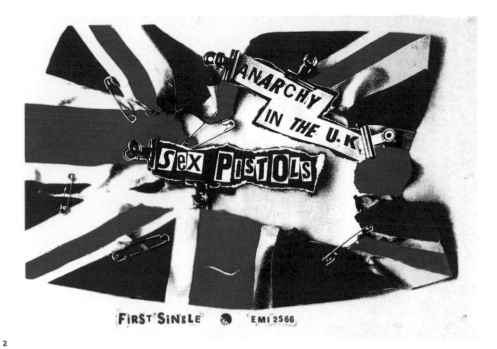

FIRST SINGLE EMI 2566

2

: NEW SINGLE ON VIRGIN RECORDS VS184 :

3

1 **God Save the Queen**, SEX PISTOLS, Virgin, 1977.
 Design: Jamie Reid. [opposite]
2 **Poster: Anarchy in the UK**, 1976.
 Design: Jamie Reid.
3 **Poster: Pretty Vacant**, 1977.
 Design: Jamie Reid.
4 **Never Mind the Bollocks, Here's The Sex Pistols**,
 THE SEX PISTOLS, Virgin, 1977.
 Design: Jamie Reid. Art direction: Malcolm McLaren.

4

1   **Music For Pleasure**, THE DAMNED, Stiff, 1977.
Design: Barney Bubbles. Illustration: Phil Smee.

2   **Autobahn**, KRAFTWERK, Vertigo, 1974.
Design: unknown.

Many commentators on popular culture have identified the stylistic profusion that followed the punk moment of 1977–8 as the first visual manifestations of postmodernity. Pictorial bricolage filled the vacuum left by the ideological hollowing out of the punk moment. Once again, the idealists proclaimed, the revolutionary potentialities of the rebel music of youth had been corralled within the marketing departments of Big Music. Although many self-identified "working class" pop-sociologists professed a serious commitment to punk's aims, they also provided the terminology to tame its effects. Subcultures expressed "the need to create and express autonomy and difference from parents" and were fast becoming research material for the expanding numbers of students studying social science subjects in universities. The moment's seminal text was *The Meaning Of Style* by Dick Hebdige (1979) which studied post-war sub cultures through the symbolic power of visual appearance. With the advent of such studies teen subcultures had the power to "deconstruct" their own appearance. Knowing how it was done was good for the generation of styles but, like any good

magic trick, tended to wreck the vicarious enjoyment of the moment.

The four most well-known designers of this period of British sleeve design are Barney Bubbles, Peter Saville, Neville Brody and Malcolm Garrett, although Saville and Brody, in particular, were to make a contribution to design long beyond the post-punk moment. Following punk's pillage of the Situationist lexicon, there was a reaching out for other graphic forms with revolutionary credentials. The work of Russian Constructivist artist/designers such as El Lissitzky, Rodchenko and Mayakovsky was widely influential, not only on their own account, but through the album sleeves of Kraftwerk, particularly *The Man Machine* of 1978 which included the credit "inspired by El Lissitzky" and featured a detail of one of his drawings on the back cover. Russian constructivist tropes – bold, simple forms (including cut-out photographic elements), a restricted range of primary colours, emphatic sans-serif typefaces and liberal use of diagonals underpinning the dynamism of the layout – are highly adaptable, as their persistence in mainstream Dutch graphic design confirms. Peter Saville, one of the most

important of the post-punk generation of British designers, acknowledges another Kraftwerk sleeve, *Autobahn* (1974) as a seminal influence on his own attitude to design. There was also a strong romantic rivivalist element amongst the diversity which, in album sleeve design, led to a fashion for allusive, moody, sometimes heroic atmospherics.

Although the results of some of these stylistic borrowings can now seem a little threadbare, the youthful co-options of this kind provided an initial armature for a considerable reinvention of typographical conventions in all manner of graphic formats – magazines and advertisements as well as design for music. In the work of the best, the results were far from a simple restatement of Suprematist stylistic conventions.

The pace for commissioning innovative album sleeve design was set by the new crop of record companies that thrived in the post-punk moment. London-based independent record company Stiff is the most celebrated of these. The company's art director, Chris Morton, marshalled the talents of a small group of notable designers which included Barney Bubbles, Hamish Orr, Eddie King and Neville Brody.

3

5

4

3 **Dazzle Ships**, ORCHESTRAL MANOEVRES IN THE DARK,
Virgin, 1983.
Design: Peter Saville Associates.
4 **James Brown**, CABARET VOLTAIRE, Some Bizarre, 1985.
Design: Neville Brody.
5 **A Different Kind of Tension**, THE BUZZCOCKS, United
Artists, 1979.
Design: Malcom Garrett. Photography: Jill Furmanovsky.

1 **Space Ritual**, HAWKWIND, United Artists, 1973.
Design: Barney Bubbles.

2 **In Search of Space**, HAWKWIND, United Artists, 1971.
Design: Barney Bubbles.

3 **Armed Forces**, ELVIS COSTELLO AND THE ATTRACTIONS,
Stiff, 1979.
Design: Barney Bubbles.

4 **Imperial Bedroom**, ELVIS COSTELLO AND THE
ATTRACTIONS, fBeat/Columbia, 1982.
Design: Barney Bubbles. Painting: Sal Forlenza.

5 **Do It Yourself**, IAN DURY & THE BLOCKHEADS, Stiff, 1979.
Design: Barney Bubbles.

Barney Bubbles (born Colin Fulcher in 1942) was an introverted and obsessive eccentric, shy of publicity to the extent that he is not credited on many of the album sleeves he designed. After studying at Twickenham School of Art in the early 1960s, he tried several design jobs including a spell working for Conran Design Group. Eventually he found more congenial work designing for the underground hippy organizations which at that time were springing up across London. Initially he worked for underground newspapers *Oz* and *Friendz*. By the late '60s he had become the designer of choice for the Notting Hill hippy community bands. Renowned for his voracious appetite for drugs – crumbling hashish on his steak and chips – Bubbles designed album sleeves for bands such as Hawkwind, Quintessence and Dr.Z. He also designed the sleeve for *Glastonbury Fayre*, a compilation of recordings of the first Glastonbury festival. His most famous sleeve design of this period was the extended visual essay in psychedelic imagery he produced for Hawkwind's *Space Ritual* (1973), a double live album with a foldout cover measuring 60 × 180cm (2 × 6 feet). His association with Hawkwind was particularly close, extending to devising their light shows and set designs, and he became almost a permanent part of their entourage.

Barney Bubbles was inclined to "sabbaticals", spending time working on farms or stacking groceries, and by the mid 1970s, the London hippy scene in decline, he had disappeared from view. In 1976 he was living in Ireland, where he might have continued to gather moss but for an accidental meeting with pub rock promoter Dave Robinson. In partnership with Jake Riviera, Dave Robinson was in the process of launching Stiff Records. Their first signing in September 1976 was the punk band the Damned. Stiff's art director, Chris Morton, who was assembling a team of designers, agreed to add Bubbles to their number. Other members of the team included Hamish Orr, Eddie King and a youthful Neville Brody.

In Stiff, Barney Bubbles found the perfect client to restart his career. His early Stiff covers for Elvis Costello, Ian Dury and the Blockheads, the Damned, and Generation X are characteristic of his late '70s output. Typically of post-punk new wave design, they are eclectic and exuberant, full of visual tricks and playful allusions to art history. Stiff's output of designs was prodigious, not just album and singles sleeves but also of point-of-sale promotions, picture discs and other promotional novelties, and provided Barney Bubbles with plenty of opportunities to experiment. When given the opportunity, as with Elvis Costello and the Attractions' *Armed Forces* (1979), he continued to demonstrate his preference for conceiving of sleeve design as a multiple-image visual essay, in counterdistinction to the tendency of many designers to relying on a single arresting image. In this Barney Bubbles was a pioneer, acknowledging an imperative that was to become increasingly important as the changeover from records to CDs gathered pace. A diagnosed schizophrenic, Barney Bubbles committed suicide in 1983.

5

3

4

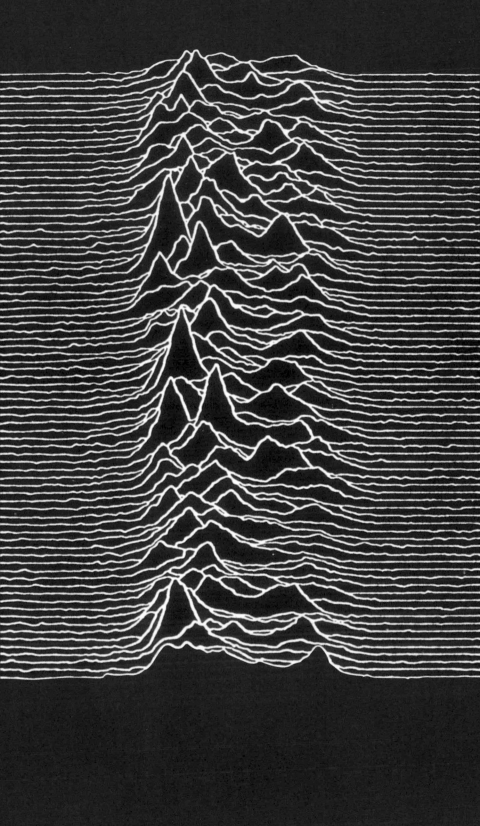

1980–89
From New Wave to Acid House

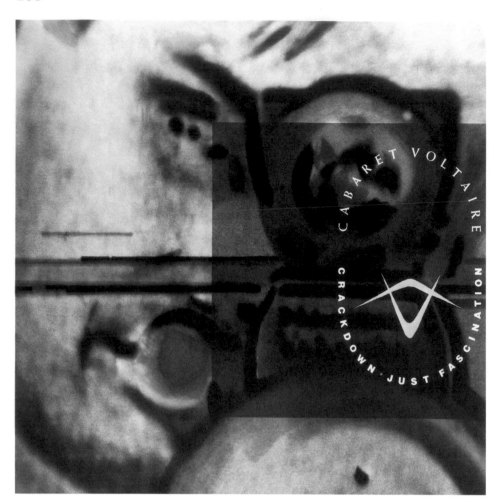

Unknown Pleasures.
JOY DIVISON, Factory, 1979.
Design: Peter Saville.
[previous pages]

Crackdown/Just Fascination.
CABARET VOLTAIRE, Some Bizarre, 1983.
Design: Neville Brody.

British design for music made a particularly strong showing during the 1980s. Although Barney Bubbles died in 1983, Peter Saville, Neville Brody, Malcolm Garrett, Rob O'Connor, and Vaughan Oliver all added their own highly original contributions to album sleeve design during the decade and gained international recognition for their innovative approaches. Neville Brody had soon largely abandoned albums for magazine design, although the way he loosened up the existing, rather stiff protocols of magazine design was incredibly influential in other graphic fields. Encouraged by the success of *i-D* magazine and *The Face*, youth-oriented magazines multiplied, celebrating the burgeoning street culture of a new generation and catering to its numerous musical tribes: technopop, ska, heavy metal, hip-hop, rap, thrash…Not for the first time the graphic subversions rising up out of this ferment found themselves readily adopted by the graphic design establishment. But this time it was no passing fad. The effect was more profound; design for music, effervescent, iconoclastic and quintessentially representative of the dismissal of stale design mores, rejoined the design mainstream for the first time in many decades. If anything is to be regretted in this process it is the possibility that, in the long view, the '80s will be seen to mark the beginning of the comprehensive re-professionalization of design for music. Anecdotal evidence does seem to suggest that throughout the '80s and into the 1990s album sleeve design has become the province of specialist design groups. And yet the odds must be against this being a permanent trend

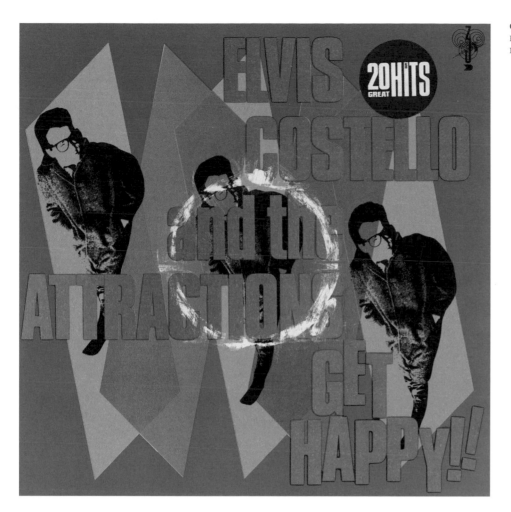

Get Happy!
ELVIS COSTELLO, fBeat, 1980.
Design: Barney Bubbles.

as long as popular music hangs on to being an untheorizable audio event. After all, music, like all art forms, has the habit of de-throning establishments at the moment of their greatest sense of self-assurance.

Early in the decade synthesizer-dominated electropop became the music of the new romantic movement, led by British bands Duran Duran and Culture Club, the latter fronted by Boy George. Malcolm Garrett, founder of design group Assorted Images, masterminded album design for both, and produced the apotheosis of the exuberant post-punk "anything goes" look. 12-inch versions of singles, often with extra tracks with special mixes, provided an increasingly important outlet for album sleeve designers. In 1983 New Order's "Blue Monday" becomes Britain's biggest selling 12-inch ever.

Album sleeve design found itself weathering two major shocks during the 1980s. The first in summer 1981 was the birth of MTV with its relentless three-minute cycle of music and visual overload. Although recording stars had made promotional films and videos in previous decades, MTV made them a vital marketing tool and, almost instantly, the production values and the degree of spectacle music videos were required to offer their audience increased exponentially. Slick, good-looking bands did well and *Rolling Stone* magazine was quick to comment that "MTV sells looks at least as much as sounds". By the mid-'80s, bands and record companies were diverting more and more of the marketing budget into music videos. Michael Jackson in particular took the music video to epic proportions. Inevitably there was a backwash

Thriller.
MICHAEL JACKSON,
Epic, 1982.
Photography: Dick Zimmerman.

Brothers in Arms.
DIRE STRAITS, Vertigo, 1985.
Design: Sutton Cooper and
Andrew Prewett.
Photography: Deborah Feingold.

which affected album sleeve design. As designer Mike Ross wryly put it at the time: "There aren't many sleeves that cost the sort of money that used to be spent on, say, those Led Zeppelin sleeves in the past. Those days are well and truly over, and if the money's available it's gambled on [the] video". Some album sleeve designers saw the writing on the wall and quickly made the transition to music video production. Some succeeded, many failed. Although stunning images were high on the list of requirements for promotional music videos, the form had more in common with television advertisements than album sleeve design.

The second shock that sleeve design had to contend with during the '80s was the arrival of the CD and its attendant jewelcase (adopted in America after the false start of the long box). Pioneered by Sony and first introduced in America by CBS in 1982, the CD was gradually to supersede the LP. The first big seller in CD format was Dire Straits' *Brothers In Arms* in 1985. Many traditionalists have decried the CD as signalling the death of album sleeve design. Events have shown otherwise, even though the plastic jewelcase into which the printed elements of CD packaging are inserted has many detractors. What the CD did herald was the increasingly rapid pace of the changeover from analogue to digital sound recording, which was to have incalculable consequences for popular music-making. It would make all the difference to the backgrounds from which future recording stars would emerge, and to what skills could be brought to music making. Playing traditional musical instruments – the archetypal guitar and drum rock band – came

Blue Monday.
NEW ORDER, Factory, 1983.
Design: Peter Saville.

Meat Is Murder.
THE SMITHS,
Rough Trade, 1985.
Concept: Morrissey.

under increasing competition from digital sound manipulation. Although everybody still had the same perfectly formed three-minute single somewhere in mind, time manipulation and the standing wave of a perfect groove meant a DJ positioned behind his decks was to become the natural successor to the keyboard player of the early 1980s' synthesizer-dominated electropop band Merging tracks together and making new sounds by "scratching" records would only be the very beginnings of ways in which dance club DJs would develop music. In time DJ superstars would subsume whole bands to themselves. This digital revolution, which has still not been fully worked through, had an equally fundamental affect on visual images and design. The consequences for design for music of computer image manipulation programmes such as Adobe Photoshop are discussed in various places throughout subsequent sections of this book.

Rave culture, one of the most notable features of the late '80s, expressed itself in design for music in a multiplicity of forms, but club flyers and acid house revisiting of psychedelic imagery are particularly notable. The increasingly dense visual fields of the club flyer, as it developed over the early years of the '90s, particularly epitomize the vast cultural shift in underground graphics which had occurred in the years since punk. Gone for the time being are the kitchen table sissors-and-paste aesthetics of "ransom-note" design. In the club flyer, most ephemeral of ephemera, we can clearly appreciate the full effects of the digital revolution on images and style.

Paid in Full.
ERIC B & RAKIM, Fourth &
Broadway, 1987.
Design: unknown.

Poster: Haçienda Club, 1983.
Design: Peter Saville.

British independent record companies which had blossomed in the post-punk new wave of the '80s received a profound setback at the end of the decade, when the distribution off-shoot of Rough Trade Records, which had been kept afloat for years by the success of other independent labels, such as Mute and 4AD records, found itself unable to meet its bills. It was eventually wound up owing £3.5 million to some 60 independent labels. Some of the larger labels managed to salvage the situation, but Rough Trade's demise signalled the close of an optimistic period when diversity was ably supported by small labels, which had added immensely to the range and quality of design for music created over the decade.

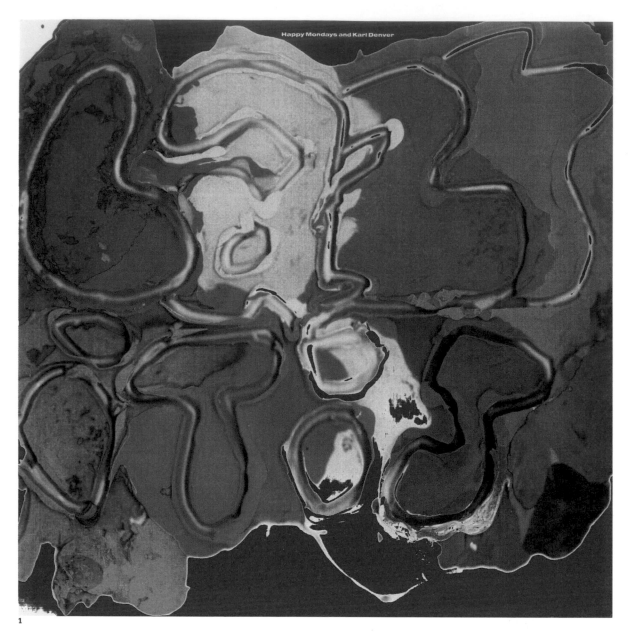

1

1 **Lazyitis**, HAPPY MONDAYS, Factory, 1990.
Design: Central Station Design.
2 **Pills'n'Thrills and Bellyaches**, HAPPY MONDAYS,
Factory,1989.
Design: Central Station Design.

2

5

3 **Poster: The Hacienda Club**, 1989.
Design: Peter Saville, Julian Morey.
4 **The Guitar and Other Machines**, THE DURUTTI COLUMN,
Factory, 1988.
Design: 8vo. Photography: Trevor Key.
5 **Power, Corruption and Lies**, NEW ORDER, Factory, 1983.
Design: Peter Saville. Painting: Henri Fantin-Latour.

3

4

During the '80s a lively, innovative music design scene developed in northern England with its epicentre in Manchester, where Factory Records and it's off-shoot, the Hacienda, were its most celebrated manifestations. The Hacienda grew to become the most legendary club of the late '80s. It came to symbolize the north of England's clubbing scene which had evolved out of the Northern Soul version of disco. Factory Records, led by the charismatic Tony Wilson, was an enlightened commissioner of design for album sleeves by talented local designers throughout the decade. The design course at Manchester Polytechnic also produced a number of key designers who would go on to make pivotal contributions to design for music during the '80s. The most notable were Peter Saville, Malcolm Garrett, David Crow and Ian Swift, all of whom made significant contributions to the post-punk ferment associated with the early years of the Manchester scene, sharing a commitment to visual innovation matched by a cool sense of formal control. For a while the inevitable drain of the best students in the direction of London was curtailed by the vitality of the music scene in and around Manchester. Although Peter Saville did move to London, he remained art director of Factory records and was highly instrumental in the success of the label and the Hacienda. Factory also numbered Martyn Atkins, Mark Farrow (later to become the designer of choice for the Pet Shop Boys), design partnerships 8vo and Central Station Design among its designers.

David Crow arrived in Manchester to study at the Polytechnic in 1980. He started the Polytechnic magazine *Fresh*. After leaving the Polytechnic he worked for Malcolm Garrett at Assorted Images before moving on to Island Records. Later he became a freelance designer. Ian Swift was at Manchester Polytechnic in 1983-86. He subsequently joined Neville Brody at *The Face* and followed him to *Arena* in 1988, where he became art director in 1990. He also designed the jazz magazine *Straight No Chaser* and was responsible for the look of Phonogram's dance label Talking Loud. He became increasingly involved with sub-cultures of the '90s, including developing a graffiti artists' support network.

Design group 8vo – Mark Holt, Hamish Muir and associate Michael Burke – was formed in 1984 on Holt's return from a freelance spell in San Francisco. Factory Communications commissioned designs for Durutti Column and the Hacienda. Their post-Saville austerity extended to regarding their work not as "design" but as "visual engineering", using only four typefaces – all sanserif – resulting in a clinical minimalism.

The style of late '80s Factory album design is generally associated with the design group Central Station Design. Two of the design group's three designers – Pat and Matt Carroll – were related to Happy Mondays band members Shaun and Paul Ryder. Their approach to design could not have been less like the cool, post-Saville look. Their most characteristic work are the Happy Mondays' sleeves *Wrote For Luck* (1988), *Bummed* (1989), and *Pills 'N' Thrills and Bellyaches* (1990). They do not have the virtue of visual consistency but an amiable home-made quality which well suits the musical approach of the Happy Mondays. Their designs were an important influence for younger designers interested in reviving a hand-drawn, kitchen table approach to design after the knife-edge cool practiced by many of the other Manchester designers during the '80s.

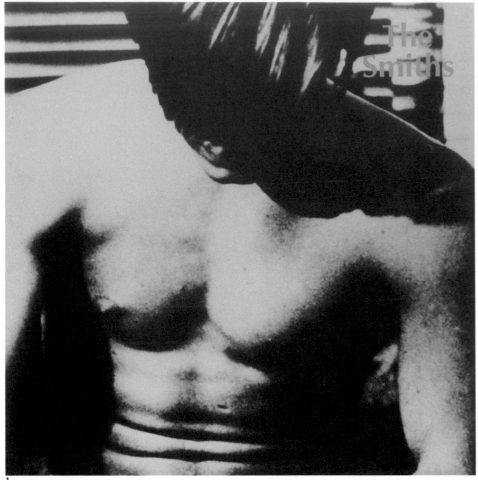

1

2

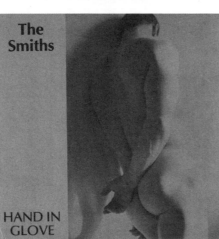

3

4

1   **The Smiths**, THE SMITHS, Rough Trade, 1984.
    Design: Morrissey.

2   **Heaven Knows I'm Miserable Now**, THE SMITHS,
    Rough Trade, 1984.
    Design: Morrissey. Layout: Caryn Gough at Ai.

3   **Hand in Glove**, THE SMITHS, Rough Trade, 1983.
    Design: The Smiths.

4   **What Difference Does It Make?**, THE SMITHS,
    Rough Trade, 1984.
    Design: Morrissey.

5   **Hatful of Hollow**, THE SMITHS, Rough Trade, 1984.
    Design: Morrissey [opposite].

Rough Trade was one of the most notable independent British record labels to emerge out of the punk foment, and one of their greatest acts during the mid '80s was The Smiths, fronted by Morrissey and guitarist Johnny Marr. As memorable as their music are the Smiths' album and single sleeves, which were designed by Morrissey as a deliberate and carefully crafted extension of the band's persona.

Steven Patrick Morrissey was born 1958 in Manchester. The Smiths, the band that launched his career, was born out of the city's vibrant post-punk scene. The band was contracted to Rough Trade, and their first single "Hand In Glove" was released in 1983. From the start, Geoff Travis, Rough Trade owner, gave Morrissey complete freedom over the design of the Smiths' sleeves. In Travis's words: "The sleeves were integral to the Smiths and Morrissey was the best man to create them. We never had any better suggestions to make". Rough Trade's art co-ordinator Jo Slee assisted Morrissey in the realization of his ideas.

The cover photograph on "Hand in Glove" is of an anonymous male model photographed by Jim French that Morrissey found in a book called *The Nude Male* by Margaret Walters. It overtly sets the tone for one of the principle themes Morrissey pursued over the Smiths' career. For the cover of their second single, *This Charming Man*, released in the autumn of 1983, he used a Narcissus-like image of a beautiful young man staring at his reflection in a mirror – a still of Jean Marais taken from the 1949 Cocteau film *Orphée*, and for their third single *What Difference Does it Make?* (1984) a photograph of Terence Stamp from the 1965 film *The Collector*. Several things are distinctive about, and common to, these sleeves. The sources of Morrissey's photographs are diverse, although often they are a still taken from a film or television programme. None are drawn from strictly contemporary sources. Although there is a sense in which the men can be seen to be a part of his

personal gallery of heroes (Elvis Presley, James Dean, George Best and Alain Delon all appear on Smiths' sleeves), they are beautiful rather than heroic. They project sexual ambiguity, an attribute which is redoubled when the sleeves are seen in series. His subtle art director's touch loads them with a homoerotic charge, intensified still further by his habit of aestheticizing his images by substituting a colour tint for the black and white of the original photograph. For the band's first album *The Smiths* (1984) Morrissey chose a close-up photograph of Joe Dallesandro from Andy Warhol's film *Flesh* which, by reputation as well as image, further emphasizes the homoerotic charge implicit in his selection process.

A second theme which emerges from Morrissey's choice of imagery has a more working class, specifically Northern edge. He used two different portraits of Salford author Shelagh Delaney on single sleeves, as well as images from two films based on her screenplays: *A Taste Of Honey* (1961) and *Charlie Bubbles* (1968). He twice used photographs of football pools winner Viv Nicholson from her book, *Spend, Spend, Spend*. For *Heaven Knows I'm Miserable Now* (1984) she is posed against a forlorn backdrop of rundown terraced houses, resplendent in her weird back-combed hairdo. He also used a portrait shot of actress Pat Phoenix from the Northern soap *Coronation Street*. All are Northern in a way which is both elegiac and mythic. Other images in Morrissey's repertoire are less specifically located, such as the group of young men on the album sleeve of *The World Won't Listen* (1987), taken from Jurgen Vollmer's book *Rock 'n' Roll Times*, or the GI taken from Emile de Antonio's film *In The Year Of The Pig* for *Meat Is Murder* (1985).

Viewed as a corpus, Morrissey's album sleeves for the Smiths are subtly allusive, poetic and convey a strange and dignified beauty. The band was disbanded in 1987.

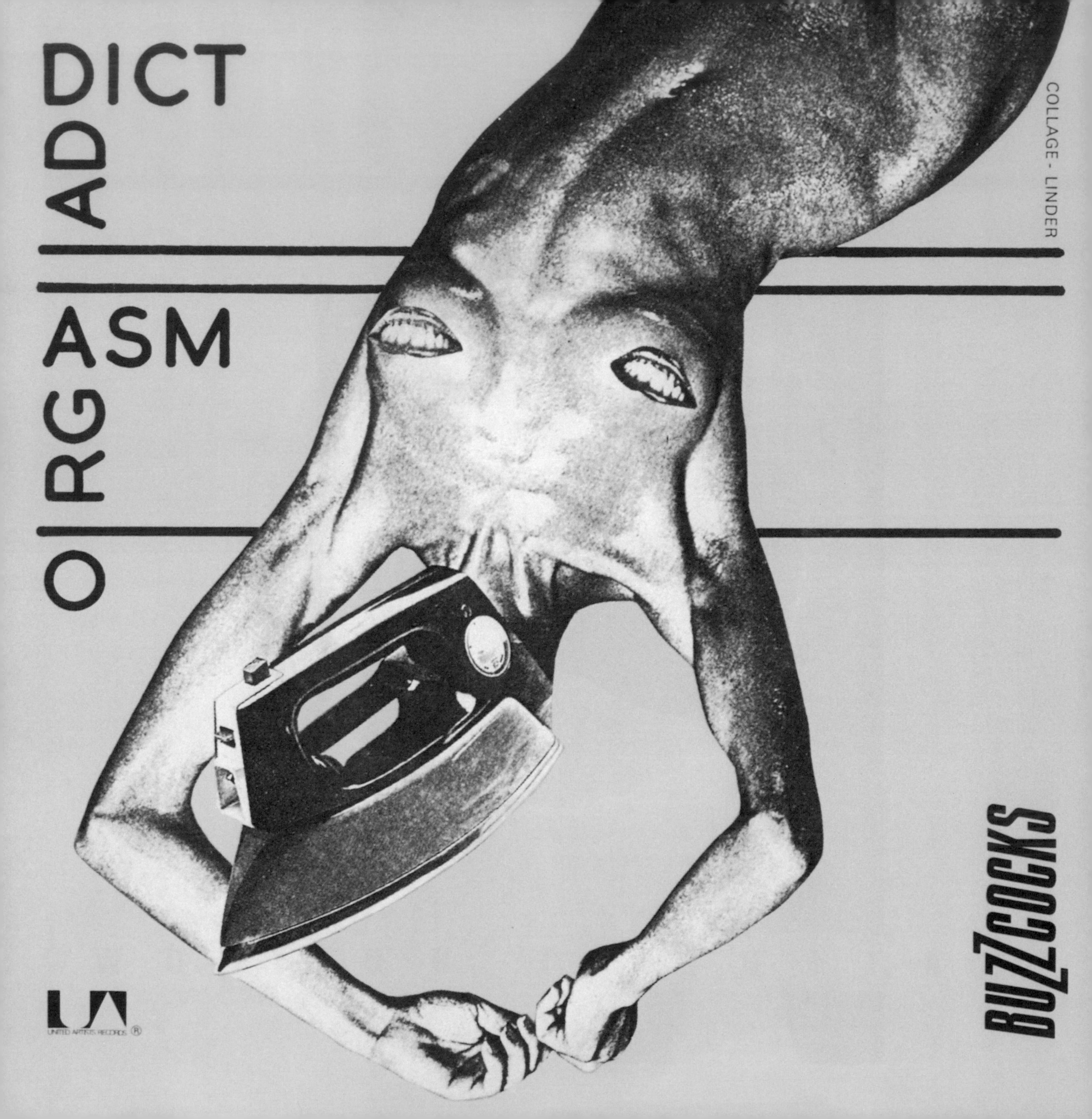
ORGASM
ADDICT
COLLAGE - LINDER
BUZZCOCKS
UNITED ARTISTS RECORDS ®

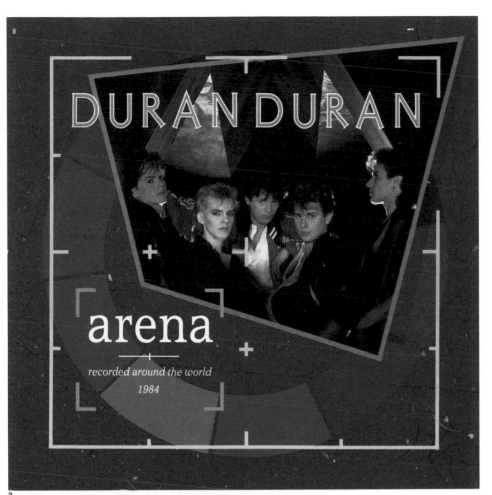

2

4

5

1 **Orgasm Addict**, THE BUZZCOCKS, United Artists,
1977. [upper cntre]
Design: Malcolm Garrett. Illustration: Linder Sterling.
2 **Arena**, DURAN DURAN, EMI, 1984.
Design: Assorted Images. Photography: Mike Owen.
3 **Family Affair**, BEF FEATURING LALAH HATHAWAY,
Ten, 1991.
Design: Malcolm Garrett for Assorted Images.
Photography: Kevin Westenberg.
4 **Colour by Numbers**, CULTURE CLUB, Virgin, 1983.
Design: Assorted Images. Photography: Jamie Morgan.
5 **The Correct Use Of Soap**, MAGAZINE, Virgin, 1980.
Design: Malcolm Garrett.

3

Malcolm Garrett was born in 1956 in Northwich, England. He studied Typography and Psychology at Reading University and then moved to the Graphic Design course at Manchester Polytechnic where he was reunited with his school friend Peter Saville. Whilst a student there he met Richard Boon, manager of a newly-formed punk group called the Buzzcocks. Boon's version of his design brief to Garrett was: "Keep the group OFF the record sleeves as much as possible... limit single design to abstraction in two colours wherever we could get away with it: establish that pattern, then disrupt it; lotsa badges (throw 'em off the stage after polite encore – build fan-base cargo cult with cheap trinkets, etc); pun fun; the appropriation of corporate ID strategies – my approach from the Theory of the Spectacle; his from trained logotypical background – and shit". The sleeve produced from this brief is one of the seminal single sleeves of punk iconography: *Orgasm Addict* (1977), which features a monotone version of a Linder Sterling montage of a naked woman with an iron for a head. (Her surreal montages were subsequently featured on Morrissey's *Your Arsenal* and Magazine's *Real Life*.)

Garrett's career went from strength to strength on the back of the post-punk, new wave acts coming to the fore in the late '70s and early '80s. He formed the London-based design company Assorted Images in 1978 (irritatingly spelt "Assorted iMaGes" at the time). Garrett's manifesto for the company was "it will use any

style; avoids fashion, ignores trends; dismisses fads; deplores dogma; remains oblivious to politics; adores American cars; eats at McDonalds; and sleeps irregularly". As a consequence of Assorted Images' work for record companies, Garrett was asked to art direct a new magazine *New Sounds New Styles* launched in 1981. It was a short-lived attempt to offer a knowing combination of style and music which failed to achieve the streetwise credibility of *i-D* and *The Face*. Garrett met Kasper De Graaf while working on the project and he subsequently joined Assorted Images in 1983. Other designers who spent spells working for the company included Keith Breeden, Jon Wozencroft and fellow Manchester Polytechnic student David Crow who worked for Assorted Images before moving on to Island Records.

Much of Garrett's earliest work is marked by his re-interpretation of 1920s Russian Constructivist design principles pioneered by artist/designers such as El Lissitzky with their emphasis on the juxtaposition of typographical elements, simple photographic cut-outs and dynamic geometrical elements such as circles and triangles. Besides the Buzzcocks, clients included Devo, Simple Minds, Duran Duran and Boy George. The relationship with Boy George and Duran Duran was particularly important as Assorted Images produced a succession of album and single sleeves for both during the period of their considerable success. Garrett's design for Magazine's *The Correct Use Of Soap* (1980) is a typical example of

the virtues of his graphic coherence, although towards the middle of the decade Assorted Images' style became increasingly baroque and over-burdened with graphic devices of every kind.

Garrett is an acknowledged enthusiast of the use of computers in design. He began to work with Apple, Scitex and Macintosh in the early '80s. In time, Assorted Images' designs began to display a less formalistic sense of abstraction with a strong illusionistic element realised through 3-D imaging computer technology. The series of sleeves for BEF are typical of this period of the company's output. In 1994 Garrett left Assorted Images to become Creative Director at AMX, one of the first UK design companies to devote itself exclusively to interactive digital TV.

Neville Brody was born in 1957 in Southgate, North London. A successful and influential graphic and typography designer with an immense range and long career at the forefront of the graphic design profession, only a comparatively brief episode in his career was centrally devoted to album sleeve design. Nonetheless, his sense of graphic invention was pivotal in defining the style of graphics for music in the '80s and early '90s.

Brody was a design student at Hornsey College in 1975 and the London College of Printing from 1977–80. On leaving college he went to work for design group Rocking Russian which immersed him in the independent music scene. Rocking Russian was run by punk survivor Al McDowell. In 1980 McDowell, in conjunction with ex-art director of *Vogue*, Terry Jones, launched *i-D* magazine which would become the great competitor to *The Face*, Brody's first magazine as art director.

Brody soon moved on from Rocking Russian and for a while worked at Stiff Records where one of his earliest sleeves was for Desmond Dekker's *Black and Dekker* (1980). He then moved again, always with a keen sense for the radical in design and music, to become art director for Fetish Records. At Fetish he was able to experiment with a graphic style which amalgamated the rough-hewn look of simple printmaking techniques with his inimitable sense of typographical architecture. Notable for his time at the label were his close working relationships with music scene radicals such as Genesis P-Orridge and 23 Skidoo. Brody designed Genesis P-Orridge's *Throbbing Gristle* album of 1982, and for 23 Skidoo, who had a recording studio at Genesis P-Orridge's Death Factory, sleeves for *The Gospel Comes to New Guinea* (1981) and *Seven Songs* (1982). Independently, he had since 1979 been the designer for Cabaret Voltaire, named after the Dada cabaret launched in 1916 in Zurich by Hugo Ball. For them he undertook single and album sleeve designs including *Red Mecca* (1981), *The Crackdown* (1983), and *The Covenant, The Sword and the Arm of the Lord* (1985).

In 1981 Brody began work for Nick Logan's *The Face*. His typographic experimentation and bold, radical page layouts changed the look of magazine design, which had now become his chief concern. In 1986 he overhauled the design of the *New Socialist* magazine before moving on to help the cooperative producing *City Limits*, the events guide to London. Subsequently he was the art director for *Arena* magazine from 1987 to 1990. Although designing for album sleeves had largely dropped away by the mid '80s, he continued to design for 23 Skidoo as they moved on from Illuminated Records to Bleeding Chin Records. Brody's typography-dominated sleeve for their compilation *Just Like Everybody* (1987) captures the coming iconography of post-industrial, typographical ethnofunk which was about to emerge from club culture.

Jon Wozencroft produced a monograph called *The Graphic Language of Neville Brody* in 1988, which was accompanied by a retrospective exhibition of his work of the same name at London's Victoria & Albert Museum, cementing his reputation. Brody still continues to experiment with new means and to push the limits of typographical design. With Jon Wozencroft he launched *Fuse*, a digital periodical published by FontShop International, to showcase experimental typefaces, and he continues to design for an international clientele.

1

2

1 **Five Albums**, THROBBING GRISTLE, Fetish, 1982.
Design: Neville Brody, from original material by Lawrence Dupre,
Peter Christopherson, Genesis P-Orridge, and Throbbing Gristle.

2 **Black and Dekker**, DESMOND DEKKER, Stiff, 1980.
Design: Neville Brody.

3 **8 Eyed Spy**, 8 EYED SPY, Fetish, 1981.
Design and illustration: Neville Brody.

3

4

4 **Baby U Left Me**, MARILYN, Phonogram, 1985.
   Design: Neville Brody.
5 **Just Like Everybody**, 23 SKIDOO, BC, 1987.
   Design: Neville Brody.

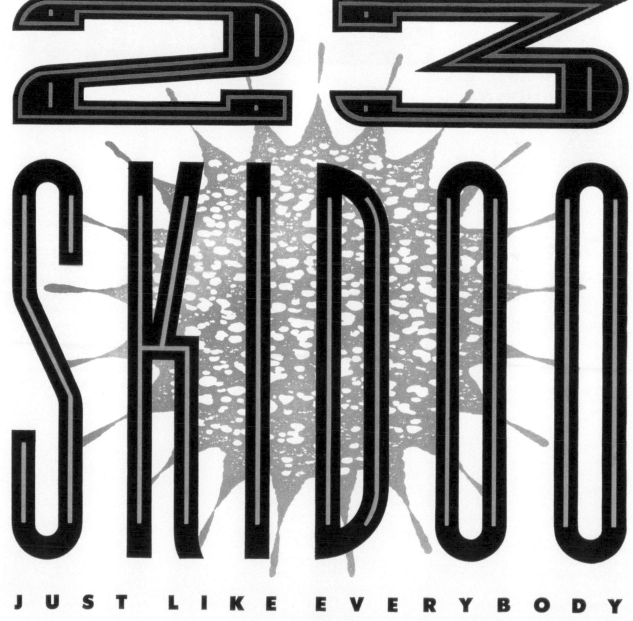

1

3

4

2

Two larger-than-life stars, Madonna (born Madonna Ciccone in 1958) and Boy George (born George O'Dowd in 1961) burst onto the music scene in the '80s, becoming icons of identity politics and giving voice to themes about sexuality, gender and identity which previously had largely only been debated in the serious press and academia. Because they approached identity politics in very different ways – being very different subversive embodiments of the theme – they offered the '80s an extremely effective popular articulation of its complexities. Through their images and stage personas they projected both the full-on crisis which masculinity was undergoing at the hands of feminism, and the schisms which would appear in feminism itself as a consequence of its essentialism, and the demonization of the male principle, which would, in turn, lead to "queer theory."

Boy George's image during his Culture Club period was a clever popularization of this loss of male essentialism then being theorized in gender studies. He first came to public notice in Britain in 1982 with the single *Do You Really Want to Hurt Me*, as celebrated for his appearance as for the band's soft melodic soul. In some senses his image was a restatement of the androgyny of David Bowie's Ziggy Stardust period, but the nuances of Boy George's stance were neither so unearthly or as intimidating as Bowie's. Furthermore there was less equivocation about the gay subtext. The design of Culture Club's sleeves was managed by Malcolm Garrett of Assorted Images in the busy

graphic style of the period, but it was the photographs of Boy George himself (usually by David Levine), always a dominant feature amongst the melange of graphic devices and typography, which made the sleeves outstanding popular representations of what the tabloid press referred to as "cross-dressing" and "gender-bending". His amiable representations of androgyny were a reflection of the dressing up widely enjoyed as part of the '80s developing club culture. There was also more than a nod to multiculturalism in the way he put his costumes together – geisha make-up, kimonos, kaftans, Peruvian hats and dreadlock styled hair with coloured paper knotted into the plaits – which was also reflected in his choice of band name. As he himself explained: "The emphasis (of Culture Club) is that everyone is part and parcel of the same race: The Human Race, whatever creed or race as it's usually defined!".

His ability to present a perfectly androgynous image when photographed and to place the glamour of transvestitism in the context of the polymorphous nature of the human race was the perfect complement to Madonna's succession of post-feminist images. The meaning of these constructed images have caused more academic theory than practically any other representation produced in the late 20th century. Camille Paglia's ringing endorsement of her project is one tiny instance of the furore she has caused: "Madonna has a far profounder vision of sex than do the feminists. She sees both the animality and the artifice . . . Feminism says 'no more masks,'

Madonna says we are nothing but masks. . ." What has received slightly less attention is the skill with which Madonna has managed the practical issues of self-image at the core of her transformation from New York ingenue, to Hollywood temptress, to post-feminist icon of female empowerment. Although it was her stage performances that caused the most headlines, her album sleeves have demonstrated her chameleon-like ability to shift image from stereotype to stereotype with consummate skill, and the sheer glamour of the images has effectively veiled the heartlessness of the mask.

1 **Like A Virgin**, MADONNA, Sire, 1984.
Design: Jeri McManus. Art Direction: Jeffrey Kent Ayeroff, Paul Greif, Jeri McManus. Photography: Steven Meisel.

2 **Rescue Me**, MADONNA, Sire, 1991.
Design: unknown. Photography: Jean Baptiste Mondino

3 **Victims**, CULTURE CLUB, Virgin, 1983.
Design: Assorted Images. Photography: David Levine.

4 **It's a Miracle**, CULTURE CLUB, Virgin, 1984.
Design: Assorted Images. Photography: David Levine.

5 **Madonna**, MADONNA, Sire, 1983.
Design: Carin Goldberg. [opposite]

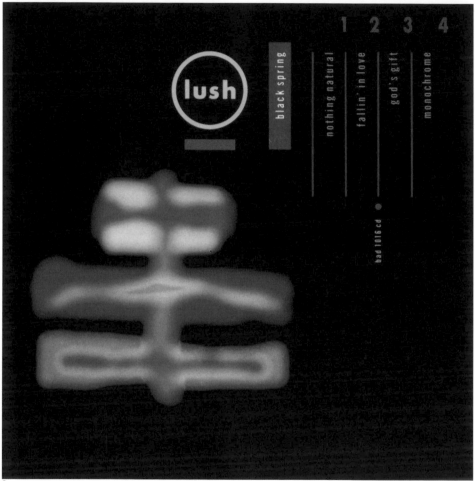

1 **Lullabies**, COCTEAU TWINS, 4AD, 1982.
Design: V23.

2 **Bossanova**, THE PIXIES, 4AD, 1990.
Design: V23. Photography: Simon Larbalestier.

3 **Black Spring**, LUSH, 4AD, 1991.
Design: V23. Photography: Jim Friedman.

4 **Pod**, THE BREEDERS, 4AD, 1990.
Design: V23. Photography: Kevin Westenberg

5 **Surfer Rosa**, THE PIXIES, 4AD, 1988. [opposite]
Design: V23. Photography: Simon Larbalestier.

Vaughan Oliver was born in 1957 in England. Although he has an exceptional range as a designer, he is closely identified with the look of 4AD, one of the most distinctive and influential independent British record companies of the '80s and early '90s. He is also associated with a resurgence in pictorial romanticism in design during the '80s, although other designers, particularly Russell Mills and David Coppenhall, are more clearly located within this stylistic territory. The character of this '80s pictorial romanticism is dark, mystical and somewhat doomed (and not to be confused with pop's lightweight New Romantics wave). Oliver's album sleeves for the Cocteau Twins' *Garlands* (1982), *Head Over Heels* (1983), *Treasure* (1984), and *Victorialand* (1986) are characteristic of his aesthetic approach at the time. They feature enigmatic out-of-focus photography with fitful, atmospheric lighting, rich colours and surfaces, all of which came to be characteristic of this new romanticist style. This strand of '80s design is sometimes seen as paralleling the contemporaneous revival of heroic figuration in painting, which sought an escape from the dry conceptualist impasse which had prevailed in art for much of the '70s. The phenomenon is best exemplified by the "New Spirit In Painting" exhibition held at the Royal Academy, London, in 1981 in which Italian and German Neo-expressionist painters like Sandro Chia, Francesco Clemente, Georg Baselitz, and Markus Lüpertz made a considerable stir.

Oliver studied design at Newcastle Polytechnic (now the University of Northumbria) from 1976–79. He subsequently moved to London where he worked for design company Benchmark. Whilst there he began to work on freelance projects for independent record company 4AD. The company had been founded in 1980 by Ivo Watts-Russell as a spin-off from the Beggars Banquet label. Watts-Russell's talent spotting (and business acumen) meant the label quickly gained a devoted following through signings such as Bauhaus, the Cocteau Twins, Dead Can Dance and Dif Juz. Meanwhile Oliver, still in need of a day job, joined the Michael Peters Group in 1981. The success of 4AD finally allowed him to leave the Michael Peters Group in 1983. He formed the design partnership 23 Envelope with photographer Nigel Grierson located in the basement of 4AD's offices in Alma Road, London. 23 Envelope's sleeve designs, as well as the labels, posters, postcards, and promotional material they also produced, quickly became an integral part of the 4AD experience, helping define the company's visual identity. Their designs for Modern English, Yazoo and This Mortal Coil became collectables in their own right, both for music lovers and graphic designers. Oliver is an accomplished art director in addition to being a designer. He has constantly extended his range by commissioning many talented photographers and illustrators. His technical command of the whole graphic process, from conceiving pictures to the final layout, is also exceptional.

By 1988 Grierson had moved on from 23 Envelope (latterly working for Tomboy Films as a director for corporate customers). Oliver established a new design partnership called v23 with calligraphic and typographical specialist Christopher Bigg. V23 had a looser relationship with 4AD than 23 Envelope, although it continued to operate from the same building. Some of v23's most accomplished designs continued to grace the album sleeves of 4AD recording artists such as The Pixies, Lush, Ultra Vivid Scene, the Breeders and His Name Is Alive. Particularly memorable of Oliver's designs of this period are sleeves for Boston band the Pixies, notably *Surfer Rosa* (1988) – somewhat reminiscent of the elaborate photographic tableaux of Joel-Peter Witkin – and *Bossanova* (1990), both produced in collaboration with photographer Simon Larbalestier. As the popularity of v23 grew, so did the amount of work the company undertook for clients other than 4AD. Book design, including Shinro Ohtake's *Tokyo Salamander: American Dream Diary 1989* and collected volumes of Oliver's own work, became increasingly important in their output, while Oliver collaborated with Roger Dean on volume 5 of *The Album Cover Album*.

Pixies

Demtro las piñones y las holas 'riqueña. Oh my golly! Oh my golly! Caminamos bagala luna caribe. Oh my golly! Oh my golly!
Besando, chichando con Surfer Rosa. Oh my golly! Oh my golly! Entonces se fue en fus madera. Oh my golly! Oh my golly!
Rosa, oh oh ohh Rosa! Rosa, oh oh ohh Rosa! Yo soy playero pero no hay playa. Oh my golly! Oh my golly!
Bien perdida la Surfer Rosa. Oh my golly! Oh my golly! La vida total es un porkeria. Oh my golly! Oh my golly!
Me hecho menos más que vida. Oh my golly! Oh my golly! Rosa, oh oh ohh Rosa! Huh! Huh! Rosa, oh oh ohh Rosa! Huh! Huh!

TIM BERNE

SANCTIFIED DREAMS

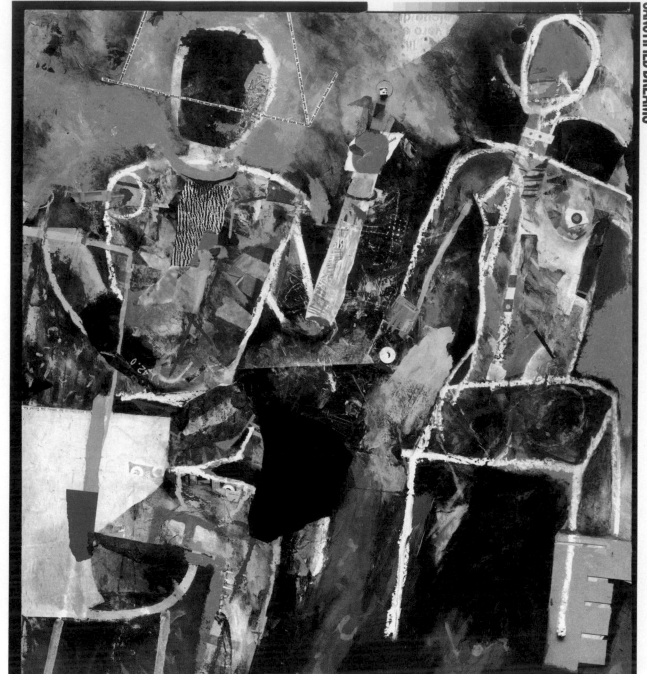

1

2

4

5

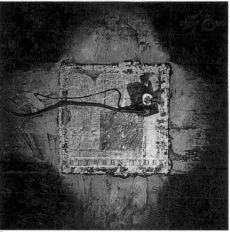

6

3

Russell Mills was born in 1952 in Ripen, England. His work as an illustrator/artist during the '80s, both for Brian Eno's Land Records, and as a freelancer, is distinctive of the pictorial romanticism in British album sleeve design which was the contrary tendency to the cool, hard-edged post-punk look of Peter Saville, Neville Brody, and Malcolm Garrett. Stylistically speaking, Mills's work has a considerable affinity with Vaughan Oliver's design output of the period. Not only did they share a stylistic outlook, they also collaborated on a variety of design projects for 4AD records and other clients. Mills also enjoyed a close working relationship with designer David Coppenhall. For a while at the end of the '80s their collaborations went under the *nom de plume* of mc2. Good examples of their joint work are David Sylvian's 5-disc retrospective *Weatherbox* (1989) and Youssou N'Dour's *Set* (1990), both for Virgin.

Mills's father was an officer in the Royal Air Force and his family moved frequently during his childhood. Long periods of his teens were spent in England, Germany and Holland, often stationed close to USAF bases. He studied at Canterbury College of Art and Maidstone College of Art between 1971 and 1974. He subsequently completed an MA in illustration at The Royal College of Art, London, in 1977. Since then he has pursued "not a 'job' but a vocation, something that is fundamental to my life". Around the mid '70s he met Brian Eno, and through their friendship he eventually became art director for Land Records, the record subsidiary of Brian Eno's publishing

and management company Opal Ltd. He was responsible for album sleeve designs for Harold Budd, Roger Eno, Michael Brook, Daniel Lanois, Djivan Gasparyan, Hugo Largo and Jon Hassell. (Land Records was closed down and the back catalogue sold off in 1991.)

Mills's main role in his collaborations was the creation of illustrative motifs. These lean heavily on a romantic fine art aesthetic, combining elements of painting, collage, montage and assemblage. His output is representative of an lush, atmospheric, old masterly vein of image-making sometimes affectionately known as "distort & distress". In Mill's case the effect is often redolent of unidentified, caballistic artefacts rescued from some mouldering country house, and suggesting a latter-day English mysticism. He often used unconventional grounds and applied unconventional materials in pursuit of a distressed and weathered appearance and a synthetic sense of age, also much beloved by certain sections of the antiques trade.

During the '90s Mills continued to be active in sleeve design, notably producing a number of sleeves for Nine Inch Nails, including *The Downward Spiral* (1994), although increasingly his energy has been devoted to his own career as a recording artist under the *nom de plume* Undark, as well as to multimedia installations.

Another illustrator/artist with a "distort & distress" attitude to album sleeve design during this period was Steve Byram, although in a more recognizably expressionistic and figurative style

than Mills. His career in design for music included a spell working as an art director for CBS during the late '80s where he co-ordinated album sleeves in many different styles, including the Beastie Boy's *Licensed To Ill* (1986). But when able to do so, he designed sleeves in a fragmented "expressionistic" fine art style, notably the Slammin' Watusis' *Kings Of Noise* (1979) and Tim Berne's *Sanctified Dreams* (1987). In 1990 he joined jazz record company JMT based in Munich, and more recently launched the Screwgun label with Tim Berne.

1   **A Broken Frame**, DEPECHE MODE, Mute, 1982.
    Design: Martyn Atkins for Town and Country Planning.
    Photography: Brian Griffin.
2   **Closer**, JOY DIVISION, Factory, 1980.
    Design: Martyn Atkins, Peter Saville. Photography: Bernard
    Pierre Wolff.
3   **Look Sharp!**, JOE JACKSON, A&M. 1979.
    Design and photography: Brian Griffin. Art direction:
    Michael Ross.

·CLOSER·

2

3

4

5

Martyn Atkins was born in 1958 in Huddersfield, England. He studied graphic design in art colleges in Halifax and Huddersfield. Subsequently he went to Manchester to work for Factory Records' creative director Peter Saville. His designs for Factory included album sleeves for A Certain Ratio and Section 25, although perhaps his most memorable project there was his collaboration with Saville on Joy Division's *Closer* sleeve (1980). Whilst Saville seems to have determined the major components of the sleeve's design, the photograph of Italian funeral statuary by French photographer Bernard Pierre Wolff, with its deep chiaroscuro and sense of figures frozen in anticipation, appears to have been influential in setting the tone for Atkins's most characteristic design work of the early 1980s, undertaken in partnership with photographer Brian Griffin.

In 1980 Atkins moved to London and launched his own company Town and Country Planning. His collaboration with Griffin resulted in a succession of images for album sleeves dominated by moody, elegiac atmospherics which capture the pictorial romanticism of the period. Prior to their work together, Griffin had produced a memorable black-and-white photograph of Joe Jackson's pointed white shoes caught in a shaft of light for the cover of *Look Sharp!* (1979). Although the subject matter is not comparable with the funereal statues of Wolff's photograph, the photograph shares the same moody sense of atmosphere captured through Griffin's use of strong light and deep shadow. Griffin and Atkins sought to replicate this quality in the *mise-en-scène* they devised for the cover of Echo and the Bunnymen's first album *Crocodiles* (1980). The album, which put the band in the forefront of the neo-psychedelic movement then sweeping Northern England, featured a group portrait of the band shot at night in woodland, the trees fitfully illuminated by garish artificial light, a kind of Technicolor *Blair Witch Project*. It was the first of a series of highly individual album sleeves they were to produce for the band picturing them in elemental settings with a strong sense of atmosphere. *Crocodiles* was followed by a twilight beach scene for *Heaven Up Here* (1981) shot on Porthcawl Beach in Wales. For their third album *Porcupine* (1983) the band was photographed at the ice-bound Gullfoss waterfall north of Reykjavik in Iceland. Equally bizarre was the shot Griffin took for *Ocean Rain* (1984), with the band photographed in a boat in a water-filled cave in St. Neot in Cornwall.

Atkins and Griffin also collaborated on Depeche Mode's *A Broken Frame* (1982). Unconfined by the need to portray the band on the front cover photograph, Griffin and Atkins produced the most enigmatic image of their collaboration: a reaper in a field of corn against a lowering sky, reminiscent both of Caspar David Friedrich and Soviet socialist realism. They attempted a variation on the same theme for the band's next album *Construction Time Again* (1983), but it fell more obviously into pastiche than *Frame*.

Atkins eventually opted to move to Los Angeles and devote his career to film and video direction, with Stylorouge taking over the management of the rump of Town and Country Planning in 1990.

1   **She's So Unusual**, CYNDI LAUPER, Epic/CBS, 1983.
    Design: Janet Perr. Photography: Annie Liebovitz.
2   **Come As You Are**, PETER WOLF, EMI, 1987.
    Design: Janet Perr. Photography: Annie Liebovitz.

Annie Leibovitz was born in 1949 in Westport, Connecticut. Of all the great photographers who have contributed to the look of rock music celebrity, she is perhaps the one to have defined its glamour with most assurance. The range of her photography is vast, touching on nearly every aspect of American popular culture. During her early years working as a freelance, mainly for *Rolling Stone* magazine, she developed a close affinity for rock music and musicians. When she first started to sell her photographs she was still a student of fine arts at the San Francisco Art Institute. She graduated in 1971, continuing her studies with photographer Ralph Gibson. She became *Rolling Stone*'s chief photographer in 1973. In 1975 she was the official photographer for the 1975 Rolling Stones American tour. She photographed the band for the cover of their 1986 album *Dirty Work*, and Mick Jagger for his 1993 solo project *Wandering Spirit*. As far as creating images for album sleeves is concerned, her most witty and inventive period was the 1980s. One of her most characterful is of Bruce Springsteen's backside set against the red and white stripes of the American flag for *Born in the U.S.A.* (1984). This was the first of a series of photographs she has taken of him for album sleeves including *Human Touch* (1992), *Greatest Hits* (1995), and *Tracks* (1998). However, perhaps her most famous photograph of a rock personality is her cover for *Rolling Stone* of a naked John Lennon embracing Yoko Ono, taken in 1980 not long before Lennon was murdered.

Leibovitz moved to work for *Vanity Fair* in 1983. Her long affiliation with *Vanity Fair*, and *Vogue*, has established her as an astute observer of American life. She has become the portrait photographer of the great and the good, often presenting them with illuminating freshness, although with the knack of not undermining their dignity. A recorder of changing times, she is the photographer of choice for the eminent of American society, and her output includes magazine, fashion, and advertising photography. Her work ranges from being official portrait photographer for the World Cup Games in Mexico in 1985 and creator of the official portfolio for the 26th Olympic Games in Atlanta, to prize-winning advertising campaigns for American Express and The Gap, and the 2000 Pirelli calendar. She said of her approach to producing the Pirelli calendar that "there is a lot of pressure not to let women down and find some way to look at women in a way that has integrity to it and this was one way to do it". This theme runs through her 1999 photographic book collaboration with Susan Sontag *Women*. Over the years she has produced album sleeve portraits of many of America's great women solo artists: Dolly Parton for *Halos & Horns* (2002), Barbra Streisand for *Timeless: Live in Concert* (2000), Judy Collins for *Judy Sings Dylan... Just Like A Woman* (1997), Patti Smith for *Gone Again* (1996), Laurie Anderson for *In Our Sleep* (1995), Cyndi Lauper for *True Colors* (1990), and Ella Fitzgerald for *Ella: Things Ain't What They Used To Be (& You Better Believe It)* (1989).

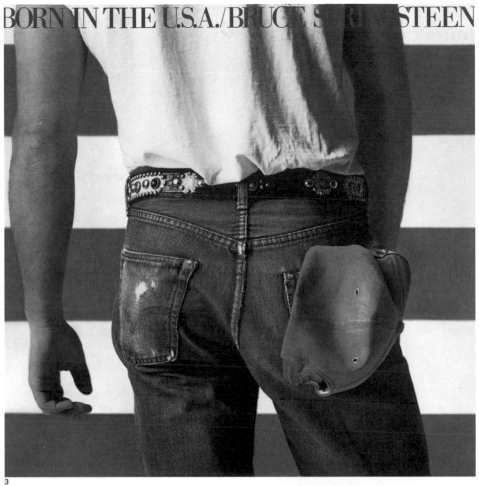

3

5

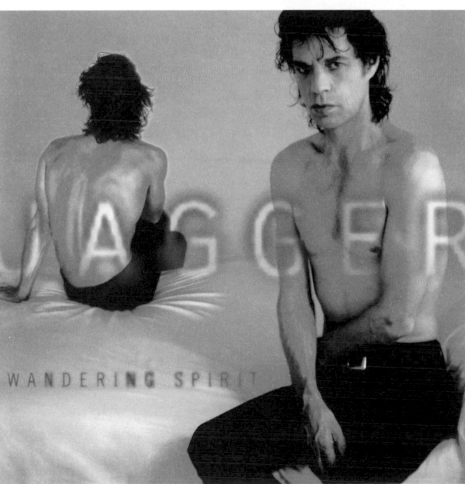

4

3 **Born in the USA**, BRUCE SPRINGSTEEN, Columbia, 1984.
Photography: Annie Leibovitz. Design and art direction:
Andrea Klein.

4 **Wandering Spirit**, MICK JAGGER, Atlantic, 1993.
Photography: Annie Leibovitz. Design: Richard Bates. Art
direction: Melanie Nissen.

5 **Gone Again**, PATTI SMITH, Arista, 1996.
Photography: Annie Leibovitz. Design: Angela Skouras.

Jan Garbarek / Ustad Fateh Ali Khan & Musicians from Pakistan

ECM

Ragas and Sagas

1

1 **Ragas and Sagas**, JAN GARBAREK / USTAD FATCH, ALI
   KHAN & MUSICIANS FROM PAKISTAN, ECM, 1992.
   Design: Barbara Wojirsch. Photography: Herbert Maeder.
2 **Sart**, JAN GARBAREK, BOBO STENSON, TERJE RYPDAL,
   ARILD ANDERSEN, JON CHRISTENSEN, ECM, 1971.
   Design: B & B Wojirsch.
3 **Azimuth '85**, AZIMUTH, ECM, 1985.
   Design: Dieter Rehm. Photography: Christian Vogt.

SART
JAN GARBAREK
BOBO STENSON
TERJE RYPDAL
ARILD ANDERSEN
JON CHRISTENSEN

ECM

2

Azimuth '85

John Taylor
Norma Winstone
Kenny Wheeler

ECM

3

4 **Voice from the Past Paradigm**, GARY PEACOCK, ECM, 1982.
Design: Dieter Rehm.
5 **Rejoicing**, PAT METHENY GROUP, ECM, 1984.
Design: Barbara Wojirsch. Photography: Rob van Petten.

GARY PEACOCK w/ JAN GARBAREK TOMASZ STANKO JACK DeJOHNETTE

Voice from the Past – PARADIGM   ECM

4

PAT METHENY w/CHARLIE HADEN & BILLY HIGGINS

Rejoicing

ECM   STEREO 817 795-2

5

ECM – Edition Of Contemporary Music – was
founded in Munich in 1969 by Manfred
Eicher. The company's visual look has been
almost entirely created by three designers:
Burkhart and Barbara Wojirsch and Dieter Rehm.
Their collective style reflects Eicher's interest in
the more challenging musical tendencies in
modern music and jazz; its roster of recording
artists including Keith Jarratt, Paul Bley, Gary
Burton, Chick Corea, Pat Metheny and Art
Ensemble of Chicago. The company's visual
output is one of the best instances of a small
record company pursuing a design policy of
consistent high quality; yet which still manages
to avoid submerging the individuality of the
recording artists under a corporate design policy,
even if it sometimes succumbs to a peculiarly
European form of high-minded design ennui.

Over its thirty years of existence, ECM's
catalogue shows a remarkably consistent approach
to design quality. The company's early album
sleeve designs reflect somewhat the muscular
formalism of American jazz album sleeves of the
1950s. However, this influence is always
modulated by the geographical proximity of the
more austere rigour of the Swiss modernist graphic
design tradition. From the first, the aesthetic mode
is avowedly elitist, and the coherence of the
company's distinctive visual repertoire is very
quickly made apparent. Muted typographical
elements of great formal precision are a frequent
characteristic. Barbara and Burkhart Wojirsch's
minimalist design for the 1971 *Sart* album is a good
example of their typo-architecture at its most
simple and refined. Moody black and white
photography, often of elemental starkness, with, for
example, desolate landscape as its subject matter,
is another frequent sleeve type. Jan Garbarek/
Ustad Fateh Ali Khan & Musicians' *Ragas and
Sagas* (1992) by Barbara Wojirsch is typical of ECM
sleeves in this vein. When colour photography is
used it tends towards chromatic simplicity or an
overall coherence resulting from a washed-out
palette. One type of image which occurs quite
often exploits the way in which everyday scenes
can, with careful framing, be photographed to
simulate the vigorous simplicity of '50s New York
abstract painting. Dieter Rehm makes a specialty
of this kind of image as in his cruciform cloud
formation for the Gary Peacock sleeve for *Voice
From The Past – Paradigm* (1982), and also in the
bisecting diagonal of the wall and shadow in the
Christian Vogt photograph on *Azimuth '85*.

In keeping with ECM's high art allegiances and
the "difficulty" of composers such as Gavin Bryars,
Steve Reich and Dmitri Shostakovich, trends in
contemporary art have been a strong influence on
the kinds of visual motifs used on the company's
album art. Throughout her career Barbara Wojirsch
has produced sleeves which feature her distinctive
freehand lettering, some of which in the 1980s was
redolent of the calligraphic forms in Cy Twombley's
paintings. Pat Metheny's *Rejoicing* (1984) is a
typical example. Recent ECM covers suggest more
allusive, dematerialized high art exemplars –
quasi-documentary photographic evidence of site-
specific installations and urban interventions of
an almost invisible nature.

WILD THINGS BY THE CREATURES

1

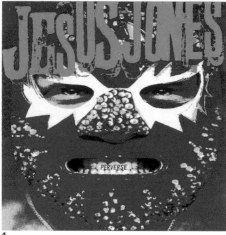

2

3

4

1   **Wild Things**, THE CREATURES, Polydor, 1981.
Design: Rob O'Connor and the Creatures. Photography:
Adrian Boot.

2   **Modern Life is Rubbish**, BLUR, Food, 1993.
Design: Stylorouge. Painting: Paul Gribble.

3   **Leisure**, BLUR, Food, 1991.
Design: Stylorouge.

4   **Perverse**, JESUS JONES, Polydor, 1980.
Design: Stylorouge. Photography: Takashi Homma. [From left to
right: front cover with artwork from inside the cd cover.]

5   **Faith**, GEORGE MICHAEL, Epic/Columbia, 1987. [opposite]
Design: Stylorouge. Photography: Russell Young.

Rob O'Connor was born in 1956 in southern England. He landed a design job at Polydor's London design studio in 1979 after studying graphic design at both Coventry and Brighton. Album sleeve assignments at Polydor included Siouxsie and the Banshees' *Join Hands* (1979), Sham 69, *The First the Best and the Last* (1980) and The Wanderers, *only Lovers Left Alive* (1981). In 1981, in search of "a greater level of creative expression and income", he left to launch his own design company Stylorouge. Stylorouge grew to become a highly successful, multidisciplinary design company with an eclectic range and an acute eye for the evocative image. It is one of the most durable design groups specializing in working for the music industry. Two decades after its launch three-quarters of its design output was still produced for record companies. As creative director, O'Connor has consistently emphasized his belief in team work and collaboration. His company is always inventive, even when required to produce endless versions of portrait sleeves for solo artists.

Initially, Stylorouge was very much a one-man band in an upstairs room on London's Edgware Road. O'Connor continued to work for Polydor artists, including Kirsty MacColl, Level 42 and Siouxsie and the Banshees, but before long had landed commissions from other record companies. Within a year he had hired Mick Lowe and Nick Ward and, by 1983, the company had moved to larger premises. By 1984 Stylorouge had produced album and single sleeves for, amongst others,

Wham, Adam Ant, Alison Moyet, Killing Joke, Paul Young and Bob Marley. The company continued to flourish throughout the 1980s. The moody, introspective image of George Michael for *Faith* (1987) is an outstanding sleeve from the late '80s. The unexpected close-cropping of Michael's portrait, unadorned by the titling, although featuring a line of gold ideogram-like figures in the bottom left corner drawn by Michael himself, captures his allusive glamour with great skill. By 1991 the Stylorouge team had grown to eleven, undertaking work for European, American and Japanese companies in the record, film and fashion industries. The company expanded into pop video production producing videos for Squeeze, Maxi Priest and All About Eve.

Although Stylorouge's range in the 1990s was as wide as ever, encompassing Sarah Brightman's *Surrender* (1992), Jesus Jones's *Perverse* (1993) and Chris de Burgh's *This Silent World* (1994), its most celebrated client during the first half of the decade was Blur. After kicking off by appropriating a Mel Ramos painting of a girl on a rhino for the 1990 single *She's So High*, Stylorouge accumulated a vast range of "British image" photographs for the band: a girl in a flowery swimming hat for *Leisure* (1991), a painting of a Mallard steam train for *Modern Life is Rubbish* (1993) and a dramatic head-on shot of greyhounds for *Parklife* (1994). These, and many more produced for singles and other publicity material, evocative of a lost, glamorized suburban childhood, are a curious mix of anti-

cosmopolitanism and art school knowingness which was to become one of the characteristics of Britpop. It is striking that the range of images produced by Microdot for Oasis record sleeves and their other publicity material during the "Britpop war" of the middle of the decade have a similar character. Notwithstanding the success of their work for Blur, Stylorouge's client list continues to cross the boundaries of all musical styles, collaborating with Storm Thorgerson on a twentieth anniversary edition of Pink Floyd's *Dark Side Of The Moon* (1993), producing the live Rolling Stones album *No Security* (1998), featuring die-hard Stones fans, the Kula Shaker album *Peasants, Pigs and Astronauts* (1999) and Geri Halliwell's *Schizophonic* (1999).

U2 The UnforgeHable Fir

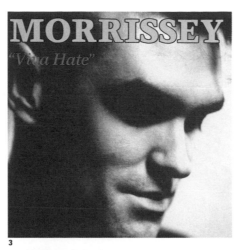

2

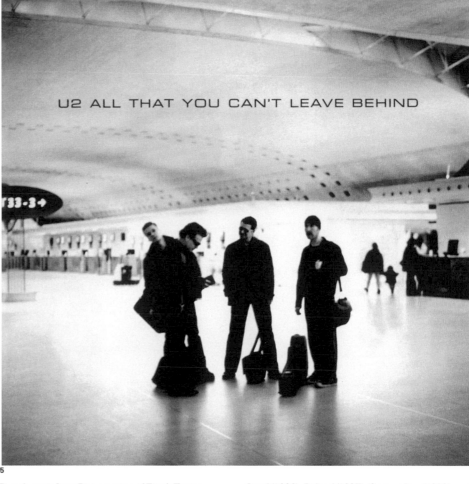

3

4

5

1 **The Unforgettable Fire**, U2, Island Records, 1984. [opposite]
Design: Anton Corbijn, Steve Averill. Photography:
Anton Corbijn.

2 **Gag**, FAD GADGET, Mute, 1984.
Photography: Anton Corbijn. Design: Savage Leisure
Centre Productions.

3 **Viva Hate**, MORRISSEY, EMI, 1988.
Design and photography: Anton Corbijn.

4 **Crossroad**, BON JOVI, Polygram, 1994.
Design and photography: Anton Corbijn.

5 **All That You Can't Leave Behind**, U2, Island Records, 2000.
Photography: Anton Corbijn. Design: Shaun McGrath at Four 5
One Design, Dublin. Art direction: Steve Averill.

Anton Corbijn was born in 1955 in Strijen, in the Netherlands. He has been based in London since 1979 from where he has pursued a highly successful career as a photographer. Initially Corbijn's career makes him seem like the archetypal rock 'n' roll photographer – working for a music paper, grabbing candid shots where he can, travelling, staying on the tour circuit while all around him drop dead. On further examination his approach is more that of a classic portrait photographer, but with a particular propensity for celebrity and a gift for creating images for album sleeves. Among his many portraits are iconic images of Captain Beefheart, David Bowie and Miles Davis.

In 1974 Corbijn enrolled in the photography course at the Intermediate Technical College in The Hague, after which he worked as an assistant to Gijsbert Hanekroot in Amsterdam. In 1976 he became chief photographer for the Dutch pop music magazine *OOR*. In 1979, he moved to London where he began work as a photographer for the British music weekly, *New Musical Express* (*NME*). In his early years in London he established himself as a versatile photographer. His photographs of the 1970s and 1980s have the raw and moody directness of documentary reportage. There is a gritty feel to his images which is enhanced by his preference for a coarse-grained, black-and-white look. His dress-down attitude has been particularly successful with male subjects.

Among his earliest album sleeves are two he produced for Fad Gadget, the monstrous Mr.

Punch-cum-Iggy Pop creation of Frank Tovey: *Under The Flag* (1982) and *Gag* (1984). In 1984 he also photographed the sleeve for Irish rock band U2's *Unforgettable Fire* with its elegiac cover image of a back-lit, overgrown folly set against a cirrus-streaked sky (and its inside sleeve of out-of-focus portrait shot of the band). His contribution to U2 album sleeves had begun with their previous album *War* (1984), for which he took the group portrait in the centre gatefold. But it was *Unforgettable Fire* which would establish him as a photographer with an almost anti-celebrity attitude to photographing stars. Despite its obliqueness, his approach has always produced images suffused with the spirit of romance. Over the next two decades he would produce (mostly in collaboration with Steve Averill) a string of distinctive album sleeves for U2: *The Joshua Tree* (1987), *Rattle & Hum* (1988), *Achtung Baby*, (1991) *POP*, (1996), *The Best Of 1980-1990* (1998), and *All That You Can't Leave Behind* (2000).

Corbijn's success as a freelance photographer allowed him to give up working for *NME* in 1984. The range of people he has sought out to photograph since then has steadily widened. His photographs have appeared in *Rolling Stone*, *Harper's Bazaar*, *Elle*, *Us*, *Vogue*, *Details*, and *Entertainment Weekly*. Throughout he has kept up a steady tempo of album sleeve work. Among his more intriguing assignments are his long-term associations with the likes of Bon Jovi and Frank Tovey, and none more so than the photographs he has taken for a succession of Metallica albums:

Load (1996), *Reload* (1997), *Garage Inc.* (1998), and *S & M* (1999). A sign of his determined interest in people as people, rather than as musical style statements, is the sheer diversity of his album sleeve commissions: *Seven Deadly Sins* for Marianne Faithfull (1999), *Don't Look Back* for John Lee Hooker (1997), *Stripped* for the Rolling Stones (1995), *Crossroads* for Bon Jovi (1994), *Rough Town* for Johnny Halliday (1993), *Automatic for the People* for REM (1991), *Under A Spanish Moon* for Herb Alpert (1998), *Into the Fire* for Bryan Adams, and *Ice Cream for Crow* for Captain Beefheart in 1982.

British rave culture crystallized around the importation of house music pioneered at a Chicago club, the Warehouse, in the mid '80s. House was eagerly embraced by the Northern Soul club scene in the north of England. The Hacienda in Manchester, which was modelled on the airy expanses of a New York Club (and which had been less than full in the first few years of its existence), was suddenly full to capacity in 1986. This was disco's illicit, punkified offspring, at several evolutionary steps removed. Even Tony Mandero got down in the mosh pit. The new club culture also reflected the experience of clubbing in Mediterranean vacation spots, Ibiza being the most archetypal with its sybaritic lifestyle, open air venues and dancing through to sunrise. In particular, Shoom in London was a pioneer rave club with its origins in Ibiza's Amnesia Club, and the innovative music mix of its resident DJ Alfredo. The arrival of house, and subsequently the Kraftwerk-influenced techno from Detroit, coincided with a widespread adoption of Ecstasy as the clubber's stimulant of choice. The combination of music, lifestyle and "E" produced a euphoric sense of community intensely experienced around successive waves of dance music innovation. House and techno led to acid house, jungle, drum'n'bass, trance, garage etc. All these dance styles were, to a significant degree, created around sampling. And DJs, rather than conventional musicians, were the pacesetters and recording stars. European house music and American hip-hop both relied heavily on sampling funk grooves and beats. Akai's S950 sampler, followed by the S1100, launched in 1988 were significant steps forward in sampler technology. The ability to timestretch – both speeding up and slowing down – looped samples of rhythm without altering the pitch became an important component of the music, as well as adding a new dimension to back-bedroom recording.

The new DJ culture spawned its own graphic form: the club flyer. They have become as significant a representation of club culture as have the 12 inch DJ record sleeve. Clubs and raves held in venues at ever-changing locations needed a line of communication with clubbers. A stack of small information sheets piled innocuously on the counter of a bar or record shop promised a clubber's gateway to nirvana. At first the flyers were simple affairs. But soon club culture began to generate its own chameleon iconography. The electronic collaging of house had already made the DJ the increasingly creative arbiter of musical taste, replacing the conventional musician or band in dance club venues. The club flyer with its short, throw-away life was the perfect visual expression of the disposable, appropriationist DJ attitude and became the visual equivalent of the cut-up pastiches, sampling and multiple overlays of the ever-mobile club culture. Flyers developed ever greater complexity, and their often baffling use of graphical overlays became the coded communications of a beleaguered, secretive subculture. In their own way they were as effective at excluding the uninitiated as were the psychedelic Haight-Ashbury posters of the '60s. Many of the young designers who learned their graphic skills

MINISTRY OF SOUNDSSIONS

MIXED BY DAVID MORALES

2

cream anthems
Thirty one of the biggest tunes in the universe

3

4

THE RETURN OF THE
HAPPY HAPPY
HAPPY HAPPY
HAPPY
SHOOM!!!
CLUB
12 thro'5 Sat. Jan.30
Fitness centre
Crown House
56-58 Southwark st.
SE1
Present invite plus £5

CHICAGO HOUSE & FRANKFURT BEAT
SPUN BY: COLIN FAVER
AND DANNY RAMPLING

All Night bar
NO RUFFIANS

5

6

1 **Flyer: Da Bomb**, 1996.
   Design: Dots per Minute.
2 **Ministry of Sound Sessions 7**, VARIOUS ARTISTS,
   Ministry of Sound, 1997
   Design: Scott Parker. Photography: Christophe Demoulin.
3 **Cream Anthems**, VARIOUS ARTISTS, Deconstruction, 1995.
   Design: Mark Farrow, Penny Boulton at Touch.
4 **Rave Base 5**, VARIOUS ARTISTS, Polygram, 1996.
   Design: Peter Hayward, Ed Holding at Mainartery.
5 **Handbill: Shoom Club**, 1987.
   Design: George Georgiou.
6 **Logo: Ministry of Sound**, 1990.
   Design: Mervyn Rands.

8

9

10

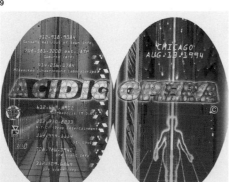

11

7 **Beat Dis**, BOMB THE BASS, Rhythm King, 1987.
Design: unknown [opposite]
8 **Balearic Beats: The Album, Vol 1**, VARIOUS ARTISTS,
ffrr, 1988.
Design: Dave Little.
9 **Bow Down Mister**, JESUS LOVES YOU, Virgin, 1991.
Design: Tony Cooper.
10 **Unsequenced**, ACID JUNKIES, Djax, 1994.
Design: J J F G Borrenbergs.
11 **Flyer: Acidic Opera**, 1996.
Design: Durica Design.

producing club flyers subsequently crossed into design's mainstream.

Acid house is an instance of the sporadic appearance of a social configuration in which a fashionable illegal drug is an integral part of an illicit youth lifestyle. The clubber's drug of choice was not (as the adoption of the smiley badge might suggest) LSD but Ecstasy, although there are striking parallels between the enclosed, secretive world of late '80s rave culture and the counter culture staked out by hippy communities in the mid to late '60s with its free-form "love-in" gatherings and drug-induced trancing. But although the taking of Ecstasy (and old-fashioned LSD) was an integral part of rave culture, "acid" was not solely a reference to the hallucinogenic drug of '60s hippies but also American slang for the appropriation of a sound or riff, a procedure immortalized in *Acid Tracks* by Phuture and *We Call It Acieed* by D Mob.

The smiley face, icon of hippy spaced-out benevolence, was recycled as the symbol of acid house. George Georgiou adopted it for flyers for the Shoom Club in early 1987. In fact, the smiley face had never really gone away. Its adaptability to every conceivable usage has made it one of the century's great icons of popular culture. But in 1986 it had been given a new lease of life by cult comic *The Watchmen* created by Alan Moore and Dave Gibbons. The smiley face image began to crop up on record sleeves, notably on 1987's ubiquitous *Beat Dis* by Bomb the Bass, and there was a memorable hare krishna version by Boy George's *Jesus Loves You* in 1991. Not surprisingly, design associated with acid house rave culture is also characterized by a revival of psychedelic design motifs. The collage techniques and endless duplications newly made possible by the arrival of the colour photocopier gave the biomorphic and optical convolutions of psychedelia a new intensity.

The role of technology would be an important factor underpinning the dynamic of rave design. By the early '90s the bed-sit punk technologies of photocopier and the cut-and-paste were being replaced by AppleMac design software. Hand-made effects achieved with enormous labour could now be achieved digitally at speed. Furthermore, computer-generated fractals allowed new twists to the worlds-within-worlds iconography which is such a characteristic of psychedelic imagery. Early AppleMac software design tools like Adobe Photoshop allowed designers to create composites of numerous layers of text and image. Illusionistic depth could be created by the superimposition of flat transparent layers of image and text like a stage set in which the scenery is painted on a series of flat gauzes. Hyper-dense skeins of information soon came to typify rave graphics. Later, as the '90s proceeded and computers became more powerful, 3-D modelling programmes such as Maya began to appear. Everywhere rave graphics took on the super-abundance of synthetic multi-vista cosmic illusionism. Typographical elements were immersed in this super-abundant visual field in a way which required the reader to "mine" information. Within this synthetic area, super-

dense 3-D images could be created which were highly tactile yet also entirely fantastical: robots, aliens and other characters often of Japanese inspiration, derived from the characters of manga pioneer Osamu Tezuka, from the later animated cartoons of anime, or from the imaginary cute creatures that inhabited the computer games of Nintendo's legendary games' director Shigoru Miyamoto.

Once the fashion for obscurantism took hold different schools began to appear. An influential early '90s DJ look was the "vacant lot" school of photography which suited the darker club sounds then prevalent. For imagery it sought out the romance of the bleak non-spaces of the urban landscape, such as bus stations and pedestrian walkways, often shot at night by sodium light. Curiously, it was a moment of convergence with the type of design which had been a staple of esoteric electronic music album sleeves for a considerable time. Out-of-focus photographic images and deconstructed typographical layouts – revisiting concrete poetry – as explored by Raygun, tomato and other exponents, were also immensely popular. All these strategies are discussed further in this book's final section.

As club culture became increasingly regulated, control passed more and more into the hands of big business. Nonetheless, the underground conjunction of clubs, alternative lifestyles and street styles, fashion and as extended through other expressions such as graffiti, continued to generate a distinctive youth design culture well into the '90s, celebrated by many illustrators such as London-based Will Barras and Lopetz of Swiss design partnership Büro Destruct.

1990–
From Techno to Napster... and beyond

Parklife.
BLUR, Food, 1994.
Design: Stylorouge.
[previous pages]

In Sides.
ORBITAL, Internal, 1996.
Design: Fultano Mauder.
Collage artists: Foul End
Trauma.

Strange Little Girls.
TORI AMOS, Atlantic, 2001.
Design: Blue Source.
Photography: Thomas Schenk.

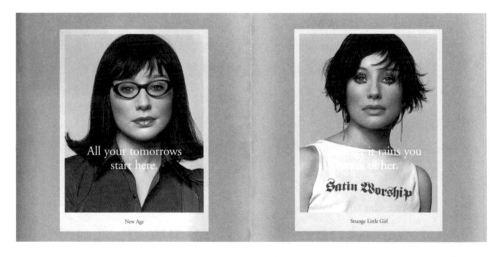

In 1992 veteran album sleeve designer Bill Claxton declared that "the art of the LP cover, I'm afraid, has pretty much vanished with the arrival of the compact disc product… I long for that big 12" by 12" space where an exciting visual image could be put that would do justice to the artist on the recording and 'turn on' the potential buyer". Such pessimism about the end of album sleeve design was defied by 1990s CD designers. Instead of mourning, many set about substantially changing the rules of album packaging, reducing the emphasis on a single killer image for the front cover, and instead turning the CD booklet into an extended visual essay paralleling the CD's musical contents. As Stefan Sagmeister, one of the '90s most notable album sleeve designers, has said of CD packaging: "apart from displaying lyrics and liner notes, they should make the consumer feel good about the band. A typical CD cover holds much more information than its vinyl counterpart. While album covers were almost like posters, CD covers are more like book design. Twenty-page booklets, transparent trays with concealed graphics underneath the CD, and elaborate printing are seen on many general releases". Sagmeister is notable for the extended visual essay and themed linking of disparate images. Other examples of this trend are the extended montage by Foul End Trauma for Orbital's *In Sides* (1996) and Blue Source's memorable pull-out of Tori Amos in a sub-Cindy Sherman series of adopted personas for *Strange Little Girl* (1997). French designer Philippe Savoir is another notable example, defining the look of the Orchestre National de Jazz by ensuring a consistent design approach to all their CDs since 1995.

Reminiscing.
ORCHESTRE NATIONAL DE
JAZZ, Verve, 1996.
Design: Phillipe Savoir/
Filifox, Paris.

Despite this new emphasis on CD design as enfolding the music with an extended sense of visual context, a number of stunning cover images appeared during the decade. There is the pair of greyhounds racing towards the viewer on Blur's *Parklife* (1994) and the menacing crab on Prodigy's *The Fat Of The Land* (1997). And then there is Marilyn Manson as a malevolent, sexually ambivalent alien on *Mechanical Animals* (1998). The sleeve of Nirvana's *Nevermind* (1991) features the single most memorable image of Seattle grunge – and it was subsequently much parodied. The image arose out of Kurt Cobain's idea of using a photograph of underwater childbirth for Nirvana's new album. The designer, Robert Fisher, researched some photographs of water births but they were too graphic. Instead the band liked a photograph he had found of a baby swimming underwater and that became the theme. It was then that Cobain came up with the finishing touch of the dollar bill on a fishing line, transforming it into a wryly cynical image of the human race's innately materialistic drive.

In America at the beginning of the decade rave culture was only just getting into its stride as house and its derivatives were reimported via the UK. In Britain, Manchester's Hacienda club was fighting a losing battle to stay open, and rave culture was being increasingly corralled by new laws, despite the success of the Megadog and Spiral Tribe events. Graham Bright's Private Member's Bill increased the penalties for organizing unlicenced raves, and the Criminal Justice and Public Order Act of 1994 further reinforced the crack-down. The effect was that British rave culture

The Fat of the Land.
PRODIGY, XL, 1997.
Design: Alex Jenkins.
Art direction: Alex Jenkins,
Liam Howlett.
Photography: Konrad Wothe/
Silvestris.

Odelay.
BECK, Bong Load, 1996.
Design and art direction: Beck
Hansen, Robert Fisher.
Photography: Bob Ludwig.

either found the going increasingly tough or it became a licenced part of mainstream youth culture. Two huge club music empires gradually emerged out of this situation: Ministry of Sound based in London, and Cream based in Liverpool. As Pet Shop Boys' designer Mark Farrow said of the Cream logo "they're kind of branding it the way that Nike would. I love it when you can take an idea to that stage, where it's just a shape and everybody knows what it is." Not only were Cream and Ministry of Sound mounting club events in outposts in the Mediterranean and the Americas, but booming record sales were an increasingly important part of their turnover. By the end of the '90s Ministry of Sound was releasing compilations at a rate not seen since the heyday of compilation labels like K-Tel, and with the same generic (albeit updated) album sleeve look.

Douglas Coupland's *Generation X, Tales for an Accelerated Culture*, published in 1991, became a key guide to '90s youth culture. In Coupland's view the young were ferociously determined not to be typecast, suspicious of marketing, overqualified, and working at Macjobs. The book became a telling prophecy of the further segmenting of popular music into sub-genres, catering to self-defining lifestyle sub-groups. Individual designers like Art Chantry in America and Trevor Jackson and Swifty in Britain assiduously followed the twists and turns of these lifestyle sub-groups organized around recreational sports like skateboarding, surfing and snowboarding, or graffiti art, or clubbing, or Kustom Kulture, all of which developed increasingly esoteric languages and conventions. Commentators duelled with names – electronica, electroclash, ambient

Mechanical Animals.
MARILYN MANSON,
Nothing/Interscope, 1998.
Design: Bau-da Design
Lab, NYC.
Art direction: Paul Brown.
Photography: Joseph Cultice.

Nevermind.
NIRVANA, Sub Pop, 1991.
Design and art direction:
Robert Fisher.
Photography: Kirk Weddle.

techno, industrial techno-thrash, pantomime horror-metal, ragga –
although the jury is still out on which of these multiplying musical
categories will be sufficiently distinct to establish their own iconographies.

Design for music post-AppleMac generated new clichés: logos
proliferated (logos design became a major taught element in art college
graphics courses), and compressed streams of lettering floated over wide
screen linear perspectives of the Zaha Hadid school of deconstructionist
architectural drawing became a fashion. By way of an antidote, there was
a resurgence of sparse, angular graffiti-inspired illustration drawing on a
hybrid heritage of cartoon/comix imagery and ideomorphic letter forms.

In smaller national markets the percentage held by home-grown
recording talent grew, accentuating the fragmentation of the recording
industry. In particular the share of international markets, particularly the
North American market, held by popular music forms from Britain
declined rapidly.

During the '90s London continued to be considered of international
importance in the world of album sleeve design, but increasingly less so
for music. A number of seminal design groups came to being in London
which went out of their way to define their character through their
interest in, and dedication to, innovative design for music. Some of them
were not above taking themselves a tad seriously. "Radical" became such
an overused term in their pronouncements it was in danger of being
devalued to the point of meaning barely more than "ingenious", and
ingenuity sometimes meant little more than the intelligent plundering of

Universal.
K-KLASS, Deconstruction, 1993.
Design: Mark Farrow.

Mo' Deep Mo' Phunky.
VARIOUS ARTISTS, Blue
Note, 1993.
Design: Ian Swift.

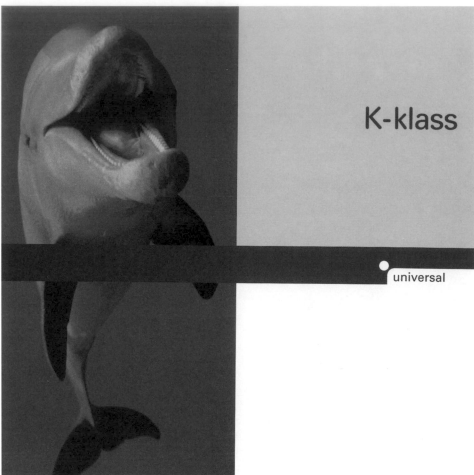

recent art history with scant attempt to shift the terms of signification. It all paralleled uncannily the development of BritArt.

As ever, small labels proliferated at a tremendous rate. Two of the most outstanding independents of the 1990s, Mo' Wax (London) and Thrill Jockey (Chicago), were both launched in 1992. Many more like them pursued their individual visions, promoting off-beat musical talent, including +cross (Tokyo), Tigerbeat6 (San Diego), Pacifier (Los Angeles), 12K (New York), Intransitive (Boston), I8U (Montreal), Sprawl (London), Active Suspension (Paris), Optical Sound (Strasbourg), Zeal (Leuven) and Bungalow (Berlin). The big multinational record companies began to show signs of distress as sales stalled. Most began re-structuring, releasing swathes of recording acts from their contracts, or not renewing them. The biggest casualty was EMI which paid Mariah Carey $28 million to walk away from her recording contract, to much public derision. Then came a further threat: downloading music files from the internet. At its height Napster, pioneer of illegal file-swapping, had 13.6 million users. Even when Napster went into liquidation following a failed attempt by Bertelsmann (owners of record label BMG) to buy the company to turn it into a subscription-paying service, it was simply replaced by other sites such as Morpheus, LimeWire, Audiogalaxy and, biggest of them all, KaZaA. In 2001 sales of CDs were down 5% from the previous year, the first decline in sales since the CD was launched. Record companies sought to discourage piracy by offering on-line incentives such as extra tracks or remixes only available by registering

Vier Stücke
CHRISTINA KUBISCH,
Editions RZ, 2000.
Concept: Christina Kubisch.
Design: Kehrer.
Photograpy: Thomas Wrede,
Mens Ziehe.

**Body Freefall, Electronic
Inform # 2.**
LUKE SLATER, Mute, 2000.
Design: Julian House at Intro.
Photography: Nigel Bennett.

through a PIN code to be found on a sticker attached to the CD booklet. And yet, if this crisis pointed to anything, it pointed to the aspect of a CD that no downloaded file could readily transfer from one user to another: well-designed and innovative packaging adding that extra visual dimension to the enjoyment of the CD. Although record companies will, no doubt, continue to adopt increasingly sophisticated encryption tools, one of the most effective weapons that record companies have against file-swapping remains the kind of CD packaging design that, as Stephan Sagmeister put it, "makes the consumer feel good about the band."

TODD TERRY PRESENTS

ROYAL ♛ HOUSE

CHAMP 1291 · Written, Produced and Mixed by Todd Terry for BENZ PRODUCTIONS · Executive Producer: Grand Wizard Tony D

5 014524 109168

E

PC

YEAH BUDDY

Design by Trevor Jackson for Bite It!
℗ 1988 Champion Records Ltd © 1988 Champion Records Ltd.
Champion Records Ltd · 181 High St Harlesden · London · NW10 4TE · Tel 01 961 5202 · Telex 295441 BUBYB Fax 01 965 3243

2

3

Trevor Jackson aka The Underdog aka Skull was born in 1968, in West London. After a Higher National Diploma course in Graphic Design at West Barnet College 1983–87 he was turned down by London colleges (including St Martin's) for postgraduate study. Instead he went to work as an assistant at the Kunst Art Company run by Martin Huxford, his former teacher.

After two months there he decided to start his own design studio Bite It!, located in Clerkenwell, London. Initially he specialized in the Afro-urban imagery which was then the coming fashion on London's club scene. Although his crude, bold and expressive forms were an immediate success, it was his work for New York rap act the Jungle Brothers in 1988 which brought him to wider notice. His designs of the late 1980s integrate typographical elements – often hand drawn – with bold, simple images realized with the quick facility of graffiti. His 1988 design for "Yeah Buddy" by Royal House is designed in what he has termed "ZX Spectrum graphics". This work shows a strong affinity to logo-like images that he refers to as "pictograms". The ideogrammatic forms – usually restricted to silhouettes – are always eloquently well-observed and ably capture the spirit of the developing rap and hip-hop dynamic. The impression given by his work of this period is its occasional similarity to Saul Bass's incisive graphic work, an acknowledged influence. His ability to convey meaningful detail through simple expressive forms also reveals his affection for comics and Hanna-Barbera cartoons. He often

worked against the technical limitations of rudimentary means of reproduction, particularly by designing with a simple photo-mechanical transfer machine when other designers could afford Macs. The growth in the market of 12-inch DJ remixes provided him with a ready market for his designs at dance labels such as Champion, 4th & Broadway, and Gee Street. He also worked for major labels WEA, MCA, Island, and Chrysalis. He produced trademark covers for the Stereo MCs, Raze, and Todd Terry. He also designed sleeves for UK-only releases of American rappers like Eric B & Rakim and the Jungle Brothers.

Immersed in the lifestyle he was designing for, it was perhaps inevitable that from being a DJ at clubs such as Megabite he would become increasingly involved in the DJ remix scene. Such was his reputation that major labels began to commission him to remix tracks for major acts, including Massive Attack and U2. Calling himself The Underdog, his remixes were highly anticipated. He went on to launch a record label under the Bite It! umbrella for which he invariably produced the sleeve designs. The mid-1990s vehicle for his own musical ideas was hip-hop act the Brotherhood, signed to Virgin in 1996, but which split after the release of their debut album *Elementalz*. Subsequent vehicles have been Skull (*Snapz*, 1999) and Playgroup (*DJ Kicks*, 2001). Meanwhile he has abandoned the playful graphic style of the late '80s and, in keeping with the times, a more austere photography-based style has taken its place.

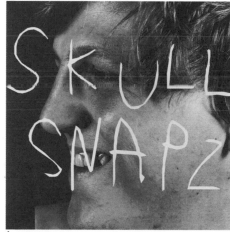

4

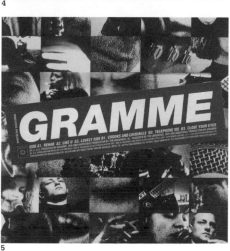

5

1 **Yeah Buddy**, ROYAL HOUSE, Champion, 1991.
 Design: Trevor Jackson for Bite It!

2 **33 45 78**, STEREO MCS, Gee Street, 1989.
 Design: Bite It!. Photograpy: Steve Speller.

3 **Moments in Soul**, JT AND THE BIG FAMILY, Champion, 1990.
 Design: Trevor Jackson.

4 **Snapz**, SKULL, Output, 1998.
 Design: Trevor Jackson.

5 **Pre-Release**, GRAMME, Output, 1999.
 Design: Trevor Jackson.

The Designers Republic was founded by Ian Anderson in Sheffield in 1986. The company came to be the archetypal designers for rave culture in the North of England in the late 1980s and early '90s. At the time the company was a five-person operation consisting of Anderson, David Smith, Nick Bax, Michael Place and Vanessa Swetman. Their design work of this period captured the ecstatic aspects of early house music through its intense melange of cyber-junk colours, layered decorative motifs, hieroglyphic emblems and fragments of recycled corporate logos. One of the terms coined to describe Designers Republic's output of this period was "American Expressionism" on account of the parodies of American corporate design the group incorporated into their output. As Anderson has said of the company's attitude to design: "I like the idea that talent borrows, genius steals. If you want to tie our style down, things like consumerism, science fiction, and Japanese culture, and any kind of packaging attracts us. There is a lot of Japanese iconography in that. It is the ultimate consumerist graphical style, wacky and odd packaging." Typical of their output of the period are Age Of Chance's single sleeve *Who's Afraid Of The Big Bad Noise* (1987) and Fangoria's *Salto Mortal* (1990). Its most famous exercise in this style was their creation of the "corporate-identity" of PWEI (Pop Will Eat Itself), as exemplified by their 12 inch single sleeve for *Wise Up! Sucker* (1989).

Anderson had no formal training as a graphic designer. Originally from South London, he moved to Sheffield to study philosophy at the University and quickly found himself involved in the local music scene. While still at college he was DJ-ing and promoting clubs, and found it cheaper and a guarantee of quality to produce his own flyers. He got further experience designing for a short-lived band he managed, and as requests to design for other bands mushroomed he launched Designers Republic on a small enterprises grant.

Although Designers Republic is closely identified with the growth of the rave and club scene, with its emphasis on a cut-up, sampling, recycling aesthetic, the company's outlook on design has continued to evolve. In the early '90s the more intense, darker implications of hardcore called for new pictorial means. In any case the company was inevitably widening its client base. It designed for Supergrass and Sleeper and most of Pulp's sleeves in the first half of the '90s.

Recent Designers Republic's clients have included Swatch, Sci-Fi Channel, MTV, Adidas, Sony Interactive Entertainment, Virgin Interactive Games, Reebok and Issey Miyake. It has also branched out into designing packaging for computer games, bringing a new degree of integration to the look of titles such as *Grand Theft Auto* and *Wipeout 3*. Nevertheless, work for the music industry continues to be central to the company's ethos. It has had a particularly close relationship with, among others, dance music labels Warp and React. The company's relationship with Warp, established in the second half of the '90s, has been particularly durable. It

inaugurated a further stylistic broadening in the company's output, some of which edges towards the design ethos of European independent niche record labels like ECM with their uncompromising, minimalist design principles. Inevitably with success Designers Republic design has become more catholic, its output encompassing many stylistic genres, some of which are more austere and refined than their earlier work. As a consequence the sense of riding the zeitgeist is somewhat dissipated in their overall output. Nevertheless, their contribution to innovation design continues to be considerable, as was acknowledged by the accolade of a special edition of the American design journal *Emigre*. Of the original members of Designers Republic only Anderson and Nick Bax still remain.

1   **Who's Afraid of the Big Bad Noise?**, AGE OF CHANCE, Virgin, 1987.
    Design: Designers Republic.
2   **Salto Mortal**, FANGORIA, Hispavox, 1990.
    Design: Designers Republic.
3   **Love Generation**, SOHO, Savage Records, 1991.
    Design: Designers Republic.
4   **Do You Like My Tight Sweater?**, MOLOKO, Echo, 1995.
    Design: Designers Republic.
5   **Randa Roomet**, PHOENECIA, Warp, 1997.
    Design: Designers Republic.
6   **Wise Up! Sucker**, POP WILL EAT ITSELF, RCA, 1989. [opposite]
    Design: Designers Republic.

1

2

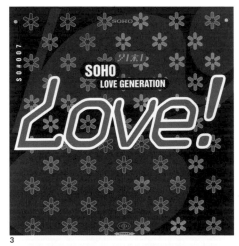

3

4

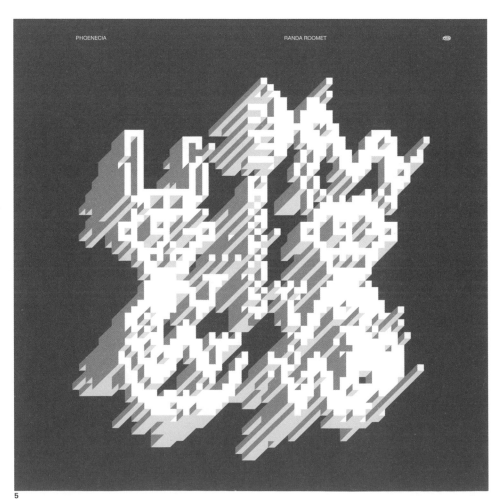

5

PT 427

5 012394 27626

D:AF F:RC120 UK

A SIDE

(R) PWEI **POWER PRODUCT**

ORGYONE

Track Two

STIMULATOR

Written by Vestan Pance
Published by BMG Music Publishing Ltd
Produced by Pop Will Eat Itself
A PWEI Production for PWEI Productions Inc. Engineered by Dave Pine

CAN U DIG IT?

DISCO MIX

Track Three

Written by Vestan Pance
Published by BMG Music Publishing Ltd
Produced by Mr X & Mr Y
Engineered by Robin Goodfellow
Wild Guitar by The Buzzard from Yeah God!

B SIDE

Sucker

* Track One

SEVEN INCH VERSION

Written by Vestan Pance Published by BMG Music Publishing Ltd
Original Recording Directed by Produced by Mr X & Mr Y
Additional Production by Flood & Mark Dodson
Original Production Directed by Robin Goodfellow
Engineered by Robin Goodfellow. Remix Engineered by Dave Pine
Wild Guitar by The Buzzard from Yeah God! Backing Vocals by Twig the Wonder

X-999

Sucker ® VERSION*

Written by Vestan Pance
Published by
BMG Music Publishing Ltd

Produced by Mr X & Mr Y
Additional Production by
Flood & Mark Dodson
Engineered by Robin Goodfellow
Remixed by Youth

Brilliant Sleeve Design & Artwork
Made In The Designers Republic
(A Telescope on Life)
Computer Sun
Phil Wolstenholme/DR

22

World-Wide Management
Craig Jennings
for Chapter 22 Management
0926 497731/497741

1 **Dicknail/Burnblack**, HOLE, Sub Pop, 1991.
Design: Art Chantry. Lettering: Courtney Love.

2 **Soundgarden**, SOUNDGARDEN, A&M, 1989.
Design: Art Chantry. Photography: Charles Peterson,
Michael Lavine.

3 **Piece of Cake**, MUDHONEY, Reprise, 1992.
Design: Art Chantry. Illustration: Edwin Fotheringham.
Lettering: Nathan Joseph Gluck.

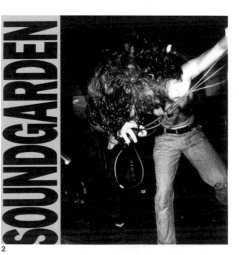

MUDHONEY

''Touch Me I'm Sick''
b/w
''Sweet Young Thing Ain't Sweet No More''   SP18

4

4   **Touch Me I'm Sick/Sweet Young Thing**, MUDHONEY, Sub Pop, 1988.
Design: unknown. Photography: Charles Peterson.
5   **Underworld**, DWARVES, Sub Pop, 1993.
Design: Jane Higgins.

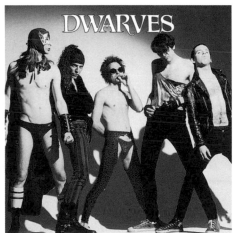

5

The story of Sub Pop (the company was originally called Subterranean Pop) is a typical, not to say quintessential, example of the vicissitudes, pig-headedness and inspiration which trail in the wake of all independent record companies. Sub Pop, which began producing small local bands in Seattle in the second half of the 1980s, became central to the development of grunge, Seattle's rock moment of the early 1990s. Although grunge was to become an over-simplified and over-hyped label attached to the lively regional rock music scene which had developed in the Seattle region, at its core it combined the obdurate, refusenik mentality of punk rock with the drive and tempos of heavy metal: sludge-punk in the pure Pacific-washed air of the Washington state littoral. Three of the major bands associated with grunge – Nirvana, Soundgarden and Mudhoney – all started their recording careers on the Sub Pop label.

Sub Pop was founded by Jonathan Poneman and Bruce Pavitt. After graduating from high school in Illinois, Soundgarden guitarist Kim Thayil and future Sub Pop founder Pavitt relocated to Olympia, Washington, with the intention of attending the Evergreen State College. The burgeoning music scene in Seattle lured them there instead. The first release on the Sub Pop label was Soundgarden's debut EP, *Screaming Life* (1987). Mudhoney, their name taken from the title of a Russ Meyer film, released *Touch Me I'm Sick* and *Sweet Young Thing (Ain't Sweet No More)* on the Sub Pop label as a very limited 7" single on brown vinyl (and initially in a plain sleeve) on August 1, 1988. Nirvana's first album *Bleach* was issued on the label in the following year. Inevitably, with success, all three bands eventually moved on to major labels, although Mudhoney continued to release on Sub Pop until 1992. Despite the disaster of losing major talent (which is always the lot of the small label) the vitality of Sub Pop's approach to the music scene helped it to weather this hemorrhaging of talent.

Sub Pop is as celebrated for its lively approach to design as it is for its catalogue. Initially the company adopted a classic post-punk approach to sleeve design, as can be seen from the toilet adorning the sleeve of Mudhoney's archetypal grunge song *Touch Me, I'm Sick*. However the company's design output soon elaborated into a range of styles, often brazenly appropriated from various pop and jazz sources. Much of the most accomplished Sub Pop work was by designer Art Chantry, himself an arch appropriationist.

Chantry was born in 1954 in Seattle. After a childhood spent in Tacoma, he studied at Western Washington University (1975–78) gaining a degree in painting as a sign of the generalist, not to say, characterless character of his university education. Chantry's start in album design came about through involvement with Seattle's free music scene magazine *The Rocket*. He began designing page layouts on a freelance basis in 1983, and in the following year became the art director, one of

6

several spells in that role at the magazine. Chantry notes of the magazine that: "It was out of *The Rocket* that a lot of the Northwest 'grunge' graphic look emerged. All the designers at Sub Pop were ex-Rocket art directors. That's why we have many of those distressed fonts that people use today".

Chantry came to know Sub Pop's Pavitt through *The Rocket*. Pavitt contributed a music review column called Sub Pop to the magazine in the mid '80s. Chantry produced his first sleeve for Sub Pop in 1989, a two-colour design for a Flaming Lips single titled *Drug Machine*. He went on to be highly instrumental in defining the visual language of grunge. However, his scope as a designer reaches far beyond a sophisticated re-engagement with the tropes of punk, even if one of the first impressions of his output is his strong adherence to the photocopier as a means, in his words, "to rot" images. For album sleeve design, more important even than David Carson, competitive surfer and high school sociology teacher of Raygun, Chantry brought the definitive '90s visual look of subculture-as-visual-pose to record shop racks. Although lacking Carson's pretensions to make type forms almost entirely autonomous from the message, and failing to offer the academic exemplification of deconstruction which both Carson's Beach Culture and Raygun did to perfection, Chantry can claim to have completed the revenge of subcultures on mainstream design. His Seattle period revealed him to be a gifted recycler, constantly deranging settled signifiers. Despite being a versatile

illustrator, he was also a voracious commissioner of others, pulling into his orbit illustrators as diverse as *Mad* magazine cartoonist Don Martin, Robert Crumb, Smool and Edwin Fotheringham.

His association with grunge led to a great demand for Chantry's services as a sleeve designer, and incidentally made him a famous advocate for many fringe activities and political causes. In little more than a decade he designed more than 500 album sleeves. In addition to his involvement with Sub Pop, he also enjoyed a close working relationship with Dave Crider of the Monomen who founded Estrus Records in 1987. In Chantry's words, "Sub Pop had that elegant, clean look that was hard-assed at the same time, and in your face, and playing games. They didn't like to put the record title on the front. Estrus, on the other hand, prides itself on its lack of subtlety. They don't want to attract the general public. They want to speak to the people they want to speak to."

In 1994 Seattle's city council pushed through an Ordinance banning flyposting. Chantry saw it as an attempt to throttle the lines of communication of the city's many-faceted underground culture. Despite a spirited resistance, it was the beginning of the end of Chantry's time in Seattle. As the epilogue to his monograph *Some People Can't Surf* notes: "In March, 2000... Art Chantry moved to St. Louis. His disenchantment with Seattle's gentrifying neighborhoods, traffic snarls, and anemic street life overwhelmed him. Most of his friends had fled. Subcultures had almost completely capitulated to Internet prosperity."

7

8

9

 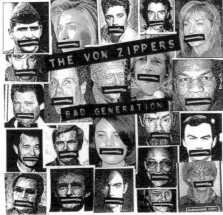

10

1 **Post**, BJÖRK, One Little Indian, 1995. [back and front]
Design: Paul White at Me Company.
Photography: Stephanie Sednaoui.
2 **Army Of Me**, BJÖRK, One Little Indian, 1995.
Design: Me Company.
3 **Life's Too Good**, THE SUGARCUBES, One Little Indian, 1988.
Design: Me Company.

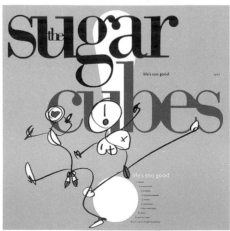

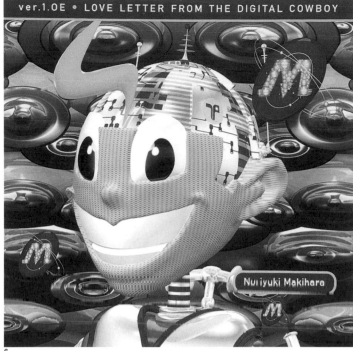

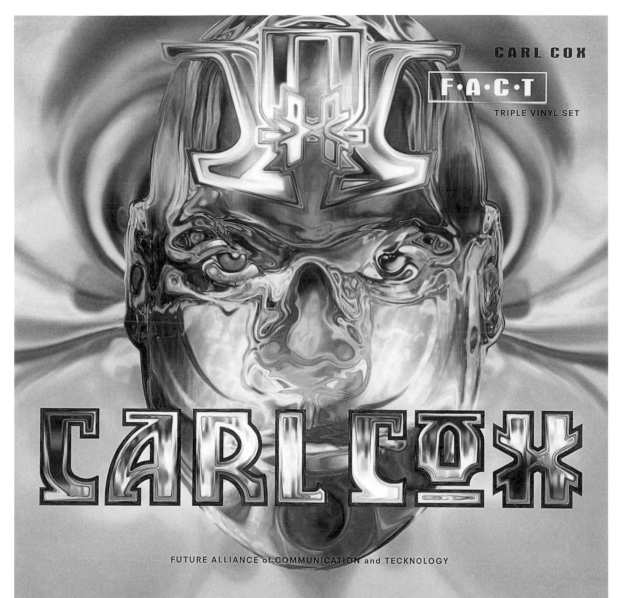

CARL COX

F·A·C·T

TRIPLE VINYL SET

CARLCOX

FUTURE ALLIANCE of COMMUNICATION and TECKNOLOGY

4

ver.1.0E • LOVE LETTER FROM THE DIGITAL COWBOY

Noriyuki Makihara

6

4 **F.A.C.T.**, CARL COX, Worldwide Ultimatum Records, 1997.
Design: Me Company.
5 **Bang Up to Date with the Popinjays**, THE POPINJAYS,
One Little Indian, 1990.
Design: Paul White at Me Company.
6 **Love Letter from the Digital Cowboy**, NORIYUKI
MAKIHARA, Warner Music, Japan, 1996.
Design: Me Company.

5

Paul White, previously a freelance designer, established Me Company in 1986. He was also one of the founders of the record company that launched Bjork's career, One Little Indian. Me Company was originally predominantly engaged in design for the music industry, a period that lasted up to the mid-1990s. Since then, and with success, it has broadened its range of clients considerably, providing design services to valuable corporate clients such as AppleMac. Me Company came to the attention of the wider public through its association with Bjork's early career in the early to mid-'90s. Paul White first met Björk in the late 1980s when she was part of Icelandic group The Sugarcubes, for which he designed a number of bold and innovative graphic sleeves. Highlights of the collaboration of White and Björk include album sleeves for *Debut* (1993), *Post* (1995), and *Homogenic* (1997). For *Homogenic*, the Alexander McQueen geisha was photographed by Nick Knight. In Bjork's words, "because we've known each other since we were teenagers, Paul knows me inside out. He takes the piss by saying that he has a special Björk box in his brain which he can just take things out of."

Perhaps the most successful and elaborate package Me Company designed for Björk was for the album *Post*. The rear cover complements the front with its computer-generated hyper-realist waterlilies and the clubbing logo typography. The portrait of Björk was shot in a London street near the bank of England on a Sunday morning. The swirling placards around her in the photograph were supposed to be giant postcards based on her choice of items, although the effect is more of banners stirred by the breeze. The coat with its airmail trimming was made by Hussein Chalayan. The photograph was taken by Stephanie Sednaoui.

During the various phases of its development, Me Company has sought to project a coherent house style, rather than project itself as a collective of individuals. It was a pioneer in the development of the machine aesthetic closely associated with the techno derivatives of house music. The key designs in this association were early sleeves for techno pioneers The Shamen, and subsequently Carl Cox's *F.A.C.T.* (1997). It had effectively pioneered the digital look associated with techno prior to the first AppleMacs becoming available to designers around 1992. The main tool

used in the creation of this machine aesthetic was the colour photocopier. It allowed for repeated cycles of montage and copying, producing the visual layering and repetitions which are such a characteristic of the style.

These laborious and largely manual processes enabled images to be produced which convincingly simulated effects which would be readily achievable once computer technology was sufficiently powerful to allow for the digital production and manipulation of images.

During the early '90s Me Company explored a number of other postmodern visual tropes, for example the subversion and recontexualization of stock photography. With Bjork's *Army Of Me* sleeve of 1992 the company adopted the widely used concept of turning a well-known celebrity into a cartoon character, producing an image with a strikingly Japanese look. The company also devised a digital persona for Japanese star Makihara for the album sleeve of *Love Letter From the Digital Cowboy* (1996). In these innovations Me Company's output parallels themes developed by the Designers Republic, and the two companies have had individual designers in common.

1   **Club Classics Vol One**, SOUL II SOUL, 10 Records, 1989.
Design: David James. Photography: Jamie Morgan.

David James was born in 1962, in Manchester. His late 1980s, early 1990s design studio David James Associates managed the difficult feat of designing for just about every genre of recorded music then fashionable, from techno through hip-hop to ambient. He produced designs for the world of club culture and for the more conventional recording stars of the music business such as Boy George, Soul II Soul and Neneh Cherry, all of whom benefit from the studied elegance of his approach to album sleeve design. This assured style was acknowledged in 1996 when he became design art director for the fashion label Prada.

James spent from 1978 to 1983 at Stockport College where he studied design and advertising. On leaving college he joined Gillette & Bevan Advertising as a junior art director. He moved to McIllroy Coates in Edinburgh in 1985, then to the Fine White Line Design Company in London in 1986. He went freelance in 1987, and launched his own design studio David James Associates where he was joined by long-time associate Gareth Hague. With the album sleeve for *Tense Nervous Headache* (1989) James engineered a change of style for Boy George, giving him a cool, distant makeover with the help of photographer Nick Knight. After the up-front over-elaborations of Assorted Images, the oblique close-up of George and top hat bathed in blue was a refreshingly stylish and minimalist image. Equally distinctive were his sleeves for Soul II Soul, most notably their *Club Classics Vol. One* (1989) album produced in collaboration with photographer Jamie Morgan.

Between them they created an elegant and expressive freizelike succession of black and white silhouetted body shapes for the outer and inner sleeve, with occasional expressive highlighting revealing moments of detail within the silhouettes.

David James Associates also produced sleeves for The Sindecut (DJ Fingers, Crazy Noddy, Lyn-e-Lyn and DJ Don't Ramp), one of the biggest UK Rap crews of the late '80s and early '90s. Two of the best are the 12-inch single sleeves "Won't Change" and "Live The Life" (both 1991). Their signature characteristic adopted for these sleeves is the insistent imagistic use of typeforms, a field that James and Hague would develop later through their typographic company Alias. For techno outfit Shades of Rhythm the "Homicide/Exorcist" 12-inch single with its pools of poured pigment, is one of several the company produced for the ZTT label.

James was the designer of choice for ambient specialists System 7 anchored by guitarist Steve Hillage and Miquette Giraudyon on synthesizer. James designed their first album *System 7* (1991) although the most memorable of a number of elegant and clever signature sleeves he has produced for the outfit is perhaps *777* (1993), for which he matched the ambient sonics with a refined liquid green logo/image amalgam.

James's restless energy and desire for new challenges have constantly led him into new areas. He launched the specialist typeface company Alias with Hague, and its clever experimentalism led to work for Mazda and Levis.

Since becoming an art director for Prada, the direction of his work has taken him away from design for music, although in 2001 Alias designed the sleeve for the Mondo Grosso album *MG4*, a recording project of Shinichi Osawa.

System 7 Altitude

Featuring Ultra Naté

2

The Sindecut Live the life Remix

4

Sweet Sensation
Shades of Rhythm

3

MG4

5

2 **System 7**, SYSTEM 7, AVL, 1991.
Design: David James, Gareth Hague.
Photography: Lewis Mulatero.
3 **Sweet Sensation**, SHADES OF RHYTHM, ZTT, 1991.
Design: David James, Gareth Hague.
Photography: Richard Burbridge.
4 **Live the Life**, SINDECUT, Virgin, 1991.
Design: David James, Gareth Hague.
5 **MG4**, MONDO GROSSO, Sony Japan, 2001.
Design and art direction: Alias. Illustration: Norio Tanaka,
Highway Graphics.

Microdot's design output of the 1990s is indelibly linked with the Oasis/Verve/Suede strand of Britpop. As with other Britpop bands, a distinctive strand of their album sleeve imagery celebrates a kind of secular Englishness which purposefully avoids overtly glamorous images, or those which already have historical or cultural weight. In particular, Microdot's design work for Oasis is caught up in the mid-'90s Britpop rivalry between Blur and Oasis, with Stylorouge batting for Blur. Considering the considerable heat their rivalry produced, it is remarkable how alike the register of their respective imagery is, employing similar vaguely nostalgic, lost childhood imagery. Although Oasis's sleeves are less overtly in this vein than Blur's, they still suggest suburban ordinariness and family life, even if the extraordinary is to be detected close beneath the surface. Single sleeves like the spectral, elegiac image of John Lennon's childhood home in Menlove Avenue, Liverpool, used on "Live Forever" (1994) and the couple on "Stand By Me" (1997) are characteristic of this uneasy sense of the suburban humdrum. These are new articulations of imagery first explored in the influential sleeves that Morrissey created for The Smiths in the 1980s. A strand of his sleeve images celebrated Northern working class culture, through the careful selection of slightly out-of-time photographs of his heroes who themselves had sought to celebrate this culture without resort to spectacle. The link is not surprising, since Oasis and Morrissey's roots are in the same Manchester milieu.

Microdot was launched by Brian Cannon at the end of the 1980s. Son of a miner, Cannon was born in Wigan in 1961. Cannon was very much part of the northern club scene at the turn of the decade, and he designed many "Revenge" flyers. Microdot's first record sleeve commission was for Kiss AMC. In Cannon's words, "It was the equivalent of a footballer scoring their first goal for a professional club." Another early client was hip-hop band Ruthless Rap Assassins. At this time he was working in a style reminiscent of Designers Republic's club work. Microdot opened an office in Manchester and Cannon met Noel Gallagher of Oasis while he was working for The Verve. His association with Oasis was formalized when he met the whole band in Autumn 1993. Cannon created the Oasis logo which was based on the Decca logo on an early Rolling Stones' record the band had seen in an album sleeve book. Inevitably, with the success of Oasis and other bands he worked for, Cannon was eventually forced to relocate Microdot's studio in London.

Among the many themes detectable in Microdot's output there is also a strand of photographic surrealism familiar from Hipgnosis covers of the 1970s, not least in two Oasis sleeves, the group shot interior on *Definitely Maybe* (1994) and the more complex setup of the country house group portrait on *Be Here Now* (1997) with its half-submerged Rolls Royce in the swimming pool. Both, in their different ways, evoke the group portrait with the open French windows on Pink Floyd's *Ummagumma* (1969). In some ways the sleeves Microdot developed for The Verve, the band fronted by Richard Ashcroft, which is often closely linked with Oasis, are the more original. Some are framed in the vein of stills from the Alain Resnais film *Last Year in Marienbad* (1961), particularly the *fête du jour* scene with the burning car in the inner sleeve of The Verve's *Storm In Heaven* (1993).

2

3

5

4

1   **Berg, Violin Concerto / Rihm, Time Chant**, ANNE-SOPHIE
MUTTER, Deutsche Grammophon, 1992.
Photography: Jorg Reichardt.

2   **Brahms, Violin Concerto / Schumann, Fantasie, op 131**,
ANNE-SOPHIE MUTTER, Deutsche Grammophon, 1997.
Art direction: Peter Schuppe, Nikolaus Boddin.
Photography: Tom Specht.

At the major labels classical music remains a
largely conventional, conservative
backwater of album sleeve design. Classical
music design is characterized by high-minded
seriousness, tropes of tradition and gravitas, in
which the classical repertoire is linked to heritage
and an established canon of masterpieces.

As far as design for music is concerned,
"classical" can be a portmanteau term covering a
rather heterogeneous musical output. The major
record labels are often roundly accused of being
only interested in a narrow classical canon
restricted to the popular favourites. Many
exponents of modern classical, new and avant-
garde musical forms are often lumped into the
classical category, even when they are radically at
odds with it. If the classical music domain is
considered from the design angle, then, it can
appear more like a warzone than a field of peaceful
co-existence. The fault line is most clearly
expressed by the fact that the recordings of many
of the 20th century's composers who have sought
to reconfigure the classical canon, sometimes
termed "new music", have traditionally been the
preserve of small specialist labels such as Mode
Records in the USA, HatHut in Switzerland,
Accord and Montaigne Auvidis in France, and
ECM and Edition RZ in Germany. Companies such
as these, which sometimes handle distribution in
a single national market, have traditionally made
progressive design a high-value adjunct to their
recordings, intensifying the ideological gulf
between the major labels and themselves.

Nevertheless, there have been occasional sparks
of originality and relatively brave episodes of
commissioning design for classical music at the
major record labels. In the mid-1990s Virgin began
a bold re-packaging of its Virgin Classics
repertoire under the art director of Jeremy Hall.
Using a small roster of designers including Sasha
Davison, Nick Bell, Paul Sonley, and Karen Wilks,
Hall steered the classical catalogue's design
toward a refined, coherent look. The results are
reminiscent of the best traditions of album sleeve
design for classical music, as exemplified by Erik
Nitsche's early-1950s re-design for Decca, although
here the binary configuration of type and image
have been subtly readjusted for the smaller CD
format. This was a notable recent instance of a
major label's moving its classical music design
toward the more rarified and considered design
look which has otherwise been the preserve of
small specialist labels.

More typical of the developments in style and
image for classical music at the major labels were
those which first began to emerge during the
1980s. These developments reflected both the
increasing attempts to find new audiences for
classical music and the growing reluctance of
some classical soloists to conform to stereotype,
an issue which was an implicit part of the then-
current emergence of identity politics. A pivotal
figure here was the young British violin soloist
Nigel Kennedy who dominated the limelight
during the second half of the '80s. His career built
on the success of his recording of the Elgar

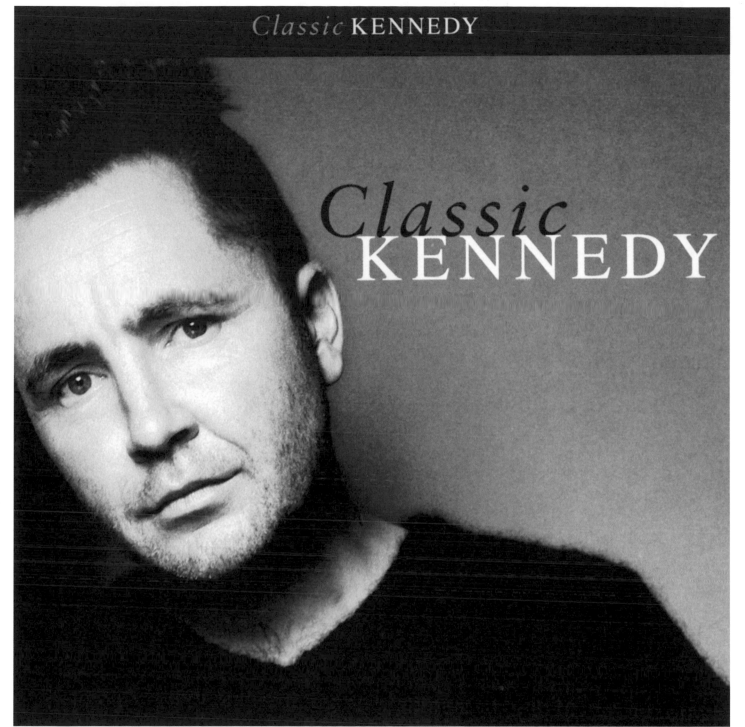

Classic KENNEDY

Classic
KENNEDY

3 **Classic Kennedy**, NIGEL KENNEDY, EMI, 1989.
Design: Paul Mitchell.
Photography: Rankin.

4 **Enchantment**, CHARLOTTE CHURCH, Sony, 2001.
Design and art direction: Jeri Heiden for SMOG.
Photography: Firooz Zahedi/JBG Los Angeles.

5 **The Violin Player**, VANESSA MAE, EMI, 1995.

5

1. *Tonight* (West Side Story) 2. *Carrickfergus* 3. *Habanera* (Carmen)
4. *Bali Ha'i* (South Pacific) 5. *Papa Can You Hear Me* (Yentl)
6. *The Flower Duet* (Lakmé) 7. *The Little Horses*
8. *From My First Moment* (Gymnopédie No. 1) 9. *The Water Is Wide*
10. *Can't Help Lovin' Dat Man* (Showboat) 11. *The Laughing Song* (Die Fledermaus)
12. *If I Loved You* (Carousel) 13. *A Bit Of Earth* (The Secret Garden)
14. *Somewhere* (West Side Story) 15. *The Prayer* (with Josh Groban)
16. *It's The Heart That Matters Most* (Christmas Carol, The Movie)

4

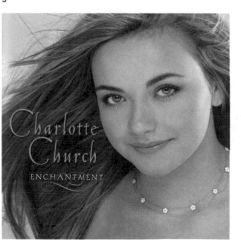

Charlotte Church
ENCHANTMENT

Dmitri Shostakovich

24 Preludes and Fugues op.87

Keith Jarrett

ECM NEW SERIES

Concerto, made when he was just 16. It created a sensation when it was released, although it was his interpretation of Vivaldi's "Four Seasons" (1989) which cemented his celebrity, selling over two million copies world wide and staying in the best sellers' charts for over a year. Record company executives began to perceive that classical music might reach a wider audience if the image of its virtuoso soloists, who were normally presented as sober geniuses, instead became racy, glamorous and charismatic performers conforming more to pop music stereotypes. Kennedy, with his post-punk coiffure of hair-gelled spikes and *enfant terrible* attitude which passed muster as recherché punk, neatly filled the bill. In 1989 he made a solo appearance on the Kate Bush album *Sensual World* and began to play and record cross-overs between rock and classical music. In so doing he helped to bring into being a new genre of virtuoso classical/rock instrumentals, making a speciality of Jim Hendrix songs such as "Purple Haze", and devising a Doors concerto. In support of this new genre, Kennedy was photographed so as to project the quirky, no-compromise self-assurance of a pop star, yet combined with an informal documentary approach, long a feature of the photographs of jazz musicians.

EMI's great rival in marketing classic music, Deutsche Grammophon, which has long been entirely unapologetic in its unreconstructed approach to album sleeve design, responded by livening up Anne-Sophie Mutter 's image, projecting her as a Valkyrie sex goddess. Although this was a successful and, relatively speaking, fairly radical step for Deutsche Grammophon, Mutter has not been interested in engaging in the kind of musical cross-overs Kennedy has explored. In fact, she has been assiduous in preserving her classical gravitas, even championing the work of esoteric modern composers such as Penderecki, Lutoslawski and Wolfgang Rihm.

In 1995, Vanessa-Mae, aged just 16 and schooled by EMI (who had learned a thing or two from the success of Kennedy) racheted up the classical/pop cross-over by going full throttle for post-Madonna glamour. She appeared on the sleeve of *The Violin Player* in classical music's equivalent of a wet teeshirt contest, frolicking in the surf with her violin in the guise of Ibiza glamour. Such was the success of *The Violin Player* that she was nominated for the "Best Female Artist" in the BRIT awards, the first classical musician and instrumentalist to be cited for what is normally a mainstream pop award. Glamour, cross-overs and packaging had well and truely put a dent in the the conservative resistance of classical music. Even the virginal Charlotte Church would be given an art director's once-over to resemble an English woodland Flora, as painted by Victorian artist John William Waterhouse, on *Enchantment* (2001).

For an appreciation of the more uncompromising design principles associated with the classical/new music canon it is necessary to look to the small, specialist labels such as Swiss company HatHutRecords, launched in 1975 by Werner X. Uehlinger. Though HatHut began as a label with its roots in jazz (primarily of the more challenging free-form kinds), its catalogue now boasts such recognized Classical/New Music names as Stockhausen, Cage, Scelsi, Haubenstock-Ramati, Tenney, and Morton Feldman. Over the years, several new label names have appeared under the HatHut umbrella to indicate the changing styles and musical attitudes of its artists, including HatArt, HatOlogy and HatNoir. After more than twenty-five years and over three hundred LP and CD releases, HatHut has garnered a reputation as one of the most adventurous and important new music labels. Over the period of its existence it has had several art directors who have been encouraged to create their own coherent "look" for the label, making music and packaging an aesthetic whole for each release. A good instance of the purity of HatHut's approach to packaging is provided in Ann Holyoke Lehman's album sleeves with their austere lettering, uneasily poised between manufacturers' utilitarian identification labels and the conventions of high-concept typography. Perhaps, not unexpectedly, they are also reminiscent of the stripped-down typography which spells out the cryptic statements of American conceptual artist, Lawrence Weiner.

With its aspiration for high art values and desire to provide a home for esoteric, uncategorizable musical projects, HatHut remains as much a paragon of small label innovation in design as it does in the actual music.

7

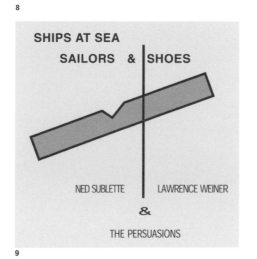

8

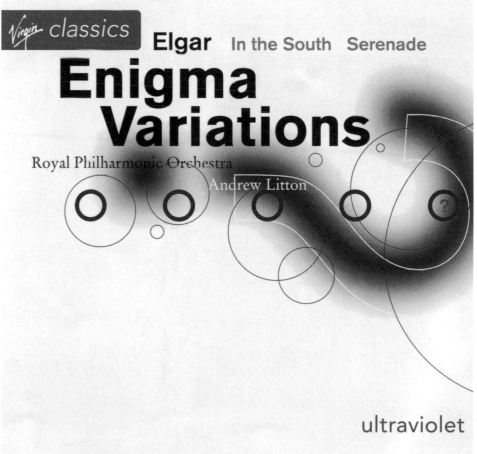

9

10

1   **Technique**, NEW ORDER, Factory, 1989.
    Design: Peter Saville Associates. Photography: Trevor Key.
2   **Joy**, GAY DAD, London, 1999.
    Art direction: Peter Saville. Design: Howard Wakefield, Paul
    Hetherington at Commercial Art.
3   **Super Highways**, THE OTHER TWO, London, 1999.
    Art direction: Peter Saville. Design: Howard Wakefield, Paul
    Hetherington at Commercial Art.

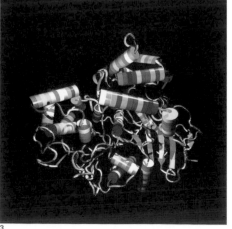

4

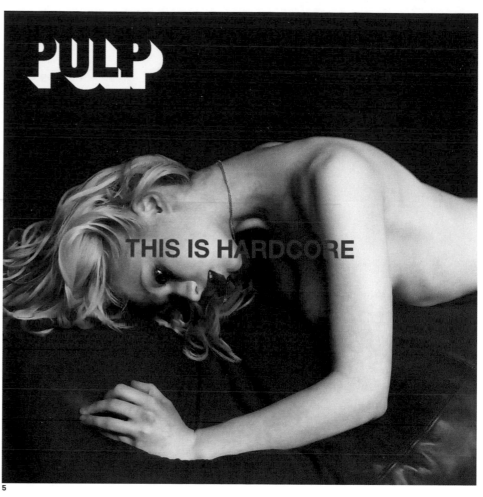

5

4   **Head Music**, SUEDE, Nude, 1999.
Design: Howard Wakefield and Paul Hetherington at
Commercial Art. Concept: Nick Knight, Peter Saville,
Brett Anderson.

5   **This is Hardcore**, PULP, Island, 1998.
Art direction: Peter Saville. Design: Howard Wakefield.
Photography: Horst Diekgerdes.

Peter Saville's contribution to music design lies in his combination of innovative typography with strong pictorial elements which he crops and frames with an elegant precision. His style neatly encapsulates the dandified alienation of English suburban youth culture in the Britpop era.

Peter Saville completed his design studies at Manchester Polytechnic in 1978. Despite being one of the founders of Factory Records, Saville moved to London the following year where he worked as art director for Virgin subsidiary Dindisc. Early work while at Dindisc included *Orchestral Manoeuvres in the Dark* (1980), Roxy Music's *Flesh + Blood* (1980) and King Crimson's *Discipline* (1981). In 1983 he would form his own design practice, Peter Saville Associates, with Brett Wickens. His new independence enabled him to clarify his relationship with Factory which was beginning to establish a reputation spearheaded by Joy Division and its subsequent reincarnation without Ian Curtis as New Order. Saville developed a signature style for both bands, designing *Unknown Pleasures* for Joy Division and *Power, Corruption and Lies* for New Order. By this time Factory was on the way to becoming the most successful independent record label ever to emerge from Manchester. It was at the centre of the late 1980s Manchester rave scene with the Hacienda Club and Happy Mondays on its books. Despite its successes, the company and the Manchester scene had suffered considerable set-backs by the end of the decade.

In addition to its work for Factory, Saville Associates undertook design work for a wide range of music world clients during the rest of the '80s, most notable being Ultravox's *Lament* (1984), Peter Gabriel's *So* (1986) and Wham's *Music from the Edge of Heaven* (1986). Saville's style of the period is characterized by sparse layouts combining sophisticated typographical elements and skilfully framed photographic images which were often restricted to black and white. The legibility of his designs signals the changing requirements caused by the switch from 12-inch vinyl album sleeve to the much smaller canvas of the 12-cm (4¾in) square compact disc jewelbox, which was well under way by the end of the decade.

In 1990 Saville joined Pentagram Design Ltd as a partner, Brett Wickens also joining as an associate. Pentagram was one of the most prestigious UK-based international design groups and numbered architect guru Theo Crosby amongst its founders.

At the time a Blueprint journalist commented that Saville and Pentagram were an unlikely pairing, and one which would have been unthinkable five years previously. As a designer working within a large international practice, Saville's skills were spread much more widely than before and for a while his individual identity was somewhat submerged. As well as designing for numerous fashion companies, he was for a time house designer for the Whitechapel Gallery, London, and also worked for the Pompidou Centre, Paris.

Saville's importance as a designer for the music industry was re-emphasized in the mid-1990s by his association with bands Pulp and Suede for whom he designed a succession of covers establishing strong visual identities for both. He began to develop an increasingly charged chromatic computer-generated illustrative style with covers like Gay Dad's *Leisure Noise* and the Other Two's *Super Highways*, both for London Records.

1

2

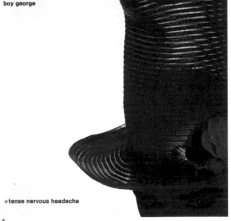

3

4

Nick Knight is a photographer of extraordinary elegance, even when elegance is under duress. Although prized by the likes of Christian Dior and Lancôme, what has caught the spirit of the 1990s most eloquently has been his ability to find beauty and strength of character in less ordinary places – as in his collaboration with fashion designer Alexander McQueen on photographs of disabled models which were featured hugely in the Tate Modern's "Century City: Art and Culture in the Modern Metropolis" exhibition in 2001. As a fashion photographer he has worked for many clients, both fashion houses and magazines such as *i-D*, *Vogue*, *Dazed and Confused*, *The Face*, and *Visionaire*. His output has also included a steady stream of commissions for album sleeves. To these he has brought the ability to form striking images out of simple means, an ability which has made him an invaluable collaborator for album sleeve designers. He has produced sleeves for, among many others, Björk, Bryan Ferry, Paul Weller, George Michael, David Bowie, and Massive Attack. More elaborate than most, and among his most stunning of his '90s images, is the portrait of Björk produced for her album *Homogenic* (1997). Concealed within the CD jewelcase is an extraordinary fold-out geisha image of the Icelandic singer, again devised in collaboration with fashion designer McQueen. Simpler, but equally memorable, is his stark, almost-silhouette image of Seal which appeared on the Michael Nash-designed album *1994*.

Knight was born in 1958, in London. He studied photography at Bournemouth & Poole College of Art & Design, on the south coast of England. When he left art school in 1982 he began to work for *i-D* magazine. He published his first book of photographs, *Skinheads*, the same year. Knight's big break came when, for *i-D*'s fifth anniversary issue, editor Terry Jones commissioned him to photograph one hundred people who had appeared in the magazine since its inception. He was originally to shoot only ten of the hundred, but he persuaded Jones to let him shoot them all. "Between us we worked out a very stripped-down way of photographing people: a white background, no assistant, two rolls of Tri-X, one 500W bulb on the background and one 500W bulb as my lighting, and half an hour for each sitter. It was a really radical, new approach to photography. In a way it was very good. It taught me how to light, or at least allowed me to perceive lighting, and it gave me an insight into a different form of photography. That was useful in terms of my development."

The project led to Knight's first foray into fashion for designer Yohji Yamamoto, who encouraged him to work in colour. "We were doing castings in the street, finding people in Portobello Road and Petticoat Lane, and it all felt real and happening and very exciting. So for three years that was my schooling in fashion."

Although Knight is usually thought of as the quintessential '90s photographer, less prescriptively he sees himself as a creator of images. When working for *i-D* he experimented with Scitex's pioneering digital printing technology, and subsequently has used his photographs as a starting point for digital manipulation by Quantel Paintbox and Adobe Photoshop, producing images which seamlessly blend painterly and photographic elements, and intensifying his use of striking colour which is a hallmark of his style. Asked about this at the end of the '90s, he responded: "Imagery is what it's about, and imagists will be the people who go into the next century. A camera will just be another tool to produce images, out of a range of tools." Some of the most innovative results from employing this attitude have come from his collaborations with Peter Saville. In particular, the series of sleeve images produced for Suede, partially based on the paintings of German artist, Paul Wunderlich.

1   **Mezzanine**, MASSIVE ATTACK, Warners, 1998.
      Photography: Nick Knight. Design and art direction: Tom
      Hingston, Robert del Naja.
2   **Homogenic**, BJÖRK, One Little Indian/Elektra, 1997.
      Photography: Nick Knight. Design: Paul White at Me Company.
      Styling: Alexander McQueen, Katy England.
3   **Coming Up**, SUEDE, Nude, 1996.
      Photography: Nick Knight. Design: Nick Knight, Peter Saville,
      Brett Anderson.
4   **Tense Nervous Headache**, BOY GEORGE, Virgin, 1988.
      Design: David James. Photography: Nick Knight.
5   **Seal**, SEAL, ZTT/Sire, 1991.
      Design: Michael Nash. Photography: Nick Knight. [opposite]

1 **Pet Shop Boys, actually**, PET SHOP BOYS, Parlophone, 1987.
Design: Mark Farrow. Photography: Eric Watson.
2 **Everything Must Go**, MANIC STREET PREACHERS,
Sony, 1996.
Design: Mark Farrow. Photography: Rankin.

Pet Shop Boys, actually.

1

2

a *deconstruction classic* remixed by hardfloor

3 **Is There Anybody Out There?**, BASSHEADS,
Deconstruction, 1996.
Design: Mark Farrow. Photography: Christopher Griffiths.

4 **Style**, ORBITAL, FFRR-London, 1999.
Design: Mark Farrow. Photography: Louise Kelly.

5 **Ladies and Gentleman We are Floating in Space**,
SPIRITUALIZED, Dedicated, 1997.
Concept: Mark Farrow. Design: Farrow Design/Spaceman.

3

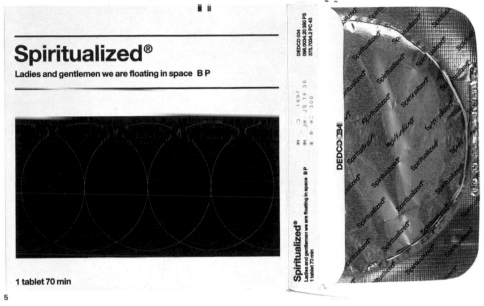

5

4

Mark Farrow was born and studied in Manchester. During the early 1980s he was part of the vibrant music scene centred on the independent Manchester record label Factory. He designed album covers for Factory acts Stockholm Monsters, Durutti Column, Section 25, Ad Infinitum, Shark Vegas, Life and A Certain Ratio as well as flyers for the Hacienda. In 1986 he moved to London and subsequently launched his own studio, Mark Farrow Design, based in Clerkenwell. Farrow was responsible for the look of Mike Pickering's dance label DeConstruction (now part of BMG Europe) where he designed for K-Klass, Bassheads and others. He has also produced compilation sleeves for 1990s superclub Cream.

One of the most elegant and cryptic of designers, Farrow always tries to reduce his designs to a few carefully honed elements. Typical of his approach to design was his response when given the task of adding to the tradition of extravagant sleeves of British band Spiritualized, led by Jason Pierce. Previous Spiritualized sleeves had included glow-in-the-dark packaging and eccentrically shaped CD boxes. For their fourth album *Ladies and Gentlemen We are Floating in Space* (1997) Farrow produced a CD which was a carefully detailed pastiche of pharmaceutical packaging with its dosage instructions and prescription sticker. It is one of the very few CD sleeves to have been put together by a pharmaceutical packaging company, and it strikes a chord with the early Damian Hirst glass vitrines filled with pharmaceutical products. Both celebrate the

aesthetic pleasures of the synthetic emotions industry, a decorative theme Hirst also employed for his one-time Notting Hill restaurant Pharmacy. This is no coincidence as Farrow's approach to album sleeve design often draws on the same Conceptual Art sources identified with the '90s "yBa" names ("young British artists") like Hirst, Sarah Lucas and Tracy Emin.

While still in Manchester Farrow's sparse, elegant style attracted the attention of Pet Shop Boys Neil Tennant and Chris Lowe. During the recording of their first album *Please* (1985) Farrow was working in their management office and came up with a white sleeve featuring a tiny picture of Neil Tennant and Chris Lowe draped with white towels which had already been printed in *Smash Hits*' news section. Farrow's approach was so much to their taste that he became the Pet Shop Boys' designer of choice, designing virtually all of the duo's album and single sleeves, tour programmes, and other ephemera since they first formed. He has created a succession of minimal white covers with pared-down portrait photographs of Tennant and Lowe. The most memorable is *Pet Shop Boys, actually* (1987) in which Lowe and Tennant are caught apparently off-guard in characteristic style: Tennant yawning, Lowe staring vacantly into the camera. The photograph was taken by Cindy Palmano in the summer of 1987 during a video shoot at the Brixton Academy for which Tennant and Lowe were required to dressed in tuxedos. The photograph seems to sum up the detached air the Pet Shop

Boys habitually projected. The disassociated sense of irony is elegantly reinforced by Farrow's understated typographical styling and the scaling and cropping of the double portrait. Among the other titles that Farrow designed for the Pet Shop Boys are *Disco* (1990), *Discography: The Complete Singles Collection* (1991), *Disco 2* (1994), *Alternative* (1995) and *Introspective* (1995), as well as singles sleeves, where *Being Boring* (1990) with portraits by the Douglas Brothers is particularly notable.

Farrow's quasi-conceptual approach to the old conundrum of how to make a portrait cover interesting has been taken a step still further in his work for the Manic Street Preachers. He has produced album designs for the band since *Everything Must Go* (1996), and his design solution for this is his most extreme neo-conceptual parody to date. He placed framed photographs of the three band members on a shelf against a blue wall and tacked a label printed with the band's name and the album title to the wall above the shelf, and then photographed the whole as an "installation". He continues to design in his signature cerebral, "fine art" style.

1   **Poster: Alex Reece at Wasserwork**, Bern 1997.
     Design: Büro Destruct.
2   **Hip Hop Don't Stop**, VARIOUS ARTISTS, Solid State, 1997.
     Design: Peter Chadwick at Zip Design.

1

2

It was inevitable that as the 1990s developed a strand of album sleeve design would emerge which set itself very much against the highly mediated productions of digital media with their manipulated photographic images and synthetic, layered spaces. Instead of being attracted to complexity, super-dense simulations and multi-dimensional spaces, some preferred alternatives which involved the most direct making processes. And for some the repudiation of digitalism was not just a response based on fashionable dissent, but had ideological meaning too.

The most obvious riposte to AppleMac design was hand-drawn, table-top illustration. Popular sources for this kind of sleeve design were anything with low art credentials: naive art, thrift store paintings, cute Japanese cartoon figures, the street shorthand of graffiti. So too were a diverse range of artists who are acknowledged masters of the throw-away, short-hand notation, from Picasso and Matisse to A.R. Penck, Keith Haring and Martin Kippenberger. At the most extreme limit of this tendency was the avowedly minimal line drawing, most compelling and effective when showing zero pretension to sophisticated representational skills. This is a reversion to a vocabulary with the directness of a doodle on a paper napkin. Generally speaking, of course, this apparently unaffected directness is deceptive. The image on the sleeve of Tortoise's *TNT* (1996) drawn on an empty CD index card by band member John Herndon tantalizes with its

knowing/naif air. Part of its attraction is the conundrum of whether it really is a quick doodle by the untutored hand of an amateur.

One of the most notable exponents of the knowing/naif approach to album sleeve design during the '90s was Kim Hiorthøy whose minimalist approach graces the album sleeves of Norwegian electronic music specialist Rune Grammofon. Born in 1971 and a Fine Art graduate, Hiorthøy was, by his mid-20s, already causing a stir with his streamlined, understated sleeve designs with their fey undertow, some reminiscent of the marginalia of Edvard Munch, particularly those for Chocolate Overdose. More recently, Hiorthøy has made a name for himself as a recording artist and his attitude to his new work

Laurent Garnier
greed + the man with the red face
(part two)

3

illuminates his approach to design: "In some ways there's no difference working with different media. Because you kind of use the same place in your head. You have some kind of abstract measures for when something works or not. It has to do with weight, flow, rhythm, mood, warm, cold, quirky and strange or hopping along or strolling gracefully."

Another distinctive contributor to the drawn sleeve is the French illustrator Seb Jarnot who is particularly associated with Laurent Garnier, the French-born DJ who was involved in the "Madchester" rave scene in the late 1980s, launching his career at the Hacienda Club. While running the Wake Up Club in Paris, he began recording tracks on the FNAC label. Following the

demise of FNAC, he and a friend, Eric Morand, started their own label, F Communications. A string of recent Garnier releases have featured minimal line drawings by Jarnot including *Greed* and *The Man with The Red Face* (both 2000). Jarnot has also produced drawings for the sleeves of Llorca's *Newcomer* (2001') and Ludovic Navarre aka St. Germain's *From Detroit to St. Germain* (1999) for Garnier's label.

Closer to graffiti, and associated hip-hop, are the angular drawing styles of London-based Will Barras and Lopetz, a member of design group Büro Destruct. Formed in Bern in 1994 Büro Destruct, like Barras, cut its teeth on club flyers, the former making a considerable name for itself by crossing the music/flyer style with Swiss design sensibility.

4

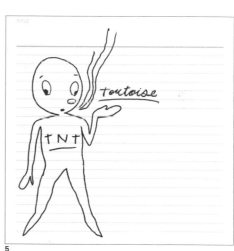

5

3 **Greed + The Man with the Red Face (Part Two)**, LAURENT GARNIER, F Communication, 2000.
Design: Seb Jarnot.

4 **Dingle Doodies**, CHOCOLATE OVERDOSE, Rune Grammofon, 1999.
Design: Kim Hiorthøy.

5 **TNT**, TORTOISE, Thrill Jockey, 1998.
Design: John Herndon.

1   **Endtroducing**, DJ SHADOW, Mo'Wax, 1996.
Design: Ben Drury, Will Bunkhead. Photography: Will Bunkhead, Barney Bunkhead.

2   **David Axelrod**, DAVID AXELROD, Mo'Wax, 2001.
Design: Ben Drury.

3   **Melodius Thunk**, ANDREA PARKER, Mo'Wax, 1996.
Design: Ben Drury and Will Bankhead. Illustration: She One.

4   **Push the Button**, MONEY MARK, Mo'Wax, 1998.
Design and photography: Ben Drury.

5   **Psyence Fiction**, UNKLE, Mo'Wax, 1998. [opposite]
Design: Ben Drury.

Ben Drury was born in 1972, in Southampton, England. He spent most of his childhood in Cornwall. After studying on the foundation course at Falmouth College of Art and Design he moved on to St. Martin's School of Art in London where he studied between 1991 and 1994. He began to design album sleeves while still at art school in collaboration with fellow-student and photographer William Bankhead. Among their clients were Global Communication, Fat Cat Records and music and sound recording independent Irdial Discs.

Drury is particularly celebrated for his art direction of British record label, Mo' Wax Records. During the 1990s the company's output was prodigious for such a small label, and Drury had overseen some 120 releases by the end of the decade. He is best known for the sleeve design of albums such as DJ Shadow's *Endtroducing* and Unkle's *Psyence Fiction*. His designs are usually realized in collaboration with others, like Futura (Drury subsequently produced a book on his work) and, of course, with his favourite photographer William Bankhead.

Mo' Wax was founded by James Lavelle, remixer, DJ and one half of Unkle, in 1992, when he was only 18 years old. Mo' Wax is one of those legendary niche labels which enjoy mercurial rises thanks to the excellence of their musical track record. Lavelle's drive, willingness to gamble with innovative talent and mania for novelty have all been distinguishing features of the Mo' Wax catalogue. The company's releases are a study in

inventive CD package design. The standard plastic jewelbox container is dismissed out of hand. Instead, almost any selection of Mo' Wax releases give the refreshing impression that the entire world has been scoured for new ways to package a CD. There is no doubt that Lavelle must be given considerable credit for this aspect of the company's releases: the constant development of new packaging solutions, the drive to try new materials, novel printing and embossing processes all reflect his wish to individuate each new release. Novelties have even stretched to action figures to accompany a new release, notably the alien figures featured on Unkle sleeves.

The label has launched an impressive and diverse roster of talent which includes DJ Shadow, Attica Blues, Rob D., Step, Palm Skin Productions and Andrea Parker. Having built an enviable reputation as an innovative label with a gift for breaking new talent, it was inevitable that the company would attract the attention of the major labels. Lavelle sold Mo' Wax to A&M records only three years after its inception, and when A&M closed in 1998 the label became part of the Beggars Banquet group. Despite these changes in ultimate ownership, Lavelle has stayed at the helm throughout the turmoil, continuing to release new projects.

Drury's involvement with Mo' Wax began when his collaborator Will Bankhead was asked to take photographs of Lavelle for *i-D* magazine in 1994. They became good friends and as a result Lavelle asked him and Drury to take over design for the

label. Bankhead provided the photography and darkroom techniques while Drury focused on the overall packaging look. Bankhead collaborated on all Drury's early designs for the label, including sleeves for Money Mark, Attica Blues, Sam Sever and Air. After a year or so he left to develop other areas of his work, and Drury became the label's sole art director. Drury still collaborates with Bankhead, whether designing for Mo' Wax, or for other labels. He runs a design studio in South London with two assistants, one for Mo' Wax work, the second for other clients.

2

3

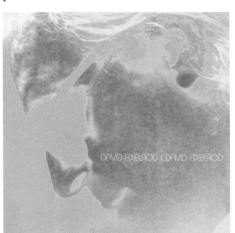

1

money mark
push the button

4

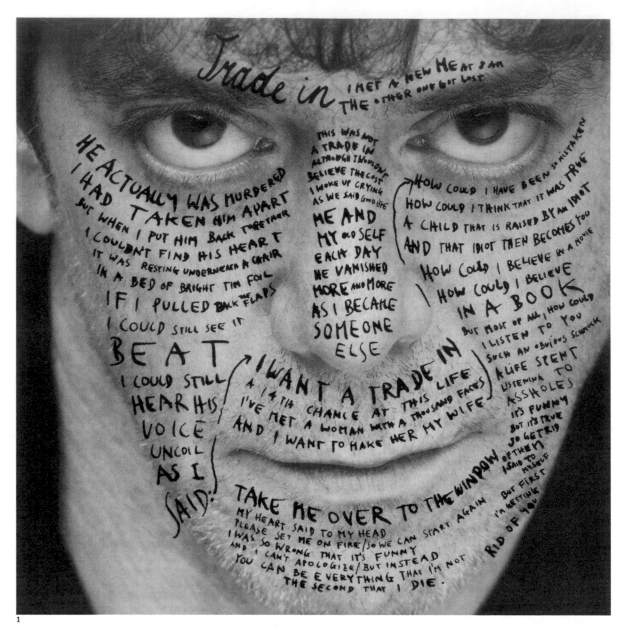

1

1 **Set the Twilight Reeling**, LOU REED, Warner Bros, 1997.
Design: Stefan Sagmeister, Veronica Oh. Photography: Timothy
Greenfield Sanders. Illustration: Tony Fitzpatrick.
2 **The Truth Hurts**, PRO PAIN, Energy, 1994.
Design: Stefan Sagmeister.

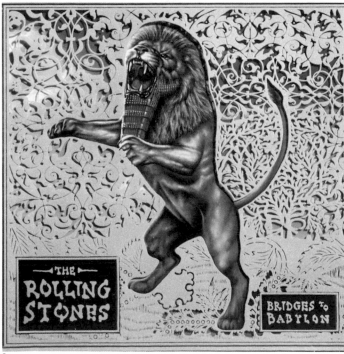

2

3 **Bridges to Babylon**, THE ROLLING STONES, Virgin, 1997.
Design: Stefan Sagmeister, Hjati Karlsson. Illustration: Kevin
Murrya, Gerard Howlands, Alan Ayers.
4 **Fantastic Spikes Through Balloon**, SKELETON KEY,
Capitol, 1997.
Design: Stefan Sagmeister, Hjati Karlsson. Photography:
Tom Schierlitz.

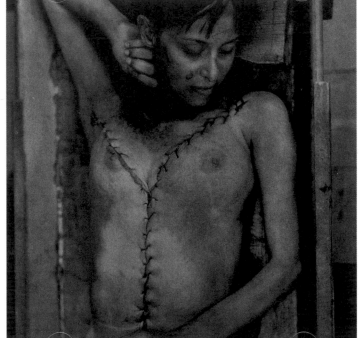

3

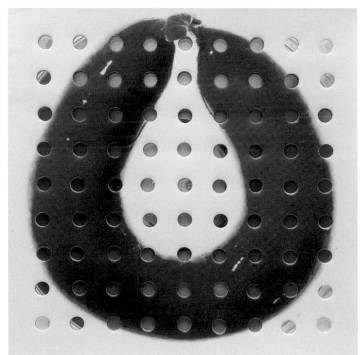

4

5

5   **Feelings**, DAVID BYRNE, Luaka Bop, 1997.
Design: Stefan Sagmeister, Hjati Karlsson. Photography:
Tom Schierlitz.
Models: Yuji Yoshimoto.

Stefan Sagmeister was born in 1961 in Bregenz, Austria. He launched his New York design studio Sagmeister Inc. in 1993. His remit was simple: "We only do music we like. It's not because we're so brilliant that we can make that choice It's more because... we only have three people here, myself, a designer and an intern, so we can afford to do what we want". His studio quickly became recognised as the most innovative New York-based specialist design studio catering for the music industry. Although Sagmeister's work for rock music luminaries Rolling Stones, David Byrne, Lou Reed and Aerosmith has brought his studio great kudos, his designs for lesser well-known clients have also sparkled, being immensely innovative and bringing a radical, fresh eye to CD packaging. He has been nominated four times for Grammies and has won many international design awards. Some of his more excessive concepts have earned him a variety of epithets including "genius", "maniac", "brilliant", "tactical" and "disgusting".

Sagmeister studied for an MFA in graphic design from the University of Applied Arts in Vienna. He subsequently studied for a master's degree at the Pratt Institute in New York while on a Fulbright scholarship. After leaving the Pratt Institute he went to work for the design studio M&Co., the design studio of Tibor Kalman (1949–99). Established by Kalman in 1979, the multidisciplinary M&Co. was at one point known as "the revolving door of graphic design" due to Kalman's restless perfectionism. His clients

ranged from the New York State Urban Development Corp. to Talking Heads, for which he and Carol Bokuniewicz designed the album sleeve for *Remain in Light* (1980). Kalman's love of brash vernacular signage, found images and humour were all characteristics which Sagmeister would later develop in his own studio's practice. Kalman closed M&Co in 1991 to launch the magazine *Colours* for Mario Toscani, creative director of Benetton, as an embodiment of the company's radical chic ethos. Sagmeister went on to be the creative director at the Hong Kong office of the advertising agency Leo Burnett before returning to New York to launch Sagmeister Inc. in 1993.

Typical of Sagmeister's inventive take on CD design is the grid of punched holes in the packaging for Skeleton Key's *Fantastic Spikes Through Balloon* (1997); as is his insertion of one of Jamie Block's favourite Rothmans Red cigarettes in the spine of the CD jewelbox of the promotional copies of his album *Timing is Everything*; as is his action-figure effigy of David Byrne for *Feelings* (1997) with its interchangeable sad and happy faces. Another celebrated design is Lou Reed's Grammy-nominated *Set the Twilight Reeling* (1987) with its hand-drawn lettering crawling over Reed's face.

Fearing that his work was losing its innovative edge, and inspired by the flexibility and experimentation of students he met when teaching a design workshop, he cleared his schedules from October 2000 to have a "year without clients". One of the exercises he set for

himself while on his sabbatical was to create a CD cover for a fictional band in just three hours. Faced by the year's layoff, Sagmeister's principle collaborator at Sagmeister Inc., Hjati Karlsson, launched his own design company Karlssonwilker Inc. with partner Jan Wilker. Sagmeister returned to designing for clients in late 2001.

Tomato came into being in 1991. The "art collective" is as famous for its attitude as it is for the images. It has produced for numerous heavyweight, anti-Globalization-activists'-hatelist multinationals of the likes of Sony, Adidas, Pepsi, Levis and Nike, all anxious to have tomato mystique rubbing off on their products. John Warwicker, tomato's ringmaster and polemicist, met Richard Smith and Karl Hyde when they were in an 1980s band called Freur, launched in 1981 while Hyde and Smith were at college in Cardiff. The group signed to CBS in 1983, and were one-hit wonders with their single *Doot Doot*. After Freur folded, vocalist Hyde and guitarist Smith formed Underworld with DJ Darren Emerson at the height of the rave scene (Emerson quit after their third album release). In 1991 they again linked up with Warwicker to launch a multimedia design group dubbed "tomato", with Steve Barker, Dirk van Dooren, Simon Taylor and Graham Wood. They were later joined by Jason Kedgly in 1994 and Michael Horsham in 1996.

Warwicker was born in 1955, he studied design at both undergraduate and postgraduate level at Camberwell School of Art. His 1980s solo career as an album sleeve designer was of some distinction. He was head of art and video at A&M Records from 1985 to '88, including a spell in California, subsequently becoming creative director at Vivid I-D from 1988 to 1991, where album sleeve veteran Nick Egan also worked. His designs included sleeves for Iggy Pop and the Rolling Stones.

Since its inception, tomato has undertaken relatively few outside album sleeve commissions, although Simon Taylor has had a close working relationship with acid jazz combos Galliano and United Future Organization, and various tomato members have worked on packaging for Unknown Public. However, few design collectives have produced an in-house band as successful as Underworld, a techno outfit which left its mark on the electronic scene of the 1990s and is still enjoying huge success. The trio's first album *Dubnobasswithmyheadman* (1993) was immediately heralded as one of the best dance albums of the decade. The sleeves for all Underworld releases have been designed by tomato. The sleeve for the first album was originally produced as part of a Hyde/Warwicker cut-up concrete poetry collaboration *mmm...*

skyscraper i love you (published 1994) and is dominated by Taylor's handprint contribution. With its 1996 single, *Born Slippy*, Underworld became one of the few techno outfits to break through to mainstream audiences. The single was taken from its second album *Second Toughest in the Infants* and featured on the soundtrack of the movie *Trainspotting*. Their third '90s album *Beaucoup Fish* was released on V2 Music in the spring of 1999. Jason Kegley made a plastic sculpture and photographed it for the cover. When asked to explain it, the members of tomato demurred. "Sometimes there's not much more to it than that," confided Warwicker. "We don't ever engage in post-rationalization. Things are sometimes just what they are."

Tomato represents some of the '90s most characteristic creative impulses, both in popular music and design. Firstly tomato represents the postmodern dethroning of high art, and the remaking of culture as fluid, do-it-yourself, immersive. Its creed is the interdisciplinary impulse to blur the boundaries between art and design (the "we're all artists now" syndrome) and, further, to bring the sonic and visual arts into

closer touch. Allied to this is the contemporary belief in professional administrations as the best way to achieve aims through semi-permanent, self-declared, work-oriented communities of a kind that have both the Beatles and the Pre-Raphaelite Brotherhood as distant ancestors. At the same time the chosen name "tomato" which, we are told, "is dictated by reference to a family of hormones – to/ma/to – found within the cerebral cortex of people who are susceptible to visions, waking dreams, sensations and feelings of weightlessness" owes more to the '90s habit of corporate branding than an acknowledgment of artistic programme or allegiances.

slack hands

GALLIANO

a.01. slack hands
a.02. slack hands (bonus beats)
a.03. slack hands (aphex mix)

United Future Organization *Loud Minority*

2

1 **Slack Hands**, GALLIANO, Talkin' Loud/Mercury, 1997.
Design: Simon Taylor at tomato.
2 **Loud Minority**, UNITED FUTURE ORGANIZATION,
Exceptional, 1992.
Design: Simon Taylor at tomato.

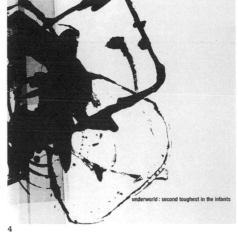

underworld : second toughest in the infants

4

3 **Dubnobasswithmyheadman**, UNDERWORLD, Junior Boys
Own, 1993.
Design: tomato.

4 **Second Toughest in the Infants**, UNDERWORLD,
Wax Trax, 1996.
Design: tomato.

3

5

5 **Steel Wheels**, THE ROLLING STONES, CBS/
Rolling Stones, 1989.
Design: John Warwicker.

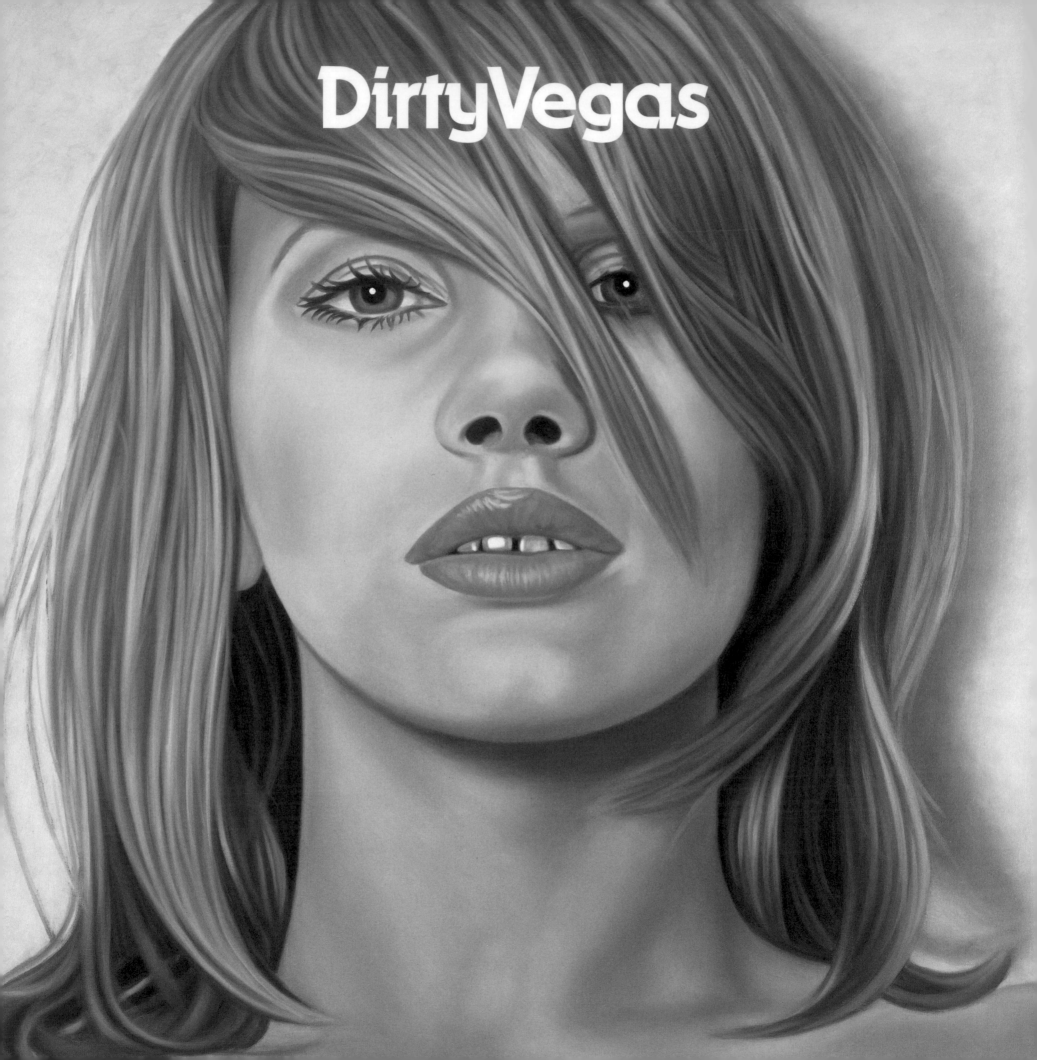

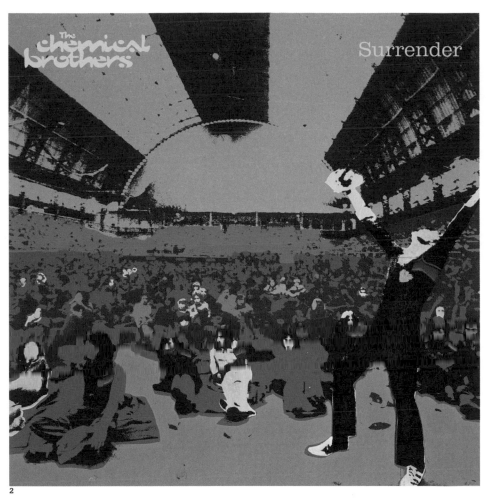

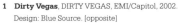

1 **Dirty Vegas**, DIRTY VEGAS, EMI/Capitol, 2002.
Design: Blue Source. [opposite]

2 **Surrender**, THE CHEMICAL BROTHERS, Virgin/
Astral Weeks, 1999.
Design: Blue Source.

3 **Different Class**, PULP, Island, 1995.
Design: Blue Source.

4 **Remedy**, BASEMENT JAXX, XL, 1999.
Design: Blue Source.

5 **A Rush of Blood to the Head**, COLDPLAY,
Parlophone/Capitol, 2002.
Design: Blue Source.

Blue Source, an upstart design company not above describing "very noisy parties" as one of their attributes, is characteristic of the 1990s breed of London-based studios who explicitly link their creative endeavours to music (music being, in their words "the core of our identity and aesthetic"). Blue Source, founded by Seb and Leigh Marling, is one of the most accomplished of the newer cross-discipline design studios with a playful, eclectic attitude to design for music. The company is well known for its clever recontextualization of stock photography and wide-ranging network of individually creative collaborators, one of the most well-known being photographer Rankin. He has worked on Blue Source album sleeve projects as disparate as Pulp's multisleeved *Different Class* (1995) and Basement Jaxx's *Remedy* (1999).

The success of *Different Class* neatly demonstrates how it is possible to rescue a potentially messy and impractical project. Donald Milne and Rankin had been commissioned to produce life-size black-and-white photographs of the members of Pulp which were then photographed as part of a variety of everyday situations. Another constraint was that the Pulp logo devised by Designers Republic was considered to be an album sleeve fixture. Blue Source arrived on the scene with the sleeve half finished. They devised a wallet to contain a final selection of twelve of the photographs, any one of which could be displayed through the cut-out window in the wallet to complete the cover image. (The idea of the alternative covers was subsequently dropped to save costs, and the wedding party photograph became the fixed cover image.) Arguably more recognizably Rankin are the "his" and "her" photographs he took for the sleeve of the single "Something Changed" taken from the album, as is the human-flesh-as-rolling-dunes image he helped to produce for Basement Jaxx's *Remedy*. Despite its popularity, both Blue Source and Basement Jaxx claim not to have been very happy with the way the sleeve turned out, Seb Marling's comment on this pointing up how fragile the relationship between recording artists and design company can become sometimes: "I think it is fair to say we had different ideas. They knew what they wanted which was very simple and straight up. We thought differently...and wanted to lead them somewhere else. Much debate was had and I think the sleeve is a product of that tension. I'm not sure any of us came out totally satisfied at the time but a lot of people like it."

An entirely different Blue Source sleeve is The Chemical Brothers' *Surrender* (1999), featuring a suite of silkscreen reinterpretations of stock photographs by Kate Gibb. The audience cover image was taken in the Olympia Grand Hall during The Great British Music Festival held over the New Year period in 1975. Blue Source has produced a number of sleeves for The Chemical Brothers relying on the recontextualization of stock photographs. Gibb's silkscreens, with their retro look of primitive, hand-cut stencil underprinting, are perhaps the most notable.

Blue Source's claim to be multi-disciplinary was extended when directorial team Rob Leggat and Leigh Marling launched Blue Source into video promos production. In their first year they directed four with great assurance, with clients including Fatboy Slim and Dirty Vegas. Their promo for Avalanche's "Since I left You" won MTV's best video award in 2002. Leigh Marling comments: "Record companies are increasingly treating their 'product' as brands. Who isn't? And a lot of our previous work in the industry has been employed in creating a strong visual identity for these acts. But structurally record companies mostly seem to operate with different people responsible for the promo and the artwork. It's currently unusual for us to be commissioned for both...although we would obviously love to get involved with projects in that way."

As Blue Source expand so inevitably does its client base. A sense of humour did not desert Leggat and Leigh Marling when asked to direct the "Where's The Cheese At" video for Pizza Hut. And only a subtle line in irony could lead Leigh Marling to explain the aim of a poster campaign for Adidas sports shoes as "to create beautiful images based on Adidas footwear technology."

1

2

3

4

1 **Exterminator,** PRIMAL SCREAM, Creation, 2000.
Design: Julian House at Intro.
2 **Vanishing Point**, PRIMAL SCREAM, Creation, 1997.
Design: Matthew Rudd, Julian House at Intro.
3 **The Noise Made by People**, BROADCAST, Warp, 2000.
Design Julian House at Intro.
4 **Life**, SIMPLY RED, Warner, 1995.
Design and art direction: Mat Cook at Intro. Photography: Zanna.
5 **The Singles 81-85**, DEPECHE MODE, Mute Records, 1998.
Design: Mat Cook at Intro. [opposite]

Intro is a London-based multi-disciplined design company producing commercials, title sequences, music promos and websites as well as designing for album sleeves. Intro's creative director, Adrian Shaughnessy, has a particularly strong association with album sleeve design, both as a practical exercise and as a theorized exercise in cultural politics. From the latter point of view he proposes the album sleeve designer as a cultural cartographer mapping the terrain in support of innovative music and subcultures. This approach informs *Sampler* and *Sampler 2*, Intro's two books of selected 1990s sleeve designs. ("They give us a chance to talk to other designers whose work we admire and who in the normal course of events we might not meet. It also allows us to express our views on design and the workings of the record industry.") Intro has created sleeves, music videos and websites for many recording acts including Howie B, Roni Size, Aphex Twin, Talvin Singh, Depeche Mode, Luke Slater, Stereolab, Simply Red, Primal Scream, Robbie Williams and Chemical Brothers. Among early work to make their name were their designs for reggae label Blood & Fire. Intro has had a particularly long-standing relationship with Primal Scream which started with their *Vanishing Point* album (1996). Intro designer Julian House devised the sleeve for the single *Kill All Hippies* as well as the now-legendary vowel-less typography for the album from which it was taken, *XTRMNTR* (2000). The Richard Hamilton influence on the *XTRMNTR* sleeve has been acknowledged by House, it being redolent of Hamilton's mid-1960s collaged interiors, such as *Interior II* (1964), in which disparate photographic cutouts, including movie stills, are combined with other elements, painted or modelled in relief, to create composite scenes in which the individual elements still retain their discreet identities. Primal Scream's relationship with Intro is highly emblematic because of the terms such as "subversion" and "provocation" that

adhere to the band, useful when trying to balance the contradictions inherent in a desire for radicality, an avoidance of the international capitalist machine and the exigencies of being a busy design company.

Intro's creative director Adrian Shaughnessy is a self-taught graphic designer. After spells with a variety of design companies, he found himself working alongside future business partner Katy Richardson. Being less than happy with their employer they decided to launch their own company with the mission statement "aesthetics first". Intro proclaims an eclectic approach ("we declare war on the dull and the dismal"), hence the appropriateness of a portmanteau name like Intro. Not too grand to coordinate *Simply Red – Greatest Hits* (1996), Intro prides itself on its co-option of a wide range of sources and styles, from mixed-media sculpture, through varied tropes of modernism, to Op-Art, Pop Art and Saul Bass-inspired soundtrack pastiches. To all of them they have brought an assured, professional touch.

Besides their many music world clients, Intro has produced designs for many other fields: Penguin Books, the Extreme Sports Channel, the Playstation 2. Intro was one of the first '90s design companies to fully embrace the concept of "cross-media", working in new media, video and film and as well as in the more traditional graphic forms. The company has won Best Design Team on two occasions at CADS, the UK music industry design awards. In 2001, in acknowledgment of their importance, Laurence King published a survey of their design, *Display Copy Only* which richly displays the full gamut of their output.

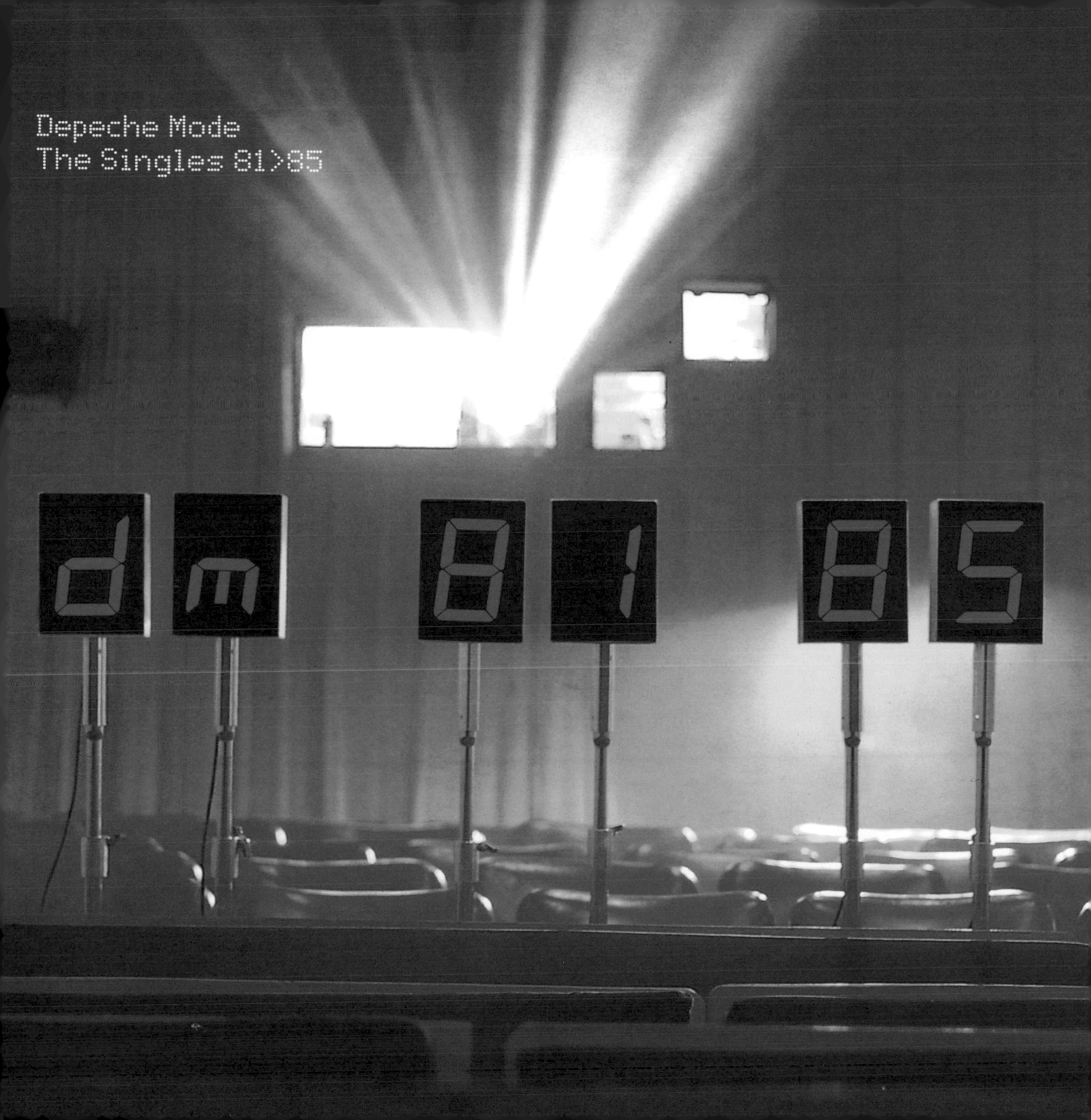
Depeche Mode
The Singles 81>85
dm 81 85

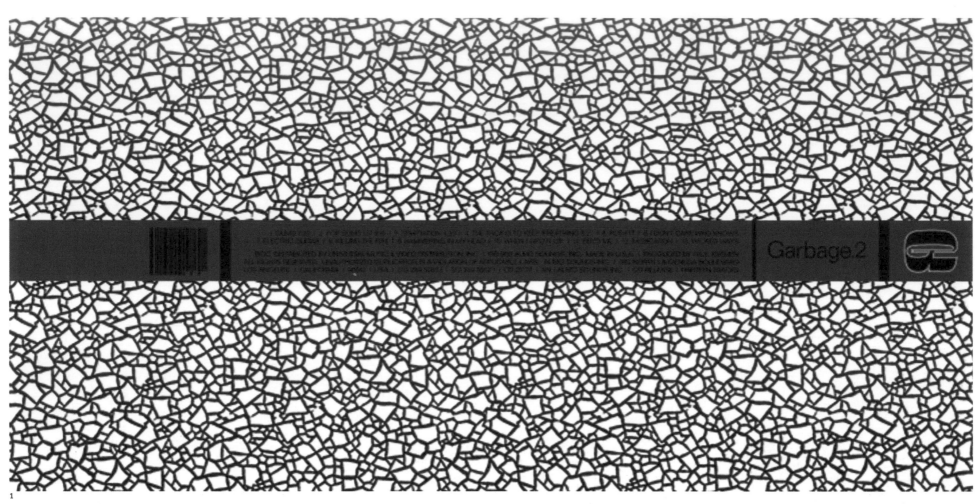

1

2

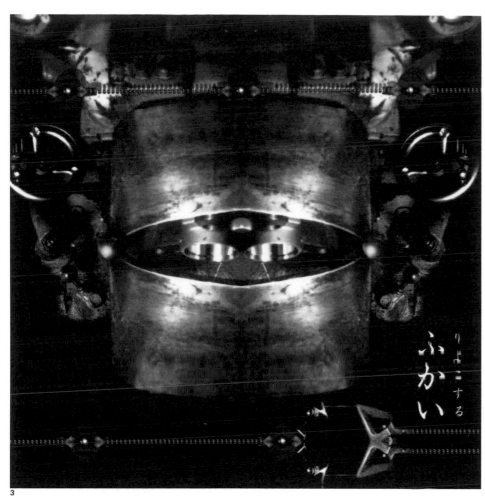

3

5

4

1 **Garbage 2**, GARBAGE, Mushroom/Almo Sounds, 1998.
Design: Carlos Segura.

2 **Machina II: The Friends and Enemies of Modern Music**,
SMASHING PUMPKINS, Constantinople (Q101 Radio), 2000.
Design: Carlos Segura.

3 **Mobile**, DEEP, Thickface, 1996.
Design: Jim Marcus at Segura Inc.

4 **Transmission From Self Pollution Radio**, PEARL JAM,
Q101 Radio, 1995.
Design: Carlos Segura

5 **Retro 101: Volume 1**, VARIOUS ARTISTS, Rhino, 1999.
Design: Segura Inc.

Segura Inc. is a paradigmatic example of a 1990s integrated design and communications company working for, and having its roots in design for music, although still supplying design and new media communication solutions for a diverse range of clients operating in many different business fields. The company is a valued supplier of design solutions for record companies from A&M, Geffen, Island, MCA, Organico Records, Synergy Records, Tommy Boy Records, Tooth & Nail Records, to Virgin and Warner Media, as well as for its own label Thickface.

Carlos Segura was born in 1956 in Santiago, Cuba. He arrived in the USA in 1965 and settled in the exile Cuban community in Miami. Like many members of the Cuban diaspora, his feelings about Cuba are equivocal: "Cuba gave me and my family nothing but shit. I am who I am today because of what America permitted me to be. Having said that, I am very proud to be Cuban in the sense that it is my family who brought me to this world, and they are the roots in me, not Cuba". His teenage years had the usual episode of being a band member, in his case playing drums.

Coincidentally, he also made his first forays into design producing flyers to promote the band. After working at a variety of advertising agencies he moved to Chicago in 1980 where he had spells at a number of design companies including Marsteller, Foote Cone & Belding, Ketchum, DDB Needham, BBDO and Young & Rubicam. Seeing little future in being an employee, he launched Segura Inc. in 1991.

Segura has made all the right moves in expanding the competencies of his original design company. He launched a highly successful digital type foundry [T-26] in 1994. Segura has said of his foundry's ambitions: "The typography that we've introduced in the market just three, four, five years ago was underground counterculture type of typography that you saw in clubs only or in underground records or experimental type projects. Now it's mainstream." Segura Inc.'s commitment to the music industry is exemplified through its own label, Thickface. It marketed [T-26] by digital direct mail, creating a short "music video" for each typeface, with the star being the font rather than a band. In 2000 Segura diversified further by launching 5inch.com to sell custom designed blank CDs and DVDs. He subsequently split up Segura Inc. into two separate ventures: Segura Interactive to focus on the internet and new media, including broadcast, and Segura Inc. which remains focused on print-related projects.

Although not particularly large, Segura Inc. has been highly influential, not least in its business model. It is an inventive, reliable supplier of design solutions to the record industry. Its work is not focused on a particular sub-section of the industry, whether hip, fashionable or not, and it has a heterogeneous client list which ranges from Duran Duran, through Willie Nelson, Christina Aguilera, Durban Poison to Pearl Jam, Garbage, Smashing Pumpkins and Tricky. Its relationship with clients, is, as Segura himself admits, sometimes less than satisfactory: "The bigger (stars) they are, the less open minded they are, so there are a lot of rules in play, especially from the label. Most of the time, we never even meet them. With smaller acts we get to meet and get to know each other." The contemporary product-based awareness of the music industry undoubtedly creates a supply situation which is precariously poised between encouraging sound product replicating highly normative values (which all design practitioners decry) and sparking the kind of unpredictable invention which is genuinely innovative. Despite such dilemmas, Segura Inc. thrives because of its openness, straightforward dealing and its ability to grasp the technical underpinnings of the world in which it operates. An admirer of Neville Brody and Stefan Sagmeister, Segura ensures that his company cuts the mustard at just about every level, and as such it perfectly exemplifies the current state of play between design companies and record labels. Things will change, the anarchic will inevitably creep back in, but for the time being – despite the rhetoric – that is how things are.

Mitchell Beazley would like to acknowledge and thank
the following designers, record companies, and photographic agencies for supplying images for inclusion in
this book. We would also like to thank the following
specialist record shops for their help and interest in this
project, including the loan of material for photography:
Harold Moores Records, London, (hmrecords.co.uk), Mole
Jazz, London (molejazz.co.uk), and Records Revisited,
New York.

Key: **a** above, **b** below, **c** centre, **l** left, **r** right

AKG Images: 18, 19l
Blue Note: 45l, 51b, 62lb & r, 65ac, 109l
Blue Source: 242-3
Jeroen Borrenbergs/Djax Records: 201cr
BuroDestruct: 234a
Art Chantry: 214l & br, 216-7
Chermayeff & Geismar Inc: 70-1
Christie's Images: 19r, 22, 23, 92, 93 br
courtesy **Irwin Chusid**: 26, 39-40
Corbis: Bettmann 16, 21, David J & Janice L Frent
    Collection 17r, Alan Le Garsmeur 17l
The Designers Republic: 212-3
Dots Per Minute: 198
Rod Dyer: 130al & 131br
Fuhrer Vienna, Hat Hut Records Ltd: 227ac
Carin Goldberg: 183
Jeremy Hall: 227r
Mick Haggerty: 132-3
Jane Higgins: 215r
Kim Hiorthoy: 235bl
Intro: 208b, 244cl, 245
David James Associates: 220-1, 230br
Seb Jarnot: 235al
Kharbine Tapabor: 20a & b
courtesy **Christina Kubisch** 209a
Mainartery: 199cr
Me Company: 218-9
Russell Mills: 187
Michael Nash Associates: 231
Robert Opie: 73, 79b, 80b, 113a, 125a
Ott and Stein: 227l
Redferns: 30a & b, 32, 45r, 68b, 72r, 78a, 81a, 85l, ac & r,
    86l, 89ar, 101b, 105, 115l & r, 125br, 131l & ar, 151l,
    153
Jamie Reid: 160-1
Simon Robinson (www.easyontheeye.net): 46r, 60-1
Sagmeister Inc: 238bl, ar & br
Peter Saville Associates: 166, 173, 175al & r, 228l & ar,
    229r
San Francisco Museum of Modern Art: Accessions
    Committee Fund 97r, Gift of Jim Chanin 98l & br, 99r
Cal Schenkel: 83r, 110-1
Segura Inc: 246-7
Alex Steinweiss: 34-7
Stylorouge: 202, 194-5
Ian Swift: 209b
Thrill Jockey: 235r
Tomato: 240l & r
Triple Earth: 227bc
V&A Images: 98ar, 104l & c
Zip Design: 234b.

Every effort has been made to credit all those who have
been involved in the design of each record cover. We
apologise should any omissions have been made.

Additional copyrights are held by:
Apple Corps Ltd: The Beatles, 88-91
Promotone BV: The Rolling Stones, 140b, 141b, 142,
    143a & b
Abcko: The Rolling Stones, 88ar, 140a, 141a.